Keys to the Secondary Classroom

Keys to the Secondary Classroom

A **Teacher's Guide** to the **First Months of School**

Rain Bongolan
Ellen Moir
Wendy Baron

CORWIN
A SAGE Company

New Teacher Center

For information:

Corwin
A SAGE Company
2455 Teller Road
Thousand Oaks, California 91320
(800) 233-9936
Fax: (800) 417-2466
www.corwinpress.com

SAGE Ltd.
1 Oliver's Yard
55 City Road
London EC1Y 1SP
United Kingdom

SAGE India Pvt. Ltd.
B 1/I 1 Mohan Cooperative
Industrial Area
Mathura Road, New Delhi 110 044
India

SAGE Asia-Pacific Pte. Ltd.
33 Pekin Street #02-01
Far East Square
Singapore 048763

Printed in the United States of America.

Library of Congress Cataloging-in-Publication Data

Bongolan, Rain.
Keys to the secondary classroom: a teacher's guide to the first months of school/Rain Bongolan, Ellen Moir, Wendy Baron.
        p. cm.
Includes bibliographical references and index.
ISBN 978-0-7619-7895-4 (cloth: alk. paper)
ISBN 978-0-7619-7896-1 (pbk.: alk. paper)
    1. High school teaching—United States. 2. Classroom management—United States.
3. Motivation in education—United States. I. Moir, Ellen. II. Baron, Wendy. III. Title.

LB1737.U6B66 2010
373.1102—dc22   2009028156

This book is printed on acid-free paper.

09   10   11   12   13   10   9   8   7   6   5   4   3   2   1

Acquisitions Editor:	Carol Chambers Collins
Associate Editor:	Julie McNall
Editorial Assistant:	Brett Ory
Production Editor:	Libby Larson
Copy Editor:	Codi Bowman
Typesetter:	C&M Digitals (P) Ltd.
Proofreader:	Wendy Jo Dymond
Indexer:	Wendy Allex
Cover Designer:	Rose Storey
Graphic Designer:	Karine Hovsepian

Contents

List of Reproducible Figures

Acknowledgments

W e are grateful for the contributions and support of the following people in the development and editing of *Keys to the Secondary Classroom:*

Kevin Drinkard and Laurie Marcellin for their substantive lesson plans for the *first two weeks of school*

John Moir, Sarah Young, and Laura Gschwend for their diligence as our local editors

Secondary mentors and outreach coordinators of the Santa Cruz New Teacher Project and New Teacher Center respectively for distinguishing the nature of *all things secondary*

And last but not least . . .

Beginning teachers! They make it possible to leverage teacher-mentor inquiry and a belief in equitable instruction for all students as important keys to identifying and implementing high-quality instruction!

Corwin gratefully acknowledges the contributions of the following reviewers:

Janet Crews
Secondary Instructional
  Coordinator
Clayton School District
Clayton, Missouri

Lori L. Grossman
Instructional Coordinator, ECH
  and Mentoring,
Professional Development
  Services
Houston Independent School
  District
Houston, Texas

Ronald W. Poplau
Social Studies Teacher
Shawnee Mission Northwest
  High School
Shawnee, Kansas

Kathy Tritz-Rhodes
Principal
Marcus-Meriden-Cleghorn
  School
Marcus and Cleghorn, Iowa

About the Authors

 **Rain Bongolan** has supported more than 120 beginning secondary teachers as a mentor for the Santa Cruz New Teacher Project. Her contributions to the profession reflect 22 years of teaching history and English at the middle school and high school levels, and her dedication to ensuring students' access to rigorous, culturally responsive instruction. For three years, Rain directed and codesigned the New Teacher Center's (NTC) English Language Learners (ELL) Institute, one of California's 24 professional development institutes. Rain consults with national organizations as well as state school districts working to improve instructional practices in adolescent literacy and English language development. She has authored several mentor- and teacher-training modules and directed grant projects for the NTC featuring practical and innovative teaching and mentoring strategies designed to advance seventh through twelfth-grade students' content literacy.

 **Wendy Baron** has taught kindergarten through Grade 6, served as a Title I reading specialist, supervised and instructed prospective teachers at the University of California, Santa Cruz (UCSC), and, for the past 20 years, has worked directly with new teachers and principals, kindergarten through Grade 12. As associate director at the New Teacher Center, Wendy oversees the Santa Cruz/Silicon Valley New Teacher Project, which supports more than 1,000 new teachers annually. She also consults with school districts throughout California and nationally on mentoring, teacher induction, and designing professional development for beginning teachers. Wendy has extensive experience in coaching, adult learning theory, group facilitation, and professional development. She is a researcher and practitioner, and she seeks continually to impact educational systems to support teacher development. Wendy is the author of several articles and book chapters, and she has produced numerous videos related to mentoring and new-teacher development.

 **Ellen Moir** is the founder and executive director of the New Teacher Center (formerly affiliated with the University of California, Santa Cruz). The NTC is committed to developing an inspired, dedicated, and highly qualified teaching force fostered by supporting communities to provide comprehensive support for new teachers as they enter the profession. For more than 20 years, she has pioneered innovative approaches to new-teacher development, research on new-teacher practice, and the design and administration of teacher induction programs. Ellen continues to work with the Santa Cruz/Silicon Valley New Teacher Project and is an advocate for new teachers across the country. Ellen has received national recognition for her work, including the 2005 Harold W. McGraw, Jr., Prize in Education and the 2003 Distinguished Teacher Educator Award from the California Council on Teacher Education. Ellen is the author of several articles and book chapters, and she produced a video series related to new-teacher development. Her work has been supported by more than 20 private foundations and donors, the National Science Foundation, and several state and federal agencies. In 2009, with renewed support from several foundations, Ellen and her leadership team re-established the NTC as an independent, nonprofit organization focused on "launching the next generation of teachers."

Introduction

Welcome to *Keys to the Secondary Classroom!* This book was written to help make your teaching life easier and, in the process, improve the academic success for your students. We hope to provide you, the teacher, with tools and resources to be able to start the school year with a solid foundation. We would like you to begin ready to enjoy your students and help them to succeed in your content area. Although our target audience for this book is new teachers, we hope to offer something of value to everyone who would like to strengthen or renew aspects of his or her teaching practice.

Preparing adolescent students for the increasing demands of our world is a complex and challenging activity. It takes great commitment, organization, subject matter knowledge, and passion. Those of you who have chosen to teach in secondary schools also have that particular gene that makes teenagers and preteens look like some of the most engaging, lively people around.

In our work of observing and supporting thousands of new teachers, we have found that the apparently seamless teaching observed in the classrooms of exemplary teachers is actually the product of hundreds of small steps. By naming and demystifying these steps, we offer more teachers the opportunity to learn and internalize the components of seamless teaching. A firm foundation in planning, management, curriculum design, and assessment frees teachers to put more energy into the creativity and soul of their practice.

We hope that, over time, your unique teaching style will emerge and that your highest vision for becoming a teacher is realized. This book offers ideas for organizing curriculum and systems that in turn will help you to realize that vision, share your strengths with students, and meet a myriad of professional expectations. We would like to help you meet high standards for all students, including those of diverse language and learning abilities.

Much of what our book has to offer is derived from the work of the New Teacher Center (NTC) at the University of California, Santa Cruz, a statewide and national center dedicated to advancing the work of those who support beginning teachers and principals. The NTC now serves principals, mentors, and teachers in more than 35 states across the United States. However, our original models for effective teaching, learning, and mentoring were based in the work of our local New Teacher Project, where dedicated teams of support providers have served thousands of local teachers since 1988. We see induction as an opportunity to shape the norms and culture of the profession. We are committed to developing teachers who are thoughtful and reflective, work collaboratively with colleagues, and approach their teaching with a questioning and problem-solving spirit. The work of the NTC includes research, and we have been able to discover and document a clear relationship between mentoring beginning teachers and student achievement gains.

In this spirit, our book attempts to offer you actual keys to the classroom, a compilation of tools and insights that we hope will create a solid foundation for a successful career in education. Here are the highlights of the chapters:

- Chapter 1, "The Adolescent Learner," describes some of the particular strengths and challenges of working with the adolescent student, along with tips for harnessing adolescent energy and steering it in a productive direction.

- Chapter 2 brings you directly into "The Nuts and Bolts of Getting Started," helping to identify the many dimensions of preparation and organization for new teachers. We walk though a step-by-step overview of preparing your classroom, materials, resources, routines, and procedures as well as identifying key people who can help. The chapter ends with a comprehensive checklist, collecting all the tasks in one place for an efficient overview.

- Chapter 3 takes us into the nitty-gritty of "Rules, Routines, and Procedures." We want to take the mystery out of setting clear expectations for student behavior, which, once established, allows us to really teach. In this chapter, we look at both prevention and intervention; positive and negative consequences; and ongoing procedures for homework, classroom management, equipment care, and more.

- In Chapter 4, we describe a variety of activities and teaching strategies that create positive classroom climates, establish cooperative norms, and allows students to build effective teams for academic work. "Community and Team Building" is an essential part of creating a positive and effective classroom environment in secondary schools.

- In Chapter 5, we take a long-range view of planning in the "Big-Picture Guide to Standards-Based Curriculum and Instruction." Before planning day-to-day, we need a bigger picture of what it is we want to teach and why. Chapter 5 presents ideas and resources for making a yearlong plan. It also provides short teaching units and themes, links curriculum to standards, and offers other considerations for planning.

- Chapter 6 brings us back to the level of "Strategies for Daily Lesson Planning and Student Engagement." In this chapter, we offer a variety of teaching strategies that can be applied across content areas to engage a wide range of students in whatever it is you want to teach. We provide a template for daily lesson planning that serves as both an organizer and a foundation for effective teaching and learning.

- Chapter 7, "Planning for the First Two Weeks of Math Class," and Chapter 8, "Planning for the First Two Weeks of English and Social Studies Class," offer step-by-step lesson plans by exemplary secondary math and language arts teachers for beginning the year. They weave together the elements of organization, rules, procedures, community building, student engagement, and content-area teaching. Feel free to borrow from and make them your own.

- In Chapter 9, we offer several concrete strategies that secondary teachers across the content areas can integrate into their teaching to improve students' abilities for *reading to learn*. How about secondary students who struggle to read grade-level text? For new and interested teachers, "Supporting Secondary Students to Read Subject Matter Text" reviews what constitutes *effective* reading skills and how you might support students to develop both general as well as subject-specific ways to use the skills.

- Chapter 10, "Teaching for English Language Learner Success," offers suggestions for identifying language needs and then offers a variety of teaching strategies geared toward improving the academic success of English learners. Larger and larger percentages of our students are struggling with both reading and writing proficiencies in academic English. Language issues are evident in immigrant students and many others who have lived in the United States for generations.

- Chapter 11 offers a closer look at the area of "Assessment of Student Learning." How do we gather ongoing information about whether students are learning what we are teaching? How do we design all our lessons with outcomes and evidence of learning in mind? In this chapter, we offer user-friendly means of integrating assessment into the daily work of teaching.

- Chapter 12, "Communication With Parents," describes simple means of making and maintaining contact with parents throughout the year. How do we make the essential link between home and school as a secondary teacher with up to 180 students? We provide you with premade parent letters in both English and Spanish to communicate on a variety of topics.

- The Epilogue's theme is "Sustaining a Passion for Teaching." As we bring the book to a close, we want to send you on your way with the knowledge that there is no better work you can be doing. How do we keep our heads and hearts engaged in what is one of the most demanding and, at the same time, satisfying professions? We want you to be able to settle in for the long haul, know you are really making a difference, and have fun at the same time.

At the back of the book, you will find a resource that includes sample class guidelines. These guidelines were developed by a teacher to be used at the outset of the school year, and they may be helpful to you as you set up your course expectations and communicate with students about how they can be successful in your course.

In addition, we have complied and included a list of well-thumbed Key Resources for Secondary Teachers. This list is organized by topical category and includes print and online resources that may be helpful to you in your practice.

The Adolescent Learner

Key Questions About Adolescents and Win-Win Teacher Responses

I know my subject and how it informs and enhances our lives. I want to teach students to appreciate these things as much as I do!

As you begin your teaching career, you bring the strengths of your subject matter knowledge and enthusiasm for wanting to share that knowledge with students. What else do you need to know and do to teach your subject effectively? Will your students be interested in what you teach? Will seemingly less interested students make it difficult for you to teach others? We invite you to consider the unique possibilities and challenges involved in engaging and instructing middle and high school students. This chapter highlights some patterns of adolescent students' behavior, their learning strengths and needs, and overarching strategies for fostering success.

WHY DO ADOLESCENTS GET SO MOODY, WILD, OR DRAMATIC?

Adolescent Learners May Exhibit Intense, Emotional, and Complex Energies in Response to a Multitude of Factors.

Do you remember your transition from elementary school to life on a middle or high school campus? Your students are now in an environment filled with two to five times the number of students that attended their former schools. They are expected to learn new ideas from several different teachers, each with a different style of teaching and set of expectations. As they gain greater independence from their parents, adolescents find themselves more actively redefining who they are in relation to others. *Peer pressure* from friends and acquaintances in school, neighborhoods, or the community at large can influence their opinions and choices of clothing, music, and what to do in their free time. Approaching young adulthood, some students work part-time or help to care for younger siblings. Some students may be coping with or helping to mediate challenging situations in their homes or neighborhoods. Many students also feel pressure to maintain exceptionally high grade point averages to raise their chances of admission to a selective four-year university.

Add these outside pressures to those happening inside their bodies! At the onset of and continuing throughout puberty, significant changes in certain types and levels of hormones trigger increases in adolescents' height and the development of their reproductive system. Barring any negative effects from thrill-seeking or other hormone-driven behaviors, major changes in the structure and function of the brain continue to occur throughout adolescence. The developmental changes that take place during adolescence dramatically act to increase the brain's efficiency and capacity for critical thinking, monitoring behavior, and making choices.

What other factors are at play? Most of today's adolescents have had access to the Internet since their preschool or early elementary school years. Many consider television, movies, music, and the Web as pivotal sources for receiving information. Current technologies provide access to global news and a wide range in music, art, languages, and images. Many students use their personal computers to instantaneously retrieve and respond to the latest information about social and cultural icons, and the day's political foes and heroes. Whether gossiping via text messages, cell phone conversations, or social networking online, more and more students are capable of connecting to one another and family members before, during, and long after school.

Imagine all these factors combined with their characteristic excitability, moodiness, sexual curiosity, impulsiveness, and the effects of occasional sleep deprivation. Your students will vary greatly in how willing they are to express or mask the influence on their thinking triggered by an incredible array of influences. Individual styles, peer influences, sociocultural backgrounds, and students' social and academic language proficiencies may also influence their responsiveness to instruction. Can't figure out why your students run so hot and cold? Chances are that they can't either! In a nutshell, the academic concepts you present, and to which you expect students to respond, exist amid their complex emotions, impulses, and input from the world.

How Can I Channel Their High-Intensity, All-About-Me Energies Toward Productive Schoolwork?

- **Introduce academic concepts by making meaningful connections to students' lives.** Whenever possible, introduce new concepts through a variety of prompts, resources, and activities that connect lesson topics and skills with students' multifaceted lives. All students have some personal knowledge to relate to what is being taught. It is your creative challenge to continually discover, or preassess, for meaningful connections between pivotal subject matter concepts, related topics, and the experiences students *bring* to your classroom. These connections create springboards for learning.

- **Use movement and peer interactions.** Increase each individual student's focus on learning with a variety of interactions. Consider what you're observing about trends in student engagement and your students' preferred learning styles. For how many students is simply hearing information sufficient? On average, do students seem more engaged when ideas are also represented visually or when they're involved in more kinesthetic or tactile, hands-on learning? How might your lessons incorporate some sociocultural styles of engagement and communication, like storytelling, cooperative group activities, rhythmic call-and-response dialogues, debates, or presentations?

    Increase focus by having students work in pairs or triads to quickly brainstorm what they know about a subject related picture, three-dimensional model, or a pivotal phrase displayed on your SMART Board, PowerPoint slide, overhead transparency, or whiteboard. As a variation, you might ask all students to stand and pair up with someone from another part of the room to discuss one homework question they've answered or problem they've solved. Draw out and affirm students' prior knowledge through these two- to five-minute stand-up meetings at any point in the lesson.

    In starting a new unit, have two or three of your more vocal students take center stage as you prompt them to *think aloud* about a unit-related concept. Engage these students in a five-minute debate about a hot-topic controversy, or ask them to describe in detail what they see in a photo or three-dimensional model. Ask how, step-by-step, they would go about answering a featured *question of the day*. Encourage their dramatic side even more by asking these learners to model a skill, demonstrate a concept, or dramatically read aloud from a pivotal text excerpt. As part of building on their prior knowledge, prompt your other students to write what is said by their peers and decide whether they agree or disagree with what they say. Eventually, more students will be willing to take a more active role in front of their peers.

- **Flex and reflect.** As you establish your procedures and expectations, it's periodically okay to share with students your own efforts to get it right. You are their instructional leader and their partner in learning. Stating your intention to support and advance their skills as learners *as well as* teach them new concepts is usually (albeit quietly) welcomed.

WHY DO THEY QUESTION THE PURPOSE OF WHAT I WANT TO TEACH?

Adolescent Learners Want to Know That What They Learn Has Value or Purpose. They Also Want to Be Taken Seriously as Students.

Students will eventually ask about the purpose or value of information presented in your class. Don't take it personally as something negative—some view it as their inherent right to question you. Soon enough you will hear, "Why do we have to learn this?" If students are less than tactful at posing this question, it may not necessarily be about defying you or about showing off in front of their peers. They are actively defining their perspectives on a range of topics. As metacognitive skills develop more rapidly during this phase, whether they'll admit to it or not, they are assessing what they know and don't know about information presented to them. Students want to know that what they are being asked to learn has some meaning, usefulness, or potential value to their lives.

All students hope you respect them as learners, including students who haven't had consistent academic success, don't appear to be working to their potential, or perceive themselves as generally disrespected in the school community. Students hope that each teacher will handle their mistakes and successes with an even and predictable hand. Ultimately, they hope that respect is consistently promoted and modeled by the adult(s) in charge.

How Can I Promote the Value of What I Teach, Including Essential Concepts That Are Difficult to Understand as Described in Grade-Level Texts? How Can I Support Struggling Readers?

- **Take time to identify and then articulate to students the "whys"** for learning each of the major concepts and skills you will need to teach. Despite the emphasis on standards and high-stakes testing, most adolescents (and many teachers) are not genuinely impressed by hearing that students are required to learn certain things. It is your responsibility to help students understand how smaller bits of information connect to larger, enduring subject matter concepts, essential questions and applications, and (better yet) how this information is connected to students' lives!
- **Model expert reading skills and help students make connections to concepts they'll encounter in text.** Despite the importance of demonstrations, visuals, and projects that engage students in learning

new content, there is no way around the fact that skillful, independent reading is still the most efficient means by which one can acquire considerable amounts of advanced-level information. Chapter 9 describes several ideas for developing students' content-literacy skills as a part of subject matter instruction. Achievement data confirm that even students with average, grade-level reading skills struggle to persist when reading to understand dense, detailed text that describes advanced subject-specific concepts. Consider this general principle: Students benefit from making connections between challenging, text-based information and larger concepts that are more interesting or meaningful to them. Support your students to make these connections by demonstrating the skills you use to think and read like a scientist, historian, mathematician, literary critic, artist, or expert of other career paths. One thing you can do is to think aloud about images that come to mind as you read a key excerpt, description, or a set of directions and procedures. Enhance reading think alouds by simultaneously displaying an enlarged version of the excerpt on an overhead transparency or SMART Board. As you encounter challenging or confusing phrases, articulate the questions that come to mind, the process for clarifying the meaning of a pivotal word, or personal experiences triggered by those phrases. As you are reading and intermittently thinking aloud, write what you are saying between the lines of text or in the margins. Ask students to write what you are writing on Post-its they can place in the margin next to the passage in the textbook. Or they can write directly onto copies of an article or excerpt from the textbook provided to them for a think aloud activity designed to develop their subject-specific reading skills.

- **Offer strong anticipatory (i.e., introductory) activities** that clearly connect new ideas to examples, resources, references, or contexts that are socioculturally relevant or familiar to your students. Enhance students' interaction with new concepts by using this language-development strategy: Provide students with graphic organizers (e.g., main idea maps or Cornell notes format) to help them quickly identify main ideas and their relationship to examples and supporting details. In leveraging these tools, you are more likely to foster initial student interest quickly, build background knowledge, and sustain engagement.

- **Show respect for students.** Affirm students' progress in learning academic concepts, successes in reaching certain goals, and improvement in behaviors that benefit them as learners. At all cost, avoid put-downs and sarcasm in your feedback to students (even if this type of back-and-forth is prevalent among some students) and use neutral, direct language to coach them toward ways to improve.

- **Respond and/or give corrective feedback** to student work as soon as possible. Make their work count. Provide and carefully walk through components of rubrics and expectations linked to major assignments, and perhaps even expectations for behavior and productive participation. Engage students in assessing their current strengths and learning needs related to these productive behaviors.

WHY DO SOME STUDENTS SEEM TO CARE ONLY ABOUT THE OPINIONS OF THEIR PEERS?

Adolescents Are Known for Their Susceptibility to Peer Pressure.

As part of gaining their independence from adults, teenagers and preteens are compelled toward peer interactions. Intense peer-group associations often act as a type of security blanket or serve as a preferred second home away from home. Generally speaking, conformity to peer-group norms regarding styles of clothing, manner of speech, and attitudes toward adults in authority can play a bigger role in the behavior of adolescents as compared to younger students. Peer-group influences can reinforce productive school behaviors and sometimes influence nonproductive ones, such as cutting or being late for class, not doing homework, or provoking conflicts with other students.

Of course, not all students are susceptible to peer pressure, or at least not to the same degree. For example, many first- and second-generation immigrant students are often fascinated by but reluctant to fully adopt the ways of more predominant student groups they view as American or *Americanized*. Many of these students tend to hold family traditions and cultural perspectives as familiar touchstones, and they consider their shared family responsibilities as priorities, at least for a while.

We caution you—although certain patterns of student behavior can be predicted, keep an open mind when you encounter some negative behaviors that may appear to have been prompted by peer-group influences. Remember that many complex factors are at play in the lives of individual students. Associating or predicting negative behaviors based *strictly* on what appears to be peer-group or sociocultural norms can result in counterproductive interactions between you and a student.

How Do I Promote More Constructive, Positive Responses and Attitudes Among Students Drawn to Negative, Peer-Pressured Behaviors?

- **Invest time in knowing who your students are and what they bring.** Each of your students brings multidimensional strengths (learning style preferences, multiple intelligences, cultural and linguistic perspectives, and individual life experiences), as well as instructional needs. Learning about these dimensions may seem daunting given the number of students you teach. The importance of considering these other types of student data is being recognized more and more by secondary educators. You may be teaching in a school organized into *smaller learning communities*, grade-level advisories, and/or student-selected *career pathway academies*. These school structures are intended to help secondary teachers collaboratively learn about the multiple dimensions of their students and use that information to plan instruction and programs that increase motivation and engagement. As an individual teacher, you can do something as simple as routinely ask students about their experiences linked to a concept you are about to teach. This signals that you value their perspectives and potential contributions. Your instruction can create another kind of draw for students when aspects about their lives are respectfully and appropriately woven into a few strategic lessons.

- **View your classroom as a place to establish a different community of peers.** Your enthusiasm, team-building efforts, meaningful questions, and even what you display on your classroom walls can help foster students' interaction with subject matter content and one another, as well as with you. Consider how your lessons and the resources you use encourage all of your students in some way to view themselves as historians, readers and writers of literature, scientists, mathematicians, artists, athletes, or tech-savvy seekers of information. Uplifting or thought-provoking pictures on your walls depicting people from the same sociocultural backgrounds as your students help to make them feel connected to the learning environment. In addition to your students' work, filling your walls with subject-related articles and visuals depicting compelling contexts, topics, and career possibilities tends to foster a level of comfort and willingness to participate.

Involve students in reflecting about some schoolwide rules, plus your own classroom rules and expectations. Plan an occasional, extended activity to foster student reflection about rules and expectations. Guiding students in reflective activities will help to raise the quality and level of response to the school's and/or your own class rules. For example, if students have been complaining about the fairness of prohibiting or limiting cell phone use during class time, it may warrant a facilitated discussion to surface the pros and cons as well as the rationale behind the rule. If they passionately argue the right to free speech in response to a reminder about expectations for using respectful language in the classroom, pause and stay neutral as you prompt students to take a few minutes to write about what might happen if free speech were taken to its outer limits. On the flip side, remember to validate students' productive, appropriate behaviors. Avoid a possible tendency even during times when students are not consistently meeting expectations to focus on only negative behaviors. (See Chapter 3 for more ideas about preassessing students' strengths, establishing a respectful environment, and setting rules.)

WHY ARE SO MANY STUDENTS LATE WITH HOMEWORK AND DEADLINES?

Adolescent Learners Tend to Be Challenged by the Concept of Time Management.

Teenagers lead busy lives. From time to time, afterschool activities, clubs, athletics, family responsibilities, part-time work, personal interests, hanging out with friends, social events, technology-driven pastimes (video games, television, Internet, text messaging), and other diversions keep them occupied and otherwise distracted from schoolwork. Most adolescents find it difficult to avoid time-management challenges. All students need some level of help to gain the know-how involved in getting things done: organizing assignments, prioritizing tasks, getting the resources or information needed to complete tasks, managing, and then spending the time needed to study. This is especially true for middle school students and high school freshmen. Even older students who seem to have it under control say they appreciate teachers who are clear (namely, those who don't assume that students automatically know) about expectations for homework, class participation, deadlines, or the length and content of an assigned paper or project.

How Do I Support Students to Become Organized and Use Their Time Wisely, Especially Related to Homework Assignments?

- **Never assume.** New secondary teachers often assume that because their students are now in their eighth or tenth year of school, they are skilled at time management. Providing students with clear expectations for short- and long-term assignments is crucial. During the first two to three weeks of school, assign students one or two of the same types of daily homework assignments until they get the routine and understand your expectations about the work. Vary the types of homework, length, and/or complexity appropriately over time. Explaining the assignment, providing students with expectations and requirements in writing, and then checking for students' understanding about each assignment are essential elements. When you assign something, convey that it counts. Build in time to each day for students to review some part of the homework assignment, and/or time for you to check that homework that was due has indeed been done (see Chapter 3, Rules, Routines, and Procedures).

- **Provide assignment calendars, a detailed syllabus, or sample projects.** Refer students to published calendars and your class syllabus at least once per week. For independent, long-term assignments, a routine check-in a couple of times per week to surface key ideas, possible problems, questions, or confusions they might have is also helpful. Given that you probably won't have examples of projects to show your students yet, consider investing time in creating one yourself. It should feature at least the titles or components of what you require for the project; the possible layout of these components; plus a separate sheet describing your expectations, types of resources to reference, and the length of written components.

- **Speak to individual students** when you notice patterns of inattention, absences, tardiness, or other evidence that a student may be performing *below* (his or her) *potential*. You may have observed that in the past the student has shown more interest in lesson topics, sharing thoughtful insights through written assignments or participating in group discussions or problem solving. Start by speaking to the student privately. Share what you've noticed about his or her past participation or previous work that is positive as well as your concerns about patterns that appear to be hindering his or her academic progress. Respectfully ask if there are ways you and/or other staff members might be able to help with certain assignments (e.g., additional bilingual or reading support, afterschool homework assistance, or access to a computer center) or other things that might be distracting the student from schoolwork. If after meeting with the student you notice that not much has changed after a while, you may want to speak to the student again, and suggest that perhaps meeting with a parent or guardian is your next step.

WHY DO SOME STUDENTS SEEM PERSISTENTLY UNMOTIVATED?

Adolescent Learners Are Generally Motivated by What They Believe Is Meaningful, Fun, and Active; Involves Choice; or Connects to Their Teacher's Passion About a Subject.

Accustomed to multiple types of input and stimuli found *outside* of class, most adolescents tend to grow restless in class when attempting to passively concentrate for long periods. Hormone-charged bodies and thoughts that drift to the life that awaits them after school sometimes make it challenging to stay focused on academic tasks. Eventually, you will inevitably hear them groan, "This is boring."

How Can I Help My Students Stay on Task? With so Much to Cover, Do I Dare Allow Time to Be Flexible and Include What They Consider Fun?

- **Divide instruction delivered through lecture, reading, or silent individual tasks into shorter segments.** Use an agenda that clearly spells out the lesson's activities. Encourage pacing with verbal cues ("Three minutes left to finish"). You need to change focus periodically to keep students' interest level high. You can always revisit concepts at another time or through various activities. Among other things, adolescents respond to teachers whom they perceive as organized. Engaging students in lessons with tasks and activities that are explained clearly and are well paced conveys this sense of organization.
- **Monitor pacing, input, and types of learning.** Post your agenda noting the main concept or objective of the day, a warm-up activity, and three or four other components of the day's lesson. Begin with a five- to eight-minute warm-up activity to get students interested in the content. Get students accustomed to answering a couple of math or science problems or responding to an interesting question, quote, word, or visual at the start of every class.

Note: This allows you to take attendance and perhaps make contact with a couple of students.

Structure lessons so that they allow students to engage in a combination of activities including the following:

- **Begin lessons with warm-ups that connect lesson concepts to students' prior knowledge. Follow warm-ups with . . .**
  - ○ Listening and responding in multiple ways to expert input or modeling (teacher or student demonstrations, lecture, video, text read aloud)
  - ○ Collaborating with other students in a variety of activities to examine the meaning of key vocabulary and concepts, or develop new representations (e.g., posters, completed graphic organizers, responses to key questions) linked to what they've read, solved, or experienced
  - ○ Individually solving problems and/or reading and responding to text
  - ○ A brief closing activity that supports students to assess or summarize what they've learned
- **Facilitate a few short, project-based assignments.** When equipped with sufficient background knowledge and the interest you've generated about a concept, students' interest can be increased even more through project-based learning. Short individual or small-group projects and presentations can be completed in two to four traditional class periods or block periods assuming students have access to the information and materials they will need to complete the task. Students can also work on these projects for homework. (Long-term or culminating projects can be worked on for a few minutes at the start of each class.) Short, in-class projects assigned at the start of a semester give you the opportunity to inform and guide students about the process, check for understanding, and raise the possibility of early and ongoing student success. In-class projects could feature their viewpoint on high-interest topics or the real-life application of an academic concept. Once projects are underway, it usually takes only a few minutes at the start of class to check for understanding about project expectations or provide additional information before turning students loose on these projects. It's still a good idea to check in with the whole group from time to time during a class period to ask some clarifying questions or offer suggestions to address confusions voiced by students. Encourage students to respectfully suggest how their peers might improve the quality of the visuals, layout, and information they plan to present to others.
- **Use quick demonstrations and multiple types of visual and auditory resources.** Using graphics, three-dimensional models, music, art, school-appropriate videos, or Web-based resources can enhance students' experience in learning a lesson's key concept. Try using various types of materials or student demonstrations to illustrate an academic concept in a nonlinguistic way (e.g., having students form a human pyramid to physically represent *hierarchy*, or ask students to line up, assigning each a negative or positive number on a number line as the basis for considering number values that are greater than or less than).

- **Recognize that active learning and choice sustains attention** for learning content that students might initially view as boring or uninteresting. In addition to discussions and responding to information presented through a variety of resources and modalities, support students to consider how they might teach this information to other audiences, including younger students, community members, or leaders. Give students assignments that involve developing their own short story, role-play activity, or questions for a game of Jeopardy. Ask students to develop a lesson for younger students, a lab experiment, or a quiz linked to a subject matter concept or skill. These tasks not only offer students with choices, but they also foster their sense of competence and connection to others.

- **Share your passion for your subject matter.** Your own dedication and passion for the content you present is a key engagement strategy. Combined with your efforts to engage and respect them as learners, your own authentic interest and curiosity about subject matter concepts are difficult for students to ignore. "Why is Mr. or Ms. _____ so excited about this topic?" Students with no prior interest in a subject will be intrigued, at the very least, by your enthusiasm and daily rediscovery of essential concepts and questions.

WHY DO SOME STUDENTS APPEAR SO CONFIDENT, EVEN WHEN THEY DON'T KNOW WHAT THEY DON'T KNOW?

Underneath It All, Adolescents Have Insecurities and, in Addition to High-Quality Instruction, Would Benefit From Receiving Additional Guidance to Increase Their Success as Students.

Despite their need to distinguish themselves from adults, most adolescents also need and want adults to guide them in the learning process, perhaps more than ever. As described earlier in this chapter, their miscalculations about things such as appropriate behavior or the time and effort needed to complete work are part of being inexperienced with a school world that has many more variables, complexities, responsibilities, and consequences for not meeting those responsibilities.

A significant number of students are often hesitant to ask for help in a direct and constructive manner. Conveying their boredom or seeming to *know it all* could mean something quite the opposite. Some students operate behind a level of social bravado meant to mask aspects of learning that are challenging to them. Students currently in the process of learning English as their second language may be reluctant to express their needs or questions in English in front of their peers. Some adolescents who have in the past felt alienated or experienced disrespect in other school communities may seem to have given up on any hope that adults will genuinely care about their success. Others may appear detached as a way of coping with rejection from potential peer-group friends, insufficient content literacy, differences in learning needs, or factors linked to at-risk situations present in their home or neighborhood. With these challenges on their mind, students may not express their needs or concerns directly, if at all.

How Do I Provide All My Students With the Guidance They Need? How Can I Promote Success?

- **Set clear consistent and reasonable limits.** Expectations about homework, due dates, appropriate language in class, and respect for materials are things that older students need and expect adults to determine. Older students perceive teachers who are lax about these things as being disorganized, "too loose," or "not like a real teacher." In these cases, students often lose respect for otherwise very knowledgeable instructors.

- **Model, model, model.** Make no assumptions about students' understanding of your expectations for work and behavior. Model the promptness, thoroughness, and respect you expect from them. Discuss study habits. Show them how an assignment should be done. Plan tasks that allow for early successes. Check for understanding regularly about your expectations. Continue to build the degree of difficulty of work and expectations over time. If you have been clear about your expectations, you can involve students in assessing their own progress and the quality of their work and overall effort. This is important when supporting them to be independent learners. Don't forget to acknowledge successes along the way.

- **Be accessible.** Talk about the value of making mistakes and reflecting on them. Selectively share some of your own mistakes. Be available for individual conferences to discuss these matters and describe other available resources (e.g., primary language instruction, tutoring, bilingual materials, simplified texts, or support from school counselors and/or teaching assistants).

2

The Nuts and Bolts of Getting Started

How do I prepare, and who might help me to get started?

In the weeks just before school starts, you'll have many things on your mind. If you're a new English teacher, you may be thinking of ways to engage students in the provocative themes of Toni Morrison's novels, Shakespeare's darker tragedies, or lyrics and essays written by today's cultural icons. If you teach history, you might be searching the Web for articles, lesson ideas, or video clips highlighting human rights issues that are sure to provoke students' opinions. If you teach math, you might be searching for or taking pictures of local monuments and public art that will help students to visualize facets of geometric shapes and their relationship to complex formulas. For your science classes, you're out collecting materials for a first-week demonstration or downloading articles about green technologies and their impact on the local environment.

As a new teacher, be prepared to make a sizable investment of time in the weeks before school starts to identify and organize many aspects of your practice. Not only will you need to continue thinking about the content of your lessons for the first week and month, you will also need to set up the nuts and bolts of teaching that most experienced teachers already have in place. Deciding on the layout of your classroom, acquiring and organizing your materials, identifying classroom procedures, and setting up systems for managing students' work will take time. The beginning of the first year of teaching is a unique time. Keep in mind you are creating an immense toolbox that you will revise throughout your career but will never have to set up from scratch again. The nuts-and-bolts considerations described throughout this chapter are based on teaching in large school communities, but the majority of the items also apply to teachers working in secondary schools with fewer than 600 students.

Middle schools and high schools are complex communities for both students and teachers. You will be a member of several groups of teachers who teach the same subject or grade level or teach students belonging to the same interdisciplinary smaller learning community (SLC) or career pathway academy. Supporting your work are dozens of other staff members—administrators, student attendance and data technicians, counselors, nurses, custodians, cafeteria staff members, computer and school network technicians, campus supervisors, home–school liaisons, student advocates, instructional assistants, athletic coaches, and librarians. You will benefit from cultivating relationships with several of these people before the school year begins. With their help, and possibly the help of a beginning-teacher coach or mentor, you will quickly learn about the ins and outs of your school and secure many of the resources you will need to get started.

Organizing resources and materials and developing key procedures prior to the start of school can mean the difference between smooth sailing and near chaos as the first action-packed weeks of school begin. This chapter will help you to organize systems for many nonteaching details that you will also be responsible for. To support your progress through the complex tasks involved in getting started, we have broken down this chapter into five parts:

1. Focusing on nuts-and-bolts questions

2. Organizing your classroom systems

3. Planning your room arrangement

4. Getting acquainted with people who can help

5. Using a comprehensive checklist of preparation tasks

Note: Don't be reluctant to ask for help. You are entering a community of teachers and learners, and everyone wants you to succeed!

FOCUSING ON THE NUTS-AND-BOLTS QUESTIONS

What Are the Nuts-And-Bolts Questions That I Need to Have Answered Sooner Than Later?

Some questions in this section are rhetorical, intended to signify questions best answered directly by school-site personnel. The school's office manager, custodians, your department chair, SLC or academy teacher leader, your new-teacher mentor, the administrator who hired you, or the person in charge of the master schedule will be able to answer many of these questions or direct you to those who can.

- ***Accessing help and information.*** Did you know administrative and support personnel are often on campus sometimes three weeks earlier than the teaching staff? This is a great time to make contact, get familiar with the layout of the campus, get answers to other key questions, and maybe even get into your classroom to start organizing it! If you aren't familiar with the school or have yet to move into the community, check out the school's Web site to view a map of the campus. Review the job titles and names of people who work in the main office to identify who might possibly help you with the ins and outs of the school system. The Web site might also post teacher resources including the staff and student handbooks as well as the student discipline policy. These resources may contain answers to several questions featured in this chapter and those linked to topics in Chapter 3, "Rules, Routines, and Procedures."

Note: You may need to establish a personal identification number and e-mail address through the district's human resources office to access certain links for teachers posted on the Web site.

- ***Connecting with a beginning teacher mentor.*** Does your district provide coaches or mentors designated to support beginning teachers? If you don't remember hearing about that when you were first hired, call the district's human resource office or check their Web page to confirm whether mentoring for new teachers is available.

- ***Anticipating professional development days.*** Did you know that most districts typically start the year with two or three districtwide or site-based professional development days? These nonteaching days are part of your total contract days. A couple of weeks before the start of school, principals typically send teachers a "welcome back" letter to announce the date, time, location, and focus of these professional development days. You may be able to set up your classroom during at least one, but not likely all, of these professional development days. Oftentimes, district Web sites will post dates for new-teacher orientations, as well as site and districtwide staff-development events that all teachers are expected to attend.

- ***Figuring out your room assignment.*** Who is able to provide information about your room assignment(s)? Are you scheduled to teach in the same room all day, or will you be expected to move to other rooms for certain periods? What preparations will help you rotate between rooms smoothly? (See Ten Tips for the Traveling Teacher later in this chapter.) Will you have a classroom specifically designed for teaching your particular subject? If not, what adaptations to your room will be needed, or what items currently in the room might need to be stored?

- ***Setting up.*** Who might provide information about or assist you in setting up your classroom? In addition to basics like your desk and chair, students' desks and chairs, storage, shelves, filing cabinets, and computers, is it possible to secure other items? How can you get additional desks and/or chair and table options for larger students who aren't able to use typical student desks? What should you do if your classroom phone, computer(s), or other technologies don't work or if heavy items need to be moved? (District safety procedures and insurance policies usually prohibit teachers and students from moving heavy items. Custodians are usually trained and certified to do this safely.)

- *Gathering textbooks and supplies.* What is the procedure for obtaining textbooks and/or teachers' editions? Which supplies are available from a centralized site supply system/room versus supplies ordered specifically for your department? Which supplies need to be ordered by individual teachers? What copy machines or services are available to teachers? Is a special code needed to use the copiers?
- *Clarifying your teaching assignments.* Who is able to give you information about your teaching assignment? Are course descriptions, teacher resources, textbooks, lists of supplementary texts, and site-developed curriculum maps available to teachers through the school's Web site or in print form? What extra nonteaching duties are expected of you?
- *Identifying daily responsibilities.* What are the essential daily tasks and/or procedures expected of all site teachers? What are the expectations and the methods for monitoring and reporting students' attendance, progress, and grades (traditional grade or roll book, electronic grade or roll book, or a combination)? Are teachers required to turn in lesson plans for the following week to site administrators?
- *Understanding discipline policies.* What are the essential district and site rules, discipline procedures, and consequences related to student behavior? Will you need to create some of your own? What documents or agreements need to be signed by students and/or parents regarding the use of the Internet or viewing commercial movies during school hours? Are there alternative settings for students who may need to leave your classroom due to serious behavior issues for a day, or two? (See Chapter 3.)

The following sections will address other chapter topics and elaborate further on some of these nuts-and-bolts questions.

ORGANIZING YOUR CLASSROOM SYSTEMS

You'll find that some teachers (both experienced and new) begin to organize their classrooms two weeks before the start of the official contract year. However, schoolwide repair and cleanup projects could make your classroom unavailable up until the first contract day! Even if you need to wait to organize the physical layout of your room, you can use the time to organize your other systems.

Procedural Systems and Record Keeping

Setting Up Your Lesson Plan Book

Use a traditional teacher's lesson plan book or lesson plan template that you can format or download from the Web. When you visit the main office, ask if teachers are provided with lesson plan and roll books. If not, these can be purchased at an office supply or teacher resource store. The traditional lesson-plan format is a table or grid spread across two pages representing a week's worth of lessons. This planning template serves as a handy visual of the scope and details for lessons you've planned for each period or block. Many teachers create a backup system. These teachers use both the traditional plan book and a binder to file hard copies of weekly lesson plan templates, single lessons, and other resources they've developed or saved on their computers.

Use the margins of a two-page weekly lesson plan template to write additional information about student events, due dates, and various teacher meetings.

Note: Even though many schools now post school event information on their Web site calendars, during the start of the year, you can't always count on this information being up to date. There may be kinks in the school's technology system that may take a while to fix depending on availability of personnel to manage the Web site.

Setting Up Your Attendance and Grade Books (Traditional and Electronic)

Teachers are expected to monitor their students' attendance daily. Teachers report students' attendance by noting absences, tardies, or period cuts. Depending on the site, teachers may complete attendance for each class using scannable rosters that are usually collected each period. Many schools manage attendance via the site's computerized student-data system that allows teachers to take roll electronically from their computers period by period. Check with the attendance or student-data technician, and use the same notation used by the school to record tardies, excused, or unexcused absences. The staff handbook usually describes these types of procedures as well.

For your record keeping, and as a backup for when this system is down, you may also want to fill in your student's names into a traditional grade book or print hard copies of the class enrollment reports generated during the first week of school. Be patient. During the first week or two, many class lists will change. Use both your hard-copy roll book and electronic versions to record completed homework and daily assignments, projects, and tests during the first couple of weeks.

More and more schools require all teachers to use the site's electronic system for grading and generating progress reports. You may want to speak with other teachers in your department or SLC about how they set up their systems.

Preparing for a Substitute

Beginning teachers are often susceptible to illness. Exposure to 60 to 160 people a day and the tendency to get inadequate rest are among the factors that will lead to your first absence. Your district may require you to establish a personal identity number (PIN) that you will you need to access many district resources including the telephone-automated process for requesting a substitute. If you weren't asked to establish a PIN at the human resources office as part of your hiring process, speak with the school's office manager to learn what you need to do get this number or anything else required to access the district's substitute-request system.

Please consider two important things about this particular nuts-and-bolts item: (1) Avoid waiting until the day that you are too sick to teach to deal with these details and (2) have a lesson plan available for the substitute. The following are three different types of substitute plans we refer to here as *business as usual*, *modified*, and *emergency*.

1. *Business as usual.* If your instructional routines and expectations are well established and your students are well underway in the current unit, your lesson plan could involve simply asking a substitute to direct students to continue working on their long-term projects or continue to do the next text-based task that they would be working on, had you been there. If you know the day before that you'll likely need to request a substitute and know that your students can carry on with a current assignment without much direction, it is still very helpful to provide the substitute with clear written directions describing what students should be doing first, second, third, and so on throughout the period.

2. *Modified.* If you know that your current unit, lessons, or types of assignments tend to involve many components, complex steps, resources, use of technology, or your input in particular, you may need to prepare a *modified* substitute plan. There's no guarantee that available substitutes will have your subject matter expertise, familiarity with certain resources, or skill in using certain classroom technologies. A modified lesson allows students to continue learning current unit concepts through assignments that don't necessarily involve the usual bells and whistles you would include. You'll probably turn to this type of plan most often, when you are able to anticipate the need for a substitute for the following day. If handouts for students are needed for the lesson, you should consider whether the substitute has enough time to make copies of these items before school starts. You may need to copy at least enough sets for a couple of periods and ask the substitute to make other copies if needed during your scheduled prep period. Check teacher Web resources, and ask teachers in your department or mentor for examples of the types of activities, resources, or graphic organizers students could use for text-based activities or analyzing videos.

3. *Emergency substitute plans.* On occasion, the business-as-usual plan might work for a day when you assumed that you would be going to work but awoke too sick to function. Call to request a substitute as soon as you can. You might want to call the school office manager as well to alert someone at your site of your situation. If the conditions for a business-as-usual plan are in place, leave a message as part of your request for a substitute, indicating that your students can continue to work on assignments already in progress. Your message might also include a request that the substitute call you at home as soon as possible to clarify certain things about the assignment or concerns you have about a particular class. However, in the case of some emergencies or a debilitating illness, you might not be able to describe any type of lesson plan over the phone. Some serious emergencies might render you unable to make the call to request a substitute! With this in mind, at the start of the year, many schools require that all teachers develop an emergency-substitute lesson plan folder and inform a designated site staff member where the folder will be located. The type of lesson you might prepare for your

emergency-substitute lesson plan folder (typically left in one of your desk drawers) usually involves stand-alone assignments; namely, activities or tasks that are not necessarily connected to a current unit or even linked to the adopted text students normally use. In that folder, you should have enough copies for students of problems to solve or articles to read, plus self-guiding graphic organizers with questions about the article for students to answer. These stand-alone substitute plans should include tasks and directions that are easy for the substitute to explain and for the students to follow.

All three plans should describe specific tasks, page numbers of resources you expect students to read, daily routines, directions for continuing a lesson or project already in progress, or for locating equipment or materials needed to complete the assignments. Remember to describe the location of your emergency-substitute lesson plan folder or materials for other types of plans as part of the message you leave through the substitute request system.

Managing Student Resources, Services, and Responsibilities

Books

Confirm with the textbook tech or librarian of any student and teacher responsibilities regarding textbooks. Students are usually assigned their own copy of the textbook for which they are responsible in case the book is damaged or lost. Students are generally expected to bring the text to class depending on the week's assignments or the instructional routines involving the text. In some schools, teachers are provided with an additional set of textbooks for students' use in class. Are bookshelves available? Will you need to find additional shelves or places to store different sets of books for the different classes you teach? Classroom texts need to be stored in a place where they can be easily accessed. Or given the limited space for movement in some classrooms, will you have a system where certain students will assist you in distributing the books from the shelves or storage area? If you are sharing a room with another teacher, you will need to plan together where books will be kept.

Note: Approach the school custodian and/or librarian as soon as you can get on campus (or at least before the day that books are issued to students) to secure extra bookcases or carts!

Materials

Where will you store student supplies like paper, pencils, pens, or markers? Do you want students to have access to these items if stored in cabinets or on your desk, or will you distribute them as needed? Will the size of your room, the number of student desks you'll have, and the abundance of students' backpacks placed on the floor limit movement and access to books and materials? After you have decided on your first-week activities, you may want to gather the materials you will need for those activities so that they are easily accessible during those hectic first days of school. If you are sharing a room with another teacher, you will need to plan together how and where items will be stored.

Collecting Student Work

Where will you store student work? With several classes and a potentially growing backlog of uncorrected work, you will need a system for collecting student work. Desk or tabletop plastic file bins for placing hanging files by period or other designations (project, team, or theme) may come in handy. Remember that easy-access systems are for current class *work in progress*, not for permanent storage.

Safety Considerations

If school safety considerations are not covered in a teacher orientation, you may want to ask your department chair or custodian about them. County, city, or district codes may specify the use of certain electrical equipment, cords, surge protectors, and designate how items can be safely stored and stacked. Laboratory and some applied arts classes have guidelines and requirements about the way in which students are to be informed about the appropriate use of materials, safety items, and utilities. You may want to consider creating some posters with guidelines that would direct students to handle equipment and materials properly.

Computer Access

What are the specifics of signed agreements describing the appropriate use of school computers and the Internet? Most districts require that students and parents agree that students will use school technology and the Internet for the express purpose of working on school assignments. Typically, access to most inappropriate sites is automatically blocked by the school's network system. Systems may also be able to track Internet use or searches through student identification numbers used to log into a system. However, many online social networks, new sites, and different ways to access them are discovered by students every day! You will periodically need to remind your students about the school policy when they are using computers in your classroom or when you give them permission to use computers located in the computer lab or library.

PLANNING YOUR ROOM ARRANGEMENT

Depending on the subject matter you teach, your room arrangement may already be determined. Technical classes (fine arts, business, and applied arts) and laboratory sciences have specific resource, equipment, and work-area needs. The number of students and the gear they will likely place on the floor next to their desks is also something to consider.

What to Consider When Arranging Your Room

Accessibility and Safety

Can student desks and chairs be arranged so that students can get to their desks easily? Make sure that bookshelves and other storage areas do not block student access as they enter or leave the room. Do some of your students use wheelchairs? How might desks and other furniture be arranged to allow enough room for students to maneuver their chairs? Check with the head custodian as to whether the layout of your room allows all students to exit it safely.

Proximity, Proximity, Proximity

Proximity is an essential classroom-management strategy. Can students' desks be arranged so that you, the teacher, can move around the room easily? What's the alternative to long rows of desks that face the front of the room, leaving you remote from nearly half your students? These questions are strategic to both arranging your room and preventing off-task behaviors (see Chapter 3).

If space allows, consider a horseshoe or U-shaped configuration for student desks. You may have to play with this a little bit factoring in the location of the door, bookshelves, and space for students to move between rows of desks. In Figure 2.1, desks are grouped around the room (rows usually three to five desks deep), with the open part of the horseshoe facing the board or the front of the classroom. This creates a space near the center of room from where you can use your LCD or overhead projector, model activities, and generally move about being no more than three to five desks away from any student in the room. An option similar to the arrangement in Figure 2.1 involves a room where the door is located in the upper right corner of the layout (toward the front of the classroom). In this case, you might move more desks to deepen the back of the room (i.e., the short side of the *U* shape), freeing space for students to enter and leave the room. Overall, with this arrangement, students face one another much more, diminishing any sense of "students versus teacher" and promoting an atmosphere for a *community of learners*. The small center-stage space also serves as a focal point for demonstrations and presentations by students.

If you decide to have the desks arranged in straight rows, you can split the rows in to two sections by eliminating one desk midway down the rows. This will create an aisle that will allow you to circulate through the classroom more easily.

If you are interested in students doing group work, consider placing desks in groups of four to six. Groupings also allow for easier teacher proximity than straight rows, create more open spaces, and, most important, allow for a variety of teaching strategies and student interaction (see Chapter 4 on community building for some cooperative learning strategies for secondary students).

Figure 2.1	Sample U-Shaped Room Arrangement

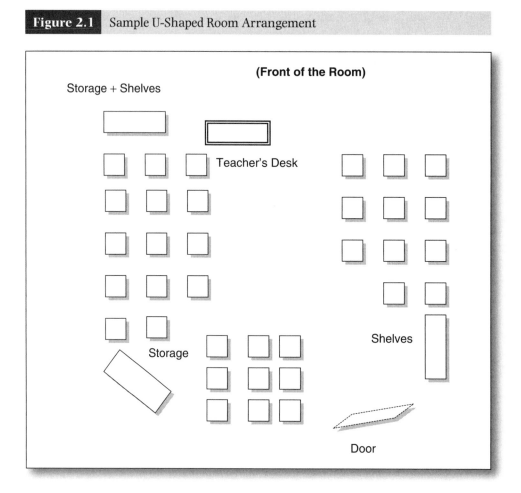

Teacher's Desk and Professional Resource Area

Some teachers like to have their desks front and center in the classroom. Others prefer to have their desks tucked in a corner of the room or by the door. If you anticipate that you may want to speak to students individually from time to time at your desk, you may want to have your desk in a less centralized area. Many teachers choose to have student materials stored away from their desk to create a sense of a more personal workspace.

Ten Tips for Traveling Teachers

Traveling or roving from class to class is a challenging proposition for any teacher. Unfortunately, new teachers are more likely to be given a rotating assignment because of their low rung on the ladder. Such an assignment is best met with good organization and a sense of humor. Over time, you will find opportunities to advocate for better teaching conditions, not just for your convenience but also for improved learning for all students. In the meantime, there are ways to make the best of it. Consider these 10 tips when solving problems related to sharing classrooms:

1. *Inquire about basic furniture.* If you are scheduled as a traveling teacher, find out if you have your own desk in each classroom, a filing cabinet, and shelf space for textbooks and other materials.

2. *Keep asking.* Every teacher should be provided with his or her own basic furniture. If you are not provided with a desk in every room, you should have at least one room or space in the department office where you can store materials or work during your prep period. Unless the issue involves lack of space, you should, in a polite and professional manner, keep inquiring about these items with your department chair, office manager, lead custodian, or perhaps the administrator who hired you.

3. *Assemble portable basics.* Some things you will need to carry from class to class: pencils, pens, markers, a few copies of discipline referrals, the day's lesson-related materials, corrected papers, extra blank overheads, lesson plan and grade book (if not part of an electronic system).

4. *Arrange for sharing.* In time, you will experience the limits to what you can do if asked to teach solely out of a bag or from a rolling cart. Another possibility is to approach the teacher or teachers assigned to the rooms in which you teach to discuss how to share the room, equipment, and storage spaces.

5. *Designate space for basics.* If there is only one desk, ask if you can use the desk to keep a box of basic supplies you will use on a daily basis. Or determine if a table or cabinet can be designated for your supplies, file boxes for student work, past lessons, other teacher resources, and the like.

6. *Make reasonable agreements.* Explore possibilities or reach agreements about the care of equipment and use of materials and wall space to display student work. If the person sharing your room is a veteran sharing it for the first time, he or she may be a bit wary of these arrangements at first. This is where your professionalism and willingness to build cooperative relationships with your colleagues come in to play.

7. *Engage in productive conversations about sharing.* Take time to listen to the concerns of the teacher with whom you will be sharing a room and ask for tips about equipment use, desk arrangement and rearrangement, materials, and basic maintenance. You both have been assigned to share the space, so be sure to voice your needs and challenges.

8. *Plan for securing the room.* Make agreements about locking up or securing the room. If you need to leave in a hurry to get to your next class, it's generally a good idea to lock the door, leaving no unsupervised students.

9. *Find out about prep time use.* Ask about the use of shared room during your prep time. Some teachers are perfectly comfortable having another teacher in the room while they are teaching. Others are not. If you cannot comfortably share the room during prep times, inquire about common department rooms or work spaces that are available for

use during that time. You may want to stock the space with some basic supplies and a place for files.

If challenges persist, if possible, meet with your new-teacher support provider or mentor to discuss related challenges or to rehearse potentially challenging conversations with other teachers or your administrator. Your mentor is likely taking note of certain challenging trends or conditions for new teachers and after a time may be discussing these observations with administrators in an effort to improve conditions overall.

10. *If a significant number of your challenges continue to center on the limitations of room sharing or traveling,* approach the department chair and/or administrator assigned to evaluate and support your professional development this year. Again, an earnest and professional conversation focused on problem solving (rather than blaming) will generally yield positive results.

GETTING ACQUAINTED WITH PEOPLE WHO CAN HELP

One of the most important keys to the secondary classroom is the strength of the relationships you build in this first month. Some sites schedule a new-teacher orientation so that this group of teachers can get acquainted with their new school community at the same time. Sometimes this support is not available in which case you may need to pursue this orientation yourself. School personnel can help you navigate the waters of a secondary school. Working as a secondary teacher means relying on interpersonal skills for dealing with a surprising number of adults. Tapping the knowledge and resources of key personnel is essential to getting what you need to operate successfully in your work community. Understanding each person's respective role is a good place to start.

Before School Starts

The following people can be very helpful to you before school starts:

New-Teacher Mentors/Support Providers

In more and more states and school districts, new teachers are automatically provided with a veteran teacher that will serve as mentor or support provider. In some cases, this mentor is also responsible to help you clear your teaching credential in the first two years of teaching. Mentors do not evaluate, but rather collaborate with you to help you be as successful as possible, often meeting with you on a weekly basis. If school is close to starting and no mentor has appeared, ask your administrator.

In the first few weeks, mentors can help you problem-solve challenges in classroom setup, rules and routines for students, acquiring materials, identifying standards and assessments, generating first-week/month ideas, and any other identified areas of need.

Site Administrators

If there isn't a formal meeting arranged for new teachers to meet administrators, *take the initiative to introduce yourself briefly to the principal and assistant principals.* These administrators ultimately approve special classroom expenditures, field trips, and future professional development opportunities. In the near future, you will be informed as to which of these administrators will be observing and evaluating your classroom practice two to four times during the year.

Office Manager or Principal's Secretary

This individual can be the most influential person at your site, often having worked at the site longer than the last three or four principals combined. They know the school history, how budgets and programs have been administrated over time, and, perhaps, have the deepest knowledge of the human resource pool.

Even though much of the following information is likely posted on the school's Web site, discussing these things with the school office manager will give you a better overall picture of school operations, procedures, possible construction projects, and whom and when to ask for assistance. If possible, set up a time to meet with the office manager or school secretary when he or she can explain things linked to the following:

- A map of the school
- A list of site personnel
- A school handbook for teachers and/or students
- Whom to contact to acquire basic start-up classroom supplies
- Whom to contact regarding procedures for discipline problems

Department Chairperson and/or SLC Teacher Leader

At any secondary school, a department chairperson can usually provide information and answer questions about important issues during the first month of school and beyond. The department chair facilitates department meetings and often sits on schoolwide committees. Many chairs are asked to advise other department members regarding standards-based curriculum, related assessments, rubrics, and securing appropriate materials. Schools organized into interdisciplinary SLCs or middle school houses, have teacher leaders who can guide and inform you about common themes, goals, and the focus of teacher collaborations. If a new-teacher orientation or walk-through does not include contact with members of your department or interdisciplinary team, arrange a time to meet with your department chair or SLC leader before students' arrival to discuss the following:

- How to acquire any teacher-created curriculum maps or units that have already been developed or used by site teachers
- The procedure for obtaining supplies and materials particular to your content curriculum, especially for the first month

- Department goals, objectives, or activities planned for the month (i.e., orientation activities for students, initial assessments)
- General guidelines regarding sharing or equipping rooms
- Information about students' cultural, academic literacy, and linguistic backgrounds

Note: Your teacher mentor may also be able to help you learn about these items as well.

Librarian

The librarian can inform you about the availability of books, research materials, periodicals, videotapes, and use of the Internet by students. *Librarians often coordinate with the textbook manager to order books that supplement the basic curriculum.* At middle schools, alternative, and smaller high schools, often, the librarian is also the textbook manager.

Textbook Manager

The textbook manager is responsible for disseminating and tracking the assignment of course textbooks. The textbook manager or "bookroom person" is also knowledgeable about teacher guides that accompany texts and other supplemental materials. You may periodically need to coordinate with this manager about obtaining widely used texts.

Lead Custodian and Room Custodian

Befriend the people who clean your room! As well as invaluable maintenance, the school custodian can demonstrate how to use the utilities in the room (phone system, heating); provide you with basic furniture when needed and remove unneeded furniture and equipment; replace and repair whiteboards, large maps, charts, mounted video equipment, or light fixtures; and, basically, help you get by in your physical room arrangement.

Attendance Technicians

Accurate attendance taking finances the school and helps to provide your paycheck. Clarify with the attendance technicians your basic daily attendance-monitoring responsibilities. In the next few weeks, attendance personnel may follow up on student absences with parent contacts.

Bilingual Support Staff

Many administrative assistants in charge of attendance and other student services are proficient in the home language of your students. If you do not speak the primary language of your students and their parents, ask the office manager which staff members are able and available to help you make home contacts.

Administrators in Charge of Discipline

This person can provide an overview of discipline procedures and forms for new staff. Before making contact, it can be helpful to review a copy of a student handbook or student rules and think of questions you might pose to that administrator about teacher responsibilities for enforcing school rules and intervening in student misbehaviors.

When School Is Underway

After the first few weeks of school, the following are also important people to know in forming a valuable team that will serve your students.

Second-Language Resource Specialists, Bilingual Resource Teachers, and Migrant Resource Specialists

These experienced classroom teachers assess and monitor the progress of students whose primary language is not English. They can offer suggestions regarding appropriate materials, special funding for resources, and information about how students are assigned to various classes. Many students who appear to speak English well fall under the domain of these specialists because they have not yet reached *academic proficiency* in English.

Special Education Teachers

Many special education students are placed for part of their day in mainstream classes, and you will be responsible for adapting curriculum to their learning needs. You may be given a list of students' names during the first week of school, or you may need to request one. Special education teachers are usually assigned to teach language arts, math, and history. They can offer insights to you as to how to promote appropriate behavior and productivity for these sometimes challenging students. *If you are a beginning special education teacher, approach the special education department chair and district coordinator prior to the start of school for the particular requirements of the program.*

Instructional Aides

If you are fortunate enough to have an instructional aide, you may not meet them until his or her contract year begins, usually when students arrive. Set aside some time to have lunch with your aide to talk about how your students might benefit from his or her guidance. Many experienced aides are quite knowledgeable about procedures, equipment, books, and routines at the site or department. Be prepared to work with them as your teaching partner, especially in facilitating group work for students with additional needs, such as struggling readers or English Language Learners.

Campus Security Supervisors

With concerns including tardiness, defiant behavior, and safety, working with campus security supervisors becomes a necessary part of school life. These individuals generally maintain a high profile to ensure students move on to class when expected or to bring students to the office to deal with discipline concerns. Introduce yourself to supervisors in charge of your part of the campus and familiarize yourself with the appropriate situations in which to use their support.

Counseling and Student Services Specialists

As problems with chronic misconduct or concerns about appropriate placement of students arise, you may need to speak to student counselors or other student-services specialists. These specialists track students' credit standing, class schedule, referrals, teacher recommendations, and special program needs. They can provide information or referrals about college, career goals, conflict resolution, drug and alcohol counseling, peer counseling, and student leadership training.

School Nurse and Other Health Services Personnel

Schools usually have part- or full-time nurses on-site. These individuals can assist students who get sick while at school, administer prescribed medications, provide first aid, and be responsible for contacting parents about sick or injured students. They also keep track of student health histories that are part of enrollment information packets, records for immunization, and lists of students with vision or hearing problems. They can provide support and referral information for students with health-related issues that affect their school performance, including drug or alcohol use, depression, or pregnancy.

USING A COMPREHENSIVE CHECKLIST

We conclude with a checklist to help you move through the preparation tasks in a systematic way (see Figure 2.2). You might want to reference it during your first few visits to the school site. The to-go list includes nuts-and-bolts items discussed in this chapter and a few other things to consider after the first couple of weeks of school. Some information and certain school documents might be available through the school's Web site. Several items listed under Curriculum Resources may be available through your state government's department of education Web site. Use the column on the far left to note things you want to know more about. As you contact school personnel, survey the contents of your classroom(s), and begin to organize resources from school or acquired on your own, use the second column to check off items you've learned about or already have in place. The last column can be used for miscellaneous notes about the items.

Figure 2.2	Nuts and Bolts To-Go List

Teacher Resource	✓	Notes and Reminders • Contact person or other support personnel • Location, guidelines, procedures, scheduling • Things to do; reminders
Classroom(s)		
❑ Room keys		
❑ School map		
❑ Bell schedules: block days, special rally, or testing days		
❑ How to operate utilities (heat, air-conditioning, phone, alarms, and other room safety features)		
❑ How to submit requests for repair or work orders for moving furniture		
General Supplies and Equipment		
❑ Plan book for semester/year		
❑ Roll book/grade book plus information for using school's electronic grading and attendance system		
❑ Teacher handbook		
❑ Course description pamphlet		
❑ Student handbook		
❑ Binder paper		
❑ Construction paper for student projects (white and assorted colors)		
❑ Easel-size poster paper		
❑ Easel-size paper stand		
❑ Overhead transparencies and pens		
❑ Miscellaneous teacher's desk supplies: pens, pencils, markers, assorted Post-its, Scotch tape, masking tape, glue, three-hole punch, stapler, staples, paper clips, and assorted binder clips (for large stacks of paper)		
❑ First-aid kit		
❑ Teacher computer and printer		
❑ Desktop computer(s)		

(Continued)

Figure 2.2 (Continued)

❏ Cart for printer or other audio-video equipment		
❏ Overhead or Elmo document projector plus cart		
❏ Additional chairs and desk set ups for relatively large, heavy-set students		
Content-Specific Supplies		
❏ Calculators		
❏ Compasses, protractors		
❏ Globes, wall maps		
❏ Storage containers, tanks (multiple sizes)		
❏ Science lab experiment supplies		
❏ Science-related safety equipment, cleaning materials, protective gear		
❏ Applied- and fine-arts class supplies; yearbook and drama club supplies		*Note*: If you teach any of these subjects or activity clubs, you should start a separate list of materials you'll need.
Student Books and Support Materials		
❏ Copies of assigned text, student workbooks		
❏ Teacher's guides		
❏ Bilingual versions of adopted text		
❏ Supplemental books (dictionaries, references, thesauri, bilingual dictionaries)		
❏ Audio-visual resources to supplement curriculum (video and DVD library, primary sources)		
❏ Written procedures or guidelines for teachers and students to obtain texts (e.g., scheduling, time limits, lost books)		
❏ Scantron or forms for automated test scoring		
Curriculum Resources		
❏ Subject matter framework		
❏ Sample syllabus of your courses		
❏ Content standards and benchmarks for students		
❏ Model or sample curriculum for courses		
❏ Supplementary resources for specific text or program adoptions (additional software with templates for teacher and student use, additional articles, worksheets, DVDs)		

Teacher Support Services		
❏ Prep or teacher work areas, restrooms, faculty lunch areas		
❏ Substitute-request system		
❏ On-site suspension areas		
❏ Procedure for contacting campus security personnel		
Important People to Meet and Work With		
❏ Beginning teacher mentors		
❏ All site administrators (in general)		
❏ Office manager and/or school secretary		
❏ Librarian		
❏ Textbook manager		
❏ Attendance technician		
❏ Administrators in charge of discipline		
❏ Lead custodian		
❏ Campus security		
❏ Special education staff		
Procedural Forms to Have on Hand		
❏ Hall pass for sending students to the suspension or detention center		
❏ Discipline referral forms; behaviors indicated for interventions by administrators		
❏ Student referral forms; teacher request for health or other services on a student's behalf		
❏ Student hall passes (to the bathroom, for errands in the office or other classrooms)		
Other Forms		
❏ Student acknowledgment or job-well-done, (half-page) forms for students and/or parents		
❏ Field trip request form and permission slips		
❏ Substitute-request verification form (usually signed after your absence)		
❏ Monthly employment verification form		
❏ Request for supplies form		
❏ Purchase-order request form		

3

Rules, Routines, and Procedures

The Basics for Daily Classroom Management

I thought the lesson was going great! But at some point, I know that many students weren't actually paying attention.

Establishing and maintaining an effective learning environment involves many components of classroom management and an understanding of other key factors. You'll soon confirm that middle and high school students can be endearing, funny, insightful, and excruciatingly challenging. Although their academic achievement levels, literacy proficiencies, and sociocultural backgrounds may differ, patterns in students' feelings about school are similar. Most began their educational histories with excitement and curiosity. Many have had consistently positive school experiences. They are generally eager to be in school and want to learn. For some, despite this eagerness and willingness to learn, school is a place of constant struggle against feelings of inadequacy, isolation, self-doubt, or sometimes boredom in response to what they believe is meaningless busywork. Some students view the classroom as an oasis from outside circumstances that may put them at risk.

All students are capable of learning. They bring their multidimensional strengths as well as their challenges to your classroom. School and nonschool experiences combined enable each one to make connections to rigorous academic concepts with some level of instructional support. Students want to be challenged and held to high standards and meaningful expectations. They would also like their teachers to support them in meeting those expectations. Although they may display indifferent or oppositional behavior from time to time, adolescents prefer to treat one another, their teacher, and the school environment with respect, and they expect the same treatment in return.

In the last few years, more and more students and their families have expressed concerns about safety issues on or near school campuses. Data indicate that secondary schools in urban communities with high crime rates, gang activity, and/or high percentages of families living at the poverty level experience more instances of fighting among students, and even violent crimes, as compared to schools in other types of socioeconomic communities. However, students attending school in other communities are not immune from this worrisome trend. The national news periodically reports incidents in suburban or small-town schools involving students committing or threatening to commit bodily harm to teachers and other students. If you teach in communities where safety has become a growing concern, you may need to take extra care in the way you create and implement preventions and interventions, as well as certain rules, routines, and procedures. Your students will value the reassurance of your intention to make your classroom a safe and respectful haven for learning.

So how exactly do you create a class environment that consistently fosters respect? Start by presuming students want to believe that you control their learning environment. Older students appreciate clear, consistent routines and rules that promote safety and respect. They are especially sensitive to issues of fairness and how they are treated in front of their peers. Before students walk through your classroom door, it is essential that you are clear as to your expectations for respectful behavior, instructional procedures, assignments, and class participation. It is also important to create opportunities for adolescents to reflect on their behavior and take responsibility for managing certain aspects of the class. As you convey that your learning environment is based on maintaining respect for one another's right to learn and upholding routines that support academic progress, your students will flourish.

The first few days and weeks of the semester are the most critical period for establishing an effective learning environment. The heart of a well-managed classroom is an engaging curriculum plus the following elements:

1. Positive student–student and student–teacher relationships

2. Preventions and interventions for student discipline

3. Explicit expectations of rules, routines, and procedures

4. Opportunities for students to reflect on their participation and learning goals and take responsibility for managing aspects of the learning environment

Consistently and equitably orchestrating these processes for your students creates and maintains an effective learning environment.

THE VALUE OF RELATIONSHIPS

Secondary teachers teach 40 to 150 more students a day than elementary teachers. Despite these daunting numbers, fostering productive, positive relationships with students is still a worthy goal. Teaching students to learn subject matter concepts is indeed your primary goal. Yet, providing opportunities that allow you and your students to learn about and acknowledge one another's experiences, opinions, interests, and challenges will help to improve conditions for learning academic concepts. Supporting all class members (yourself included) to consider one another's perspectives, as well as academic content, conveys a motivating belief that all of your adolescent students are intelligent and capable and care deeply about people and ideas.

There are many ways to promote respectful relationships with adolescent students before, during, and after instruction. Success lies in the consistent and respectful manner in which you greet and address students, appropriately reference aspects of their lives or perspectives during instruction, and organize the classroom to be an inviting and comfortable place to learn. Such actions foster positive relationships and are like money in the bank as you support and challenge students to reach high academic goals.

PREVENTION AND INTERVENTIONS BEFORE DISCIPLINE

To develop a specific set of rules, routines, and procedures, we suggest that you consider how the concept of preventions and interventions impact the overall management of your class. When teachers focus on preventions, the need for interventions and further disciplinary actions involving school administrators often decreases. Start the year by concentrating on implementing each of the preventions listed in Figure 3.1. Except for times when a high-priority school rule is broken (see Removal and Administrative Intervention), save the interventions toward the end of the list for when you have reached the end of your patience and goodwill.

Note: Implementing our recommendations in the later section, Rules, Routines, and Procedures, is one form of prevention.

Preventions

Preventions are routine actions teachers orchestrate to prevent off-task behaviors, keep a class focused and engaged, and promote a mutually respectful learning environment.

1. Noncontingent Reinforcements (Relationship Builders)

Displaying culturally relevant posters with images of teenagers, as well as utilizing activities, contexts, cultural icons, and topics featuring positive

| **Figure 3.1** | Quick List of Preventions and Interventions |

Preventions

1. Noncontingent reinforcements (relationship builders)

2. Positive parent contact

3. Room arrangement and proximity

4. Implementation of rules, routines, and procedures

5. Attention signal, wait time

6. Check for understanding—whole class

7. Target talk—acknowledging expected behaviors

8. Praise, prompt, leave

9. Use of instructional time, pacing, and engagement

10. Neutrality

Interventions

1. Check for understanding—individualized

2. Verbal limit setting

3. Broken record

4. Change setting

5. Parent contact

6. Removal and administrative intervention

aspects of students' lives, demonstrates your awareness of students' experiences and interests. A quick acknowledgment (preferably not in front of the entire class) of a student's accomplishments in other endeavors also builds positive relationships. Greeting students casually when you see them in the quad, at your door before class, or during afterschool events helps build your relationships in an important way. At the start of the semester, you might stage partner interviews or group poster projects linking their experiences to a subject-related topic (see Chapter 4). Some schools encourage teachers to communicate with students and their families via the school's e-mail system. Although e-mail contact is primarily intended to inform parents of student's academic progress or to allow parents to communicate with teachers, it may also be permissible to use e-mail to send quick congratulations or encouragement to students.

Note: We encourage you to review your school's policy and guidelines regarding the appropriate use of school e-mail for communicating with students and parents.

Your room décor could also include a few items that represent your dimensions as an individual. As students walk by pictures of you and the people, places, and events you hold dear, they get a sense of who you are beyond the person who puts them through academic paces. From time to time, you might selectively share an anecdote about something that happened over the weekend or recall how a friend, family member, or you as a student their age reacted to a topic, dilemma, or problem examined in class.

2. Positive Parent Contact

Building relationships with students and their families by acknowledging positive student behaviors can also be a key prevention strategy. A positive parent contact can take less than a minute and make a big impression on students and parents alike. Considering students from among all your combined classes, think of 8 to 10 who, based on the last couple of weeks, deserve some type of positive acknowledgment. Half of the students could be those who have recently turned in some exceptional work; the other half might be students who have struggled with some aspect of learning but have recently demonstrated remarkable improvement. If you don't speak the home language of a student's family, you might approach a staff member who does to assist you in leaving a brief message. Invest a few minutes a week to complete and send preformatted "job well done" notes, write a few strategic e-mails, or leave phone messages to parents or guardians about their students' accomplishments. (See Chapter 12 on communicating with parents for sample parent notes in English and Spanish.)

You may find that parents or guardians tend to participate less frequently in activities like back-to-school nights, open houses, or schoolwide fundraising events once their children are in middle or high school. The reasons vary and may include the belief that these students are "old enough" to navigate the system independently or because parents also have younger children who need their attention more. Don't give up on school events as an opportunity to make positive parent contacts! For back to school night, you might want to prepare a one-page handout that briefly introduces who you are, your professional preparation, the name and focus of the courses you teach, your general expectations for students, your contact information, and your hopes for working collaboratively with parents. Before you distribute it, request that a willing colleague, your mentor, or your friend proofread the page for any awkward passages or ideas that you don't intend to convey. On the day after the event, provide copies of the page to students whose parents could not attend.

Go ahead and ask! If your students are with their parents at afterschool games, club activities, or fundraising events, ask them to introduce you. Depending on their availability during school hours, some parents will accept your invitation to chaperone field trips. Others may be able to help organize schoolwide fundraising efforts or participate in school activities connected to their hobbies, interests, cultural traditions, or work in the community. Remember to ask!

3. Room Arrangement and Proximity

How you arrange your classroom can eliminate a number of potential problems in classroom management. Without saying a word, your proximity to students prevents a number of misbehaviors. In a traditional seating arrangement of straight rows facing front, the dynamic is clear: them versus you. Students can hide behind one another, and if you aren't constantly moving up and down rows, students toward the back can easily tune you out. What are some alternatives?

- *Horseshoe or U-shaped desk arrangement.* See Chapter 2 for a visual of this U-shaped configuration (Figure 2.1), which leaves a space in the middle of the room where (1) the teacher can move around and be no more than a few feet away from anyone and (2) students can get up and model a procedure or skill. As students face other students, that sense of students versus the solitary teacher is diminished.
- *Small groups.* Some teachers will place students together bringing four to six desks into small groups. This arrangement also allows for easy teacher proximity around the room. It has the additional advantage of allowing for a variety of teaching strategies where students assist one another and work together in cooperative groups.

In some classrooms, the room arrangement is dictated for you, by such things as lab tables, computer stations, or table islands. This is challenging when you attempt to use proximity to focus students' attention. Some of you may have classrooms equipped with a SMART Board and a wireless pad that allows you to manipulate board input from any part of the room. Short of that, you can create different focal points for small-group instruction using chart paper and an easel as your board. In these larger, lab-type rooms use the board at the front of the room and the chart stand or overhead projector at the back, allowing you to teach from both ends of the room. Make sure there is adequate space between rows and clusters of desks through which you can move easily around the room, and pause for a while, continuing to teach or direct students as you stand near those who are tempted toward off-task behavior. Be prepared to be everywhere!

4. Defining and Practicing Rules, Routines, and Procedures

Many new teachers assume that adolescent students should "know better" by this age and begin without establishing rules or specific routines and procedures. Often, teachers expect that the strength of the content combined with their enthusiasm for teaching it will provide enough structure and focus for students. Unfortunately, this is rarely enough. Rules of behavior and expectations for learning need to be presented from the start, taught rather than told, and reviewed periodically throughout the quarter, semester, and year. We discuss specifics about rules in detail later in this chapter.

5. *Attention Signal and Wait Time*

Attention signals including chimes, bells, or gongs are becoming increasingly popular among secondary teachers. When you engage students in small-group work or other active tasks, it is helpful to have a distinct attention-getting sound other than your voice to signal time to stop everything and listen to instruction or directions. In some contexts, middle school teachers might combine the use of a chime or clapping three times immediately followed by counting down (starting from 10) until all students are quiet. (Hopefully that's by the time you are down to the number 1.)

Suddenly pausing instruction or using what is referred to as "wait time" is often an effective way to refocus students' attention. When employing wait time, your abrupt silence and body language should convey that you are momentarily stopping all instructional action until students are focused only on you. When using an attention signal combined with wait time, the idea is to pause after the signal (perhaps up to 20 seconds), waiting until you have students' complete attention before speaking. When you are first establishing this prevention, and students respond to it appropriately, commend them on their response to the procedure. If students do not respond quickly, neutrally repeat your expectations about the attention signal and your confidence that their response will improve the next time.

6. *Check for Understanding*

Once you have established certain rules, routines, and procedures, you can decrease misbehaviors by taking a moment to *check for understanding*. Use this method during the first month to help students internalize your rules, routines, and expectations for their behavior. It can also decrease off-task behaviors by helping students to remember what they need to do to complete an assignment! Here are a few ways to check for understanding:

- *Who can tell me?* (a twist on the traditional approach)
  - Whenever possible, help students focus by providing a hard copy or displaying an outline of directions for completing a task. If you can only provide directions verbally, or even when you can refer to visuals, checking for understanding minimizes confusion about assigned tasks, a common reason given by students for not paying attention. Covering up or asking students not to look at the directions for a moment say, "Raise your hands if you can repeat the directions for this assignment." If all hands are raised, say, "Good! Now turn to a partner, and in less than one minute, the taller student will repeat the directions to his or her partner. The other partner should speak up if he or she wants to add or correct something." If you ask the question and only some hands are raised, ask those students to keep their hands raised while you select one of them to repeat the directions to the class. Without commenting on what the first student says, ask another student to add or correct the directions just stated. Ask another student to do the same until the directions are complete and

accurate. End by quickly restating the directions. The whole process should take less than five to six minutes.

- *Thumbs-Up* (especially effective for middle school)
  - ○ Here's a way for students to confirm their understanding of ideas or directions without saying a word. Pose a total of four or five true/false questions about an assignment to which students are to respond with *thumbs-up* or *thumbs-down*. Here are two examples: "This next assignment needs to have a minimum of a three-paragraph response" (true—thumbs-up, false—thumbs-down). "You have the option of working with a partner" (true—thumbs-up, false—thumbs-down). Conclude this check for understanding with a quick summary of the directions in written form highlighted on the board, on an overhead transparency, or in the textbook.

- *Fist to Five* (also effective for middle school)
  - ○ By holding up zero to five fingers, students demonstrate whether the directions or concepts were clearly presented. "If the explanation (or directions) were absolutely clear, show me by holding up five fingers. Almost clear, four fingers . . . zero, not clear at all." If most students hold up four to five fingers, ask a person holding up five fingers to restate the explanation or directions. If at least half of the students have three fingers up, you will need to reexplain the concepts or directions and write them in some form for the whole class to see.

7. Target Talk—Acknowledging Expected Behaviors

Often, teachers become overly focused on misbehaving students. A key prevention is to remember to praise or give *targeted talk* to acknowledge a student or group performing tasks as expected. Positive public acknowledgment of students helps to further establish and maintain your stated expectations. Try to acknowledge pairs, triads, or clusters of students, as most adolescents are generally uncomfortable about being singled out, even for positive behaviors.

When a teacher provides targeted talk or acknowledgment of specific behaviors, this becomes more helpful to students than a simple, "Good job!" Target talk helps students know what they did correctly so they can recreate that behavior. For example, "70% of our class turned in yesterday's assignment with all of the worksheets attached. Good job." "Thank you to those students who began the bell assignment before the tardy bell rang." "I noticed that a number of groups are working on the extra credit assignments. I commend your efforts!" "Yesterday, all of you were engaged and completed the first two group-work tasks on the agenda before I was ready to move on to the next thing!"

8. Praise, Prompt, Leave

This strategy can be particularly effective for students who are especially challenged if required to focus on something for longer periods. After you've checked students' understanding about an assignment, and you make your way around the room as students work on the task, support persistently unfocused students by using your proximity to

- praise—acknowledge specific aspects of the work students are doing correctly.
- prompt—point out the next task or encourage them to continue their efforts, "Now, find one more example to support your idea."
- leave—reinforce that the next move is up to the student as you continue your way around the room to support others.

After a few minutes, come back around to further that student's progress with the same praise-prompt-leave approach.

9. Use of Instructional Time, Pacing, and Engagement

Often, the best manager of adolescent energy is instructional pacing and engagement (see Chapter 1 regarding adolescents and time-management challenges). Transitioning through four to six different types of learning activities in a 55-minute period or 80-minute block period keeps students moving and interested. Posting and referring intermittently to a daily agenda of outcomes and tasks supports pacing for you as well as your students (see Routines later in this chapter). When students are working on long-term projects in class, you can break up the time with student progress reports, short segments when new input is presented either by you or through a short article or video clip. A teacher's engaging lessons, enthusiastic modeling, use of varied resources, and passion for the content also contribute toward keeping students on task and focused on learning.

10. Neutrality

Try to use a neutral tone when acknowledging or stating expected behavior or when addressing challenging behaviors. Neutrality can be near impossible when frustration is high. However, when you react with emotion, students hear the tone and not the directions. Your impact will be greatest when you deliver your intended message with the type of clarity that anger often obscures.

Interventions

The majority of students will respond to preventions, most of the time. However, for various reasons, there may still be a few who resist following rules, routines, and procedures. Even if you have been alerted to certain at-risk students ahead of time, it's best to establish preventions for your class as a whole, as outlined earlier. You need to develop the willingness of the majority of students to maintain an effective learning environment. With the majority of students focused in a well-managed class, you will be better able to give more-challenging students the particular attention they may need. Consider the following interventions to refocus attention to learning.

1. Individualized Check for Understanding

Some students may need you to talk to them individually and with neutrality to clarify your expectations for behavior. Ask the student to relate the understanding he or she has about expectations for appropriate language, behavior in a group, and the like. If the student offers no clarification, this is your opportunity to restate your expectations, in the spirit of supporting that student to be successful in your class. As soon as the student shows evidence of attempting to follow your expectations, give him or her positive feedback to reinforce a step in the right direction.

2. Verbal Limit Setting

This particular intervention generally works with younger students, and in some secondary settings, it may not have the same impact. However, if you have implemented many of the preventions listed and have fostered positive relationships among the majority of students in a class, the occasional use of verbal limit setting can be effective.

When a particularly resistant student or group of students cannot sustain expected behavior, using a neutral tone of voice, you may need to state something firmly to the student(s). In essence, you want to set or quickly reinforce a limit to a certain behavior. "Please put away the photo album from home and get back to the assignment." "Please remember to use respectful language in class." "Make it possible for students to concentrate on these word problems. Please stop the side conversations." As you do this, you are defining what is not acceptable and restating what is acceptable.

Note: Setting limits on students' use of cell phones in class has become an ongoing problem in many schools. Most schools expect students to turn cell phones off while in class, but verbal limit setting will probably be necessary on occasion. See ideas listed under Rules, Routines, and Procedures.

3. Broken Record

You may find yourself needing to repeat certain directions or verbal limit-setting statements with an individual student who is insistent on debating you in front of the whole class. This method is also one that generally works with younger students who don't necessarily have a history of acting out. If done in a neutral manner and in classes where you know that your expectations are widely known and accepted by other students, it may be effective with older students who may need extra reminding. With each of these students, we hope that you have previously tried checking for understanding and verbal limit setting. Using the broken-record approach means neutrally, without engaging in an argument or raising your voice, repeating a rule or expectation known to all students in response to any ongoing arguments by an individual student. It is very important to state it as neutrally as possible and to pause to regain your composure and give the student a chance to comply between your broken-record statements. Avoid arguing, defending the expectation, closing in on the student, or involving other students in the exchange. Remember that if your other students understand the rules and your expectations for the most part, the issue is probably not about the soundness of either.

4. Change Setting

High school teachers are more apt to forego the broken-record method and decide that it is time to ask students to move to another part of the classroom to keep certain students from distracting others. You might even ask the student to move in a friendly but exasperated tone of voice. In some cases, you may need to speak to a student individually (i.e., not in earshot of the rest of the class), stating neutrally that the move is a temporary solution that would benefit the student and others. If a student is not, necessarily, defiant but seems unable to work productively during class, approach the student, and request that he or she speak to you for just a moment just outside your classroom. Quickly ask what the problem is. Restate the expectation for working productively during class, and suggest that the student has the choice of coming to your classroom at lunchtime or after school to make up for time wasted or return to class and refocus his or her energy immediately.

Some middle school teachers make an informal arrangement with the teacher next door or a *buddy teacher* for students who need to have a different setting for a few minutes or a class period. In this case, students can be sent with an assignment to work in the other teacher's classroom. This allows both teacher and/or student a cooling-off period and reserves using the administration as a resource for the most serious offenses.

5. Parent Contact

Parent contact was listed earlier as a positive prevention, and it can come into play as an intervention. The goal of positive parental contact is to foster parents' willingness to become team members in maintaining an effective learning environment. If a student is chronically breaking rules or is uncooperative, it may be time to make a parent contact to address inappropriate behaviors by the student:

1. Share a key expectation or rule linked to a set of behaviors

2. Describe the difficulty the student is having with your expectation and behaviors

3. Represent the contact (usually by phone) as an opportunity to problem solve how to support the student to be more successful in your class.

If you do not speak the same language as your students' parents, there are usually office personnel or bilingual teachers who can help you make these contacts. If you are unable to find translators on site, ask an administrator for some assistance.

6. Removal and Administrative Intervention

Earlier in this chapter, we noted that *students want to believe that you control their learning environment. If a student is misbehaving in such a way or to such an extent that he or she has compromised this belief among your other students, it may be time to consider (temporary) removal from your classroom as an intervention.* If a student is not necessarily aggressive toward you but is clearly not responding to preventions, other interventions, or repeated requests to follow your class rules, you may want to consider the option of removal. Call a campus supervisor to escort the student to the detention center. During your prep time or after school, you will probably need to make another parent contact and/or set up a face-to-face meeting as soon as possible with the parent, student, and possibly a site administrator.

Note: How the school's detention center works and what teachers should do if they need a student to go there is something to look into as part of your initial nuts-and-bolts tour of the school!

If a student is insubordinate toward you to the degree of cursing, threatening, or posturing at you, it is time to call the office to request that an administrator or campus supervisor come to your room and escort the student directly to the office. In either of these cases of removal, you will probably need to fill out some type of school detention or suspension form describing your reasons for having the student removed.

It is important that you review the school handbook or other documents describing the school's discipline policy, schoolwide rules, specific consequences for breaking those rules, and what teachers are required to do if students break these rules in their presence. In other words, do not attempt to deal with the following types of situations on your own. Behaviors and school rules that fall under this category typically involve students (1) fighting with or threatening to hurt another student, (2) being under the influence of or possessing drugs or alcohol in school, (3) refusing to follow student dress-code policies designed to deter promotion of gang activity or drug use, (4) speaking to or taunting another student in a manner that conveys sexual harassment (see policy specifics), (5) possible theft, (6) carrying weapons, (7) intentional destruction of school property, and (8) outright insubordination toward or threats made to a teacher.

Note: The increase in plagiarism is a growing concern in middle and high school communities. Some schools have addressed this matter in their schoolwide rules and consequences. In addition to related guidelines about plagiarism described in the student handbook, other schools address this topic as part of first week or first month community-building activities. Eliciting students' opinions through short essay prompts about why students plagiarize or ways to avoid situations that may result in plagiarizing may help to facilitate discussions that support students to make different decisions.

RULES, ROUTINES, AND PROCEDURES

Rules

Rules apply to behaviors that are expected at all times in your class. There need not be many basic rules, but they should be focused on protecting the rights of all students to learn and their teacher to teach. Remember that you will also be responsible for maintaining schoolwide rules. To be able to refer to rules to reinforce expected behaviors, students should have a copy of the rules and the rules should be posted in the classroom in large enough print so that students can read them from their desks. Figure 3.2 provides an example of classroom rules and bulleted details, which are optional for posters or handouts.

Figure 3.2	Examples of Class Rules

Treat all people in this class with respect.

- Remember that all students in this class have the right to learn and that the teacher has the right to teach.

- Ask yourself, "Will what I'm about to say or do positively contribute to learning?" "Will my words and actions show respect for other students, the teacher, and myself?"

Attend every day, and do your best at all times.

- Be here and participate! Focus on your work and the ideas you're learning. Ask questions if you are unclear about certain assignments or ideas. Persist!

- Avoid distractions and disturbances (i.e., turn off cell phones and music devices).

- Be thoughtful and thorough about assignments. Aim to complete and turn in homework assignments, long-term assignments, and group and individual tasks on time.

Come prepared each day with the appropriate materials.

- Bring your books and materials to class! Think about materials you will need tomorrow, this week, and next!

Take care of materials associated with this class.

- Treat books, tools, displays, furniture, and other resources with respect. They are your tools for learning.

Student Involvement in Creating Classroom Rules and Expectations

Of course, there are rules that apply to all students, schoolwide. And establishing a set of rules for your classroom is your prerogative. At the start of the semester, some teachers involve students in creating some class rules and expectations or reflecting on some you may have already identified. This can be a valuable use of time; students often have more buy-in and are more willing to self-monitor when they are able to think through the purpose of each rule from their point of view. It is a powerful learning experience for students to see their peers use commonsense thinking to contribute to a decision usually made by an adult. If you choose to involve students, consider the following steps:

1. *Define expected behaviors.* One way to get a big-picture view of rules is to have students divide a sheet of paper in thirds, labeling the three sections *students*, *teachers*, and *parents*. They can write two or three ideas in each

column about what are expected behaviors for successful students, effective teachers, and parents who want to support their children as students.

2. *Pool ideas and knowledge.* Ask students to share their ideas about expected behaviors with a partner. Each set of partners then teams up with another set to form a group of four. The task of the group is to come to consensus about what it considers the two most important expected behaviors for students, teachers, and parents.

3. *Collaborate to define and prioritize rules.* Each group presents its report on expected behaviors to the class while the teacher records ideas on an overhead or poster paper. Guide students to detect common patterns in the group reports. You will likely see many ideas that you would have arrived at if you had designed your classroom rules and expectations.

4. *Participate as teacher.* Add to the list your ideas of items the students missed. Thank each class for their input, reminding them that you will determine the final list of rules and expectations that will serve all the classes you teach. Over the next few days, incorporate the rules into your preventions, checking for understanding frequently and noting positive behavior identified in the rules.

Consequences

If a student has broken one of the eight types of site-based rules listed under Removal and Administrator Intervention, you are probably required to have an administrator deal with the student directly. Remember, if rules are established in a classroom environment that has preventions, interventions, strong relationships, and engaging curriculum, the need for consequences decreases. However, some students may be truly resistant to following rules and meeting your expectations. If you send a letter home to parents at the beginning of the year describing your course, grading system, and other items, you might include a list of your rules and consequences. Here is a sample progression of consequences:

1. If a student persistently does not follow class rules and expectations, you may do the following:
   a. Speak to the student individually, clarify the rule, and warn of further consequences
   b. Refer the student to detention center during class or have the student come back to your classroom for detention during lunch or after school to finish assignments that were not completed because of misbehavior during class time

2. If the student does not go to detention as expected, you should contact the student's parent or guardian by phone to discuss the misbehavior and the student's refusal to go to detention.

   Note on the phone that if the student's behavior does not change, you plan to initiate a behavior contract that lists specific expectations and behaviors organized so that the student can rate, from one to five, how he or she is doing as far as expected behavior for each day the contract is in effect. Your school may already have a contract form including items intended to address the student's current behavior regarding schoolwide expectations (e.g., cutting classes.) Let the parent know that if such a contract is necessary, you will notify the parent by phone or e-mail that the student has signed a contract and you will update the parent as to the student's progress.

3. The student should show you the contract at the end of the week so you can discuss progress being made. If there is no significant change in student behavior, you should arrange to meet with the student, parent, and a site administrator to problem solve and find other ways to ensure the student will improve his or her behavior.

   Note: If at any time a student becomes insubordinate or threatening in reaction to any of these consequences, "go past Go" and ask that a campus supervisor or site administrator come to your classroom to accompany the student to the office for possible suspension.

Note to alternative education teachers: Many alternative education schools with a large number of at-risk students have their own internal systems for supporting students to change their behavior. These schools often adopt schoolwide incentive programs for referring, encouraging, or warning students regarding their behavior. At-risk students often need additional counseling support to examine the causes of their behavior and an explicit plan to address each behavior that impedes their success. A long-range plan for behavior management may be a larger task for a team of adults to design rather than an isolated effort by a single teacher.

> Keep records of consequences and interventions for individual students. This will become important if you participate in a parent conference. You can note interventions on individual cards or on a page in your roll book.

Administrative Intervention

As noted earlier, you may need to ask an administrator to intervene to support you in carrying out more-serious consequences to student misbehaviors. Because administrators support teachers in their discipline process, they generally expect the teacher to have documented other items related to school expectations, such as any unexcused absences or tardies and previous actions or consequences (e.g., conferences with the student, detention, parent contacts, contracts, and meetings with the parent and student).

Some infractions are appropriate to refer to administrators immediately such as suspicion of drug use or fighting and others described earlier under Removal and Administrative Intervention.

Routines

A routine refers to a set of actions occurring on a daily basis in a classroom, usually directed by the teacher. Examples of a teacher's daily classroom routines include the following:

- Prepare for class by completing a lesson plan, gathering necessary materials and documents, as well as creating graphics and additional resources as needed.

- Take attendance and make announcements particular to your class about upcoming deadlines, assignments, reminders about the proper treatment of materials, equipment, and the like.
- Make schoolwide announcements generated by other staff members or students about items of concern outside your class.
- Write the agenda on the board or overhead, as well as the transition work, bell work, warm-up assignments, homework assignments, and other timely reminders. Refer to these items verbally as appropriate during the period.
- Provide students with bell work or another transition activity to complete as they enter the room each day.
- Check homework for quality or completion. Students self-correct homework or turn it in for teacher correction.
- Check intermittently for understanding regarding any rules or directions that may need special attention or reinforcement.
- Follow schoolwide routines at prescribed times during the day like a common binder check and all-school sustained silent reading (SSR), if instituted at your school.

Procedures

A procedure is generally a set of sequenced student actions related to a specific task with minimal teacher involvement. Teachers will want to teach a number of procedures that students are expected to follow to complete tasks, such as the following.

> A self-directing transition should take students about five to eight minutes to complete, allowing you to take roll, make a few individual contacts with students who might need extra assistance or encouragement, and complete a quick homework check.

Beginning-of-Class Transitions (Warm-Ups or Bell Work)

A posted task or set of tasks with self-explanatory directions supports students to transition from a previous class or break into your class. During the first week of school, you can expect students to master the procedure of beginning the transition or bell-work assignment as soon as the tardy bell rings. Students can expect that the directions for the bell-work assignment are clear and self-explanatory and that all necessary materials are accessible. Bell work should be done quietly with no conversation.

Avoid teaching new concepts or skills as bell work. The task should generally be an extension or review of a concept already covered in class. It can also be an idea that students can access from personal experience and link to learning objectives.

Following are some examples of bell-work assignments in various content areas:

- Copy today's agenda. Using our textbook's glossary, define the following words (list five or six).
- From yesterday's reading, describe in a paragraph the context and meaning of the quote "A rose by any other name would smell as sweet."

- Reread the first page of Chapter 4. In a paragraph, describe the advice you would give to any of the leaders involved in this conflict?
- Using these 12 words from our presentation on the circulatory system (list the words), write five or six sentences. You may use your notes.
- Solve the first three problems on Page 83. In complete sentences, explain how you solved one of the problems.
- Rewrite the following sentences, changing the verb form to the past tense.

Journals—Quick Writes

Quick writes engage students to access their prior knowledge and connect life experiences to a concept the teacher will explore. In this procedure, students are given a visual, word problem, prompt, or quote from a text and are asked to write a response for five to seven minutes. Students may be asked to share their responses with a partner, to save their entry for later reference, or to turn it in to be reviewed by the teacher.

Assigning Homework

Homework is assigned to provide students with additional practice, preparatory review, or elaboration of concepts. Homework should not be used to teach new concepts. At the beginning of the semester, explain your homework policy to parents, recommending that they encourage and monitor their child's efforts. Many teachers do not make a homework assignment for each day of the week. Instead, a set of assignments may be due in a week's time. Some schools encourage or require teachers to post homework assignments online. Students and parents can access a teacher's Web page for weekly homework assignments and long-term projects.

How much time per day should students spend on homework? For middle school students, several surveys indicate a daily total of 60 to 90 minutes of homework from all subjects combined. This may expand to a few weekend hours per quarter for special projects. For high school, depending on the number of accelerated classes a student takes, the daily total homework time for all classes combined ranges anywhere from 90 minutes to more than three hours, with homework on most weekends. Another formula suggests that students should be given a total number of minutes of homework equivalent to 10 times their grade level. A ninth grader would therefore receive an average of 90 minutes of homework daily. Remember, you are not the only teacher assigning homework!

Homework and Accountability

For the sake of accountability, many teachers quickly check homework for completion only. At the next level, teachers can monitor accuracy and quality via daily whole-class correction of assignments. You may choose to correct only key assignments during the week and record students' grades. Encourage students to keep and organize their homework assignments, as they may be helpful for test review.

The type of assignment, how you monitor and record grades or points for the accuracy and quality of students' homework is different from points given for having simply completed homework. You can determine a point system (e.g., two points per day for each assignment completed on time multiplied by the number of assignments given per week), and how these completion points are factored into the overall value of homework to students' overall grade. One method for monitoring homework completion is to have a check-off column in the grade book or electronic grading program for daily assignments. Another system that makes accountability clear is to create a *stamp sheet*, where each day you can stamp a square to verify that the student completed the assigned homework. The stamp sheet can be three-hole punched and contain enough squares for a month's worth of homework. Collect and use the information on the stamp sheet to calculate what predetermined percentage of points toward a grade students will receive for homework completion.

Some teachers have combined homework accountability with encouraging punctuality (see Figure 3.3). These sheets become valuable records when a parent or administrative conference becomes necessary with resistant students. Monitoring homework and punctuality can become a student job and does not need to be a time-consuming task for the teacher.

Figure 3.3   Sample Stamp-Sheet Template

Student's Name: Period:					
Date	*Monday*	*Tuesday*	*Wednesday*	*Thursday*	*Friday*
Homework Completed Yes/No					
On time to class? Yes/No					

Equipment Use

For each of the following content areas, check with your department chair about the existing policy or recommendations related to the appropriate use, cleanup, and storage of equipment. If appropriate, include these expectations in your course syllabus, and post them in your classroom as a reminder to students.

- *Science.* During the first week of class, it is important to review any safety requirements and procedures related to the use of materials, sharp implements, and highly sensitive and expensive equipment in science labs. Many science teachers give a guided tour of the various types of equipment that, if handled improperly, may lead to injury or contamination.

- *Physical education.* The introduction of each individual sport is usually accompanied by information about equipment, its appropriate use, and storage. Provision of muscle-building weights or other equipment should be accompanied by some expectations for appropriate weight, use, and supervision (peer spotters). Having these procedures explicitly outlined and posted is helpful.
- *Computer technology.* Teachers of these classes outline explicit expectations about how the technology should be used. At the start of the year, many computer classes have students sign an agreement about the use of the equipment, including appropriate use of the Internet.
- *Shop, home economics, and agricultural and mechanical sciences.* Students should be given explicit direction regarding the appropriate and safe use of all heavy equipment or electrical appliances.
- *Visual arts.* The introduction of each art medium, such as clay, sculpture, or painting, should be accompanied by an explanation of the appropriate use, clean up, and storage of materials.

Figure 3.4   Checklist for Daily Classroom Management

Checklist for Daily Classroom Management

You will need to be prepared ahead of time with the following:

Preventions and Interventions

—— *An attention-getting signal (e.g., bell, chime, counting down)*
—— *A menu of preventions and positive intervention strategies*
—— *A class list with phone numbers and parent names*
—— *Notes for positive parent contacts, translated into home language when possible*

Rules

—— *Three to four classroom rules, posted in a visible location*
—— *Existing schoolwide rules, also posted*
—— *Knowledge of the school discipline policy*
—— *Copies of existing notices for detention referrals*

Routines and Procedures

—— *Completing bell-work/warm-up assignments at the start of the period*
—— *Checking attendance and punctuality*
—— *Transitioning from one activity to another*
—— *Assigning and collecting homework*
—— *Caring for equipment*

4

Community and Team Building

Activities for the Secondary Classroom

I know community building is important, but how can I do this with so many students and so little time to teach content?

Community-building activities help create a classroom climate that supports students to learn subject matter content collaboratively. Besides the academic concepts you present, students benefit from opportunities to grapple with these concepts with their peers. Despite their social nature, adolescents may not automatically know how to work productively in groups. For students to work well and take risks with one another, there first needs to be a climate of mutual respect in the classroom. Students need the opportunity to practice listening skills. They need to learn to respect one another's individuality and experiences, as well as to draw on one another's strengths.

Once the class climate is conducive to teamwork, cooperative skills still take structure and practice. In this chapter, we lay out a variety of team-building and cooperative activities, some intended only for the beginning of the year, others to be revisited and practiced throughout the year.

Making time at the beginning of the year to get to know your students is more than a *feel-good* task. Chapter 3 (Rules, Routines, and Procedures) and Chapter 6 (Strategies for Daily Lesson Planning and Student Engagement) highlight how learning more about your students and drawing on student's prior knowledge is an essential ingredient of both creating an effective environment for learning and planning engaging lessons. The more you know of your students' interests and experience, the better bridge you have for making your instruction more meaningful to them. The better students learn to work with one another, the more partners for teaching and learning you will have in the room.

ACTIVITIES FOR THE BEGINNING OF THE SCHOOL YEAR

NAVIGATING THE SCHOOL WITH GIVE-ONE-GET-ONE

Purpose

To identify information about the school that may be unfamiliar to students, to review what students know, and to share information

Note: This activity is particularly useful for a group of students new to the school, such as sixth or seventh graders for middle or junior high, ninth graders for high school. Prompting students to generate three ideas linked to a particular unit or concept, Give-One-Get-One can be used throughout the year, for both team-building and academic work.

Materials

- Graphic organizer
- Worksheet, overhead transparency, or SMART Board display
- School handbooks

Time

Approximately 15–20 minutes

Introduction

- Give students the school handbook, and allow time to read through.
- Tell students, "The purpose of this activity, Give-One-Get-One, is to help you be successful at our school. In a few minutes, you'll have an opportunity to share information about the school and learn from others."

Activity

- Give each student the Give-One-Get-One worksheet (Figure 4.1). Ask them to record three things they know about the school, such as start time, rules, library hours, and so on.
- Model the process using the overhead. Ask students to generate a few items and record them randomly in three boxes.
- Tell students, after they record their three pieces of information, they will get up and exchange information with other students. For example (model this with a student or two), go up to a classmate, introduce yourself, and share one idea. That person would then share one of his or her ideas with another person. Both write them down, thank one another, and then move on to exchange ideas with another classmate. If both participants have exactly the same information, have them generate a new idea together and record it in one of the boxes.
- Let students know your expectations for their behavior as they are milling around. Students need to sit down when they have completed all 12 squares.
- Check for understanding.
- Call time when the majority of students have filled out their worksheets.

Closure

- Ask students to share some of the information they received about the school. Use a method to call on students at random such as *equity sticks* (Popsicle sticks labeled with each student's name, drawn at random).

Figure 4.1   Give-One-Get-One

Give-One-Get-One

Name: Date:

Subject: Period:

Directions: Write three pieces of information in any square. Exchange information until all 12 squares are filled.

INTRODUCING ACADEMIC VOCABULARY WITH WORD SPLASH AND NUMBERED HEADS TOGETHER

Purpose

To define subject matter or school-related vocabulary that may be unfamiliar to all students

Note: This activity is especially effective as a follow-up to a reading assignment and can be used at the beginning of the year to explore a school handbook or other information about school procedures and logistics.

Materials

- Vocabulary words listed on a chart or overhead
- Worksheet of vocabulary words (one per group)

Time

Approximately 15 minutes

Introduction

There are many things in our school handbook that can support your success. Today we're going to define some important terms using an activity called Word Splash (Figure 4.2).

Activity

- Assign students to groups of three and ask them to number off, 1, 2, and 3.
- Explain that during the next seven minutes, the group will try to define as many terms as possible.
- The paper must be passed around the group, so each person records the definition of an equal number of words. At the end of the allotted time, a number will be called, and the student with that number will need to stand up and be prepared to define the designated term.
- Check for understanding.
- Give students seven minutes to define the terms. Monitor for equity of recording and defining of terms so that one person is not doing the majority of the work.

Closure

- Using the *numbered-heads* strategy, ask students to define the terms. For example, ask all ones to stand. Call on a Number 1 student to define the term.
- Ask students if there were any other terms that were unfamiliar to them that were not listed on this Word Splash.

Figure 4.2	Word Splash Sample

WORD SPLASH

Group Members:

Date: Period:

Directions: Define as many words as you can in the allotted time.

blood   heart   rhythmic   pressure   muscle   pump   clrculation   artery   valve

WHAT ARE OUR SIMILARITIES AND DIFFERENCES?

Purpose

To get a sense of students' backgrounds, experiences, and interests, to compare and contrast

Materials

- Graphic organizer. The questions for the first example are general and can be used as a team-building activity at the beginning of the school year for an advisory or homeroom class. The questions in the graphic organizers that follow it are subject specific.
- Pairs of playing cards or another way to select random pairs

Time

Approximately 20 minutes

Introduction

- Tell students that today they are going to learn more about one another and determine ways that they are similar and different.
- Model the process by putting the graphic organizer up on the overhead projector.
- Ask a student volunteer to come up and be your partner. Talk about each question, and determine whether your responses should be recorded under the similarities or differences column.

Activity

- Pair up students randomly.
- Give each pair one graphic organizer. (see Figures 4.3 through 4.8)
- Remind them to share their responses to each question and then determine in which column to record their answers.
- Give 10 minutes for students to complete the task.

Closure

Ask students the following:

- What are some similarities in your partnerships?
- What are some career interests?
- What impact do people want to make in the world, or what difference do they want to make in people's lives?

Figure 4.3   What Are Our Similarities and Differences?

WHAT ARE OUR SIMILARITIES AND DIFFERENCES?

Partner 1:   Partner 2:

Period: Date:

	Differences Partner 1	Similarities	Differences Partner 2
1. Where have you traveled?			
2. What are your hobbies or interests?			
3. What is your favorite food?			
4. What are some possible careers for you?			
5. What impact or difference do you want to make in the world?			
6. What is something you are interested in learning this year?			

Figure 4.4   What Are Our Similarities and Differences About Learning History?

WHAT ARE OUR SIMILARITIES AND DIFFERENCES ABOUT LEARNING HISTORY?

Partner 1:   Partner 2:

Period: Date:

	Differences Partner 1	Similarities	Differences Partner 2
1. Do you usually like learning about history or current events? (Yes/No) Why or why not?			
2. Describe one thing that you usually have to do in history classes that you *don't* like to do.			
3. If someone offered to pay your expenses to live somewhere else for a year, where would it be? Why are you interested in that place?			
4. What types of stories from the newspaper, on the Internet, or television news is most interesting to you? Why?			
5. If you had to choose, would you rather think about the past, present, or future? Why?			

Figure 4.5 What Are Our Similarities and Differences About Learning Math?

WHAT ARE OUR SIMILARITIES AND DIFFERENCES ABOUT LEARNING MATH?

Partner 1:   Partner 2:

Period: Date:

	Differences Partner 1	Similarities	Differences Partner 2
1. Do you usually enjoy learning math? (Yes/No) Why or why not?			
2. Describe one thing that you usually have to do in math classes that you *don't* like to do.			
3. Describe the last time you needed to figure out the cost or weight of something or measure the distance or size of something?			
4. Complete this sentence: "The best math teachers are ones who ..."			
5. Name one possible career or job you would like to have in the future. What might you need to know or do in the job that has something to do with math?			

Figure 4.6 What Are Our Similarities and Differences About Learning Science?

WHAT ARE OUR SIMILARITIES AND DIFFERENCES ABOUT LEARNING SCIENCE?

Partner 1:   Partner 2:

Period: Date:

	Differences Partner 1	Similarities	Differences Partner 2
1. Do you usually enjoy learning science concepts? (Yes/No) Why or why not?			
2. Describe one thing that you usually have to do in science classes that you *don't* like to do.			
3. If you had to choose, would you rather study about the human body, animals and nature, how mechanical things work, chemical reactions, or issues having to do with the environment?			
4. Complete this sentence: "The best science teachers are ones who ..."			
5. Name one possible career or job you would like to have in the future. What might you need to know or do in the job is connected to a scientific concept or topic?			

Figure 4.7 What Are Our Similarities and Differences About Learning Literature?

WHAT ARE OUR SIMILARITIES AND DIFFERENCES ABOUT LEARNING LITERATURE?

Partner 1: Partner 2:

Period: Date:

	Differences Partner 1	Similarities	Differences Partner 2
1. Do you usually enjoy learning in your English literature class? (Yes/No) Why or why not?			
2. Describe one thing that you usually have to do in English classes that you *don't* like to do?			
3. If you had to choose, would you rather read fiction or nonfiction? Why?			
4. Complete this sentence: "The best English literature teachers are ones who . . ."			
5. Name one possible career or job you would like to have in the future. What might you need to know or do in the job connected to comprehending reading materials?			

WHAT ARE OUR SIMILARITIES AND DIFFERENCES ABOUT LEARNING A NEW LANGUAGE?

Partner 1:   Partner 2:

Period: Date:

	Differences Partner 1	Similarities	Differences Partner 2
1. Do you usually enjoy learning a new language? (Yes/No) Why or why not?			
2. Describe one thing that you usually have to do in language classes that you *don't* like to do.			
3. If you had to choose a language to learn other than the one you learned as a child, which one would you choose? Why?			
4. Complete this sentence: "The best language teachers are ones who ..."			
5. Name one possible career or job you would like to have in the future. What might you need to do in the job that may require you to speak or read a language other than first language?			

PARTNER INTERVIEWS

Purpose

To surface students' interests, backgrounds, and experiences and to develop communication skills and build community. This activity is recommended for homeroom or advisory classes. Career academy teachers might modify this activity by adding a question or two related to their specific career pathway.

Materials

- Survey
- Graphic organizer
- Pairs of playing cards or other way to create random pairs

Time

Approximately 15 minutes to complete the interviews on Day 1. Determining similarities and differences could happen on Day 2.

Introduction

Tell students, "We are a diverse group of individuals with varied backgrounds, interests, and experiences. Today, we're going to spend some time getting to know one another. I also want to know more about who you are so I can connect the school curriculum with your lives."

Activity

- Tell students that they will have seven minutes each to interview one another, before they introduce their partners to the class.
- Explain the process before moving students into pairs.
- Students will be paired up randomly and determine who will be 1 and 2.
- Student 2 will interview Student 1, listening and recording his or her responses on the survey sheet.
- Model the process with a volunteer.
- Pair students and give them the survey (Figure 4.9).
- Ask them to determine 1 and 2.
- After five minutes, let students know there are two minutes remaining.
- After seven minutes, call time, and switch roles.

Closure

- Model how to introduce a partner with a volunteer. Say the student's name and one or two things about him or her that you've just learned.
- Either call on each partnership to introduce one another or go around the room and have students introduce one another while seated.

Figure 4.9 Partner Interviews

PARTNER INTERVIEWS

Partner 1:   Partner 2:

Period: Date:

What is something you like to do or are good at doing?

What is your family background and culture? What is a family tradition that you enjoy?

What experience stands out for you that changed your life or had a significant impact?

What is a future plan or goal you have?

DEVELOPING NORMS FOR COOPERATIVE GROUPS

Purpose

To establish norms for cooperative group work and to develop criteria for students to self-assess their participation in group work

Materials

- Paper for two charts, "What don't you like about . . . " and "Expert groups"
- Graphic organizer worksheet

Time

Approximately 30–45 minutes (can be done in two parts)

Introduction

- Share a quote that speaks to group work, such as,

  In a very real sense there is no such thing as organizational behavior. There is only individual behavior. Everything else flows from that.

  —Stephen Covey, author

- Ask students to share with a partner what they think the quote means. Get some ideas from the room.
- Tell students, "We will be working in cooperative groups throughout the school year. We will need norms for how to work together."
- Ask students to think individually about their experience in groups, and record on the graphic organizer, "What don't you like about working in groups with other students?"
- Ask students to share a few ideas. Record on a chart.

Activity

- Form groups of three. Ask students to number off 1, 2, and 3.
- Post roles: ones will be recorders, twos will be facilitators, threes will be reporters.
- The facilitator's role is to ensure everyone in the group has an equal chance to contribute, possibly going around the circle until each person is out of ideas.
- Stop the groups after three minutes, and ask **threes** to stand up and share some of their group's ideas. Record ideas on the chart.
- Give groups three to five minutes to talk about the underlying causes for these behaviors (listed on column on the right) that bother us while twos record on the worksheet.
- Threes stand up and share some underlying cause. Record on chart.
- Say, "Given what we don't like about group work, what would a positive group experience be like? Or how would an *expert group* act? What types of things might they say?" Record ideas on a separate chart labeled "Expert Groups."

Closure

Tell students, "This is our goal—to have every group you work in be a high-functioning, expert group. During the year, we will take time to reflect on our group work using these ideas, or norms, we have created."

| Figure 4.10 | Cooperative Groups |

COOPERATIVE GROUPS

Name: Group:

Date: Period:

What don't you like about working in groups with other students?	*In your opinion, why do some students do things you don't like when they're working in a group? (underlying causes)*

WHAT I *KNOW*, WHAT I *WANT* TO KNOW, WHAT I'VE *LEARNED* (K-W-L)

Purpose

To find out what students know about the subject and what they want to learn

Materials

K-W-L chart

Time

Approximately 15 minutes

Introduction

- Tell students you want to hear from them what they already know about this subject and what they want to learn. You'll use this information to guide your planning throughout the year. Use this same form when you begin a new unit of study. At the end of each unit, you'll ask them to reflect on what they learned.
- Model the process with the whole class first:
  1. Draw a chart with three columns.
  2. Label them Know/Want to Learn/Learned.
  3. Invite students to generate a few items under each of the first two columns.

Activity

- Give each student his or her own K-W-L worksheet (Figure 4.11).
- Allow about five to seven minutes for students to generate personal lists of what they already know (in general about the subject or a specific topic) and what they want to learn.

Closure

- Ask students to share some of the things they know and want to learn. Record them on the chart used at the beginning of the lesson.
- Collect worksheets for your information.

Figure 4.11   What I *Know*, What I *Want* to Know, What I've *Learned* (K-W-L)

WHAT I *KNOW*, WHAT I *WANT* TO LEARN, WHAT I'VE *LEARNED* (K-W-L)

Name: Date:

Subject: Period:

Directions: Brainstorm what you know about the subject and what you want to learn.

What I Know	What I Want to Learn	What I've Learned

WHAT ARE YOUR MULTIPLE INTELLIGENCE STRENGTHS?

Purpose

To identify ways different students learn and to understand learning preferences that come easily to students and those that take more work

Materials

- Multiple intelligences survey
- Multiple intelligences scoring sheet
- Multiple intelligences signs (on 8½ × 11 paper)
  - Linguistic
  - Mathematical
  - Spatial
  - Musical
  - Bodily/Kinesthetic
  - Interpersonal
  - Intrapersonal
  - Nature

- Recording sheet with discussion questions
- Chart requirements

Time

Approximately 45 minutes (can be split into two sessions)

Introduction

- Ask students, "Which would you prefer?"
  - Working on a number problem
  - Writing a poem about your feelings
  - Reading a book
  - Taking a walk in nature
  - Talking with friends
  - Listening to music
  - Dancing or bike riding
  - Designing

- Tell students, "Each of us learns in different ways. Understanding yourself and the way you learn will help you be more successful in everything you do. In this activity, you will explore the multiple intelligences, learn about your preferences, and how your classmates are similar to and different from you."
- Give students the multiple intelligences survey (Figure 4.12) and review the eight types. Ask students first to predict their intelligence preference and write it on the back of the survey. Next, ask students to quietly self-assess to find their dominant intelligence using the scoring sheet (Figure 4.13).

Activity

- Tell students that in a minute, they will go to an area in the room and meet other students that have a similar dominant intelligence. Point out where each group will meet.
- Ask each intelligence type, one at a time, to move to their new group.
- Once in their groups, students will sign their names to the multiple intelligence sign.
- Students number off one through four, and assign roles based on those numbers:
  - Ones–Facilitators
  - Twos–Recorders
  - Threes–Chart makers
  - Fours–Reporters

Group Directions

- Facilitators will be facilitating a discussion in which every student will have an opportunity to respond to each question. The facilitator ensures equity of participation and task completion.
- Recorders will write down the groups' responses to the following questions:
  - What do you like doing the most in school?
  - What is most challenging for you?
  - What would you like others to know about your kind of intelligence?
- Chart makers supervise the creation of a chart (they don't need to do all the work) that has the following three elements:
  - The name of the intelligence
  - A graphic that represents the intelligence
  - A motto for the group
  - Post the chart on the nearest wall

Closure or Day 2

- Ask the reporter from each group to share a few things students in this group like to do, find challenging, and would like others to know about their kind of intelligence.
- Ask chart makers to share their intelligence chart.
- Ask students to write (in their journal would be best) the following:
  - What did you learn about yourself that was surprising or unexpected?
  - What did you find out about your classmates that was interesting?
  - What intelligence(s) would you like to develop more?
  - Invite students to share a few of their responses.

Figure 4.12	Multiple Intelligences Survey

MULTIPLE INTELLIGENCES SURVEY

Name: **Date:**

Period:

Each of us is intelligent in many ways. To help you discover your intelligence strengths, take the following survey. Put an *X* next to each statement that expresses a statement that is mostly true for you. Leave it blank if the statement is untrue or you are unsure whether it characterizes you

1. _____ I like to design and/or draw things.
2. _____ I enjoy singing or humming.
3. _____ I play a musical instrument (or would like to).
4. _____ I like to work with numbers.
5. _____ I like to memorize poems, stories, facts, and the like.
6. _____ I like to dance, and I pick up new steps quickly.
7. _____ I notice how people are feeling, and I like to help others.
8. _____ I enjoy listening to stories and reading books.
9. _____ I can easily determine directions (north, south, east, west).
10. _____ I enjoy watching nature shows and programs about exploration.
11. _____ I can understand the directions that come with gadgets.
12. _____ I like to play word games, such as Scrabble and crossword puzzles.
13. _____ I am coordinated (ride a bike, ski, surf, skate, dance).
14. _____ I like doing experiments.
15. _____ I find it difficult to sit still for long periods.
16. _____ I like to go to science museums, planetariums, Exploratoriums, and the like.
17. _____ I enjoy building and/or creating sculptures.
18. _____ I enjoy tongue twisters, rhymes, and puns.
19. _____ I notice changes in the seasons, stars, moon phases, and tides.
20. _____ I sometimes get a song, melody, or advertisement stuck in my head.
21. _____ I like to measure, sort, and organize things.
22. _____ I like to look at shapes of building and structures.
23. _____ I notice sounds in my environment, such as dogs barking and sirens.
24. _____ I love nature, animals, and the outdoors.
25. _____ I like to write in a diary or journal.
26. _____ I make friends easily.
27. _____ I am often a leader when I am in a group.
28. _____ I like to work on things by myself rather than in a group.
29. _____ I usually know what's going on with my friends and family.
30. _____ I am pretty independent.

Figure 4.13   Multiple Intelligences Scoring Sheet

MULTIPLE INTELLIGENCES SCORING SHEET

Name: Date:

Period:

Directions: Find out your dominant intelligence(s) by putting an *X* next to each number you checked off on your self-assessment.

Linguistic	*Logical/Mathematical*	*Musical*	*Spatial*
___5	___4	___2	___1
___8	___14	___3	___9
___12	___16	___20	___11
___18	___21	___23	___22
Bodily/Kinesthetic	*Interpersonal*	*Intrapersonal*	*Nature*
___6	___7	___25	___10
___13	___27	___26	___19
___15	___29	___28	___24
___17		___30	

Which intelligence(s) had a score of three or more?

Which intelligence(s) had a score of zero or one?

What is your dominant intelligence?

Figure 4.14   Intelligence-Alike Groups

INTELLIGENCE-ALIKE GROUPS

Intelligence:

Names of people in group:

Discussion Questions:

- What do you like doing the most in school?

- What is most challenging for you?

- What would you like others to know about your kind of intelligence?

ACTIVITIES TO USE THROUGHOUT THE SCHOOL YEAR

INDIVIDUAL HISTORY FOR LEARNING _____

Purpose

To surface students' past experiences and attitudes related to learning your subject's key concepts

Materials

- Survey

Time

Approximately 15 minutes

Introduction

- Start this lesson by sharing a negative learning experience, or something that impacted your desire and/or ability to learn about the subject you teach. Then share a positive experience or something that enhanced your desire and/or ability to learn this subject's key concepts.
- Tell students that today they will be reflecting on their histories for learning concepts related to this subject and uncovering attitudes, experiences, and ideas that have influenced them along the way.

Activity

- Ask students to fill out the survey (Figure 4.15) individually.
- Form groups of four and ask students to number off 1, 2, 3, and 4.

Round-robin share—Ask students in their group to share their responses to the survey, one question at a time. After each member has responded to the first question, they start with the second question, then the third, and so on.

Closure

- Ask ones to stand and share something group members enjoy about the subject.
- Ask twos to share something group members find challenging.
- Ask threes to share ways students currently use learning from this subject in their lives.
- Ask fours to share future use of this subject.
- Collect papers.
- Return students to their original seats.

Figure 4.15 My Individual History for Learning _____

MY INDIVIDUAL HISTORY FOR LEARNING _____

Name: Date:

Period: Subject

Directions: In the boxes below, write about your current viewpoint and past experiences involved in learning about this subject.

What do you like about this subject?	*What makes this subject difficult to learn sometimes?*
What do you remember as the best class activity or project you did for this subject?	*What do you remember as the worst activity or project for this subject?*
Among the ideas, facts, or skills you've learned about this subject, describe one you'll never forget.	*In general, how might you use what you've learned about this subject in the future?*

QUOTE DISCUSSION

Purpose

To develop students' ability to reason and communicate effectively

Materials

- Quote
- Journal or other paper to record

Time

Approximately 30 minutes

Introduction

Ask students, "What is a quote? Why or how do you believe quotes are chosen?" Record students' ideas on the board, poster paper, SMART Board, or overhead transparency.

- Ask if anyone can repeat a quote that is important to him or her? Record a few or have a few ready that you can share that you think will be provocative or interesting to your students. Explain that, today, students will be responding to a quote individually and then discussing it with their peers.

Note: The quote activity can be used throughout the year to introduce a new unit or concept. Use quotes related to the new unit or concept taken from current events articles, the news, popular song lyrics, or movies.

Activity

Post the quote on the board and ask students to respond in writing:

- What does it mean to you?
- Give an example of the quote's meaning in real life.
  - Model this procedure with one of the student-generated quotes.

Discussion Process

- Tell students they will form random groups of three to share their responses.
- Once they are in their groups, they will number off 1, 2, 3, and 4.
- Ones first share their responses and examples. Next, twos share and then, threes.
- Encourage the members of each group to ask questions of one another and build on one another's ideas. Model this process.
- Each group then generates a new example to illustrate the quote, and all group members record it in their journals.

Closure

- Ask the students to elaborate on their original responses by incorporating ideas generated during the group discussion.
- Student share responses. Promote equity of participation by using *equity sticks* (Popsicle sticks labeled with student names that are pulled randomly).
  - Ask, "How did hearing other students' responses expand your thinking?"

- *Alternative*: Provide several quotes, and ask students to select the quote that speaks to them. Form discussion groups based on student-selected quotes.

SAMPLE QUOTES

Whether you think you can or think you can't—you are right.

—Henry Ford, founder of Ford Motor Company

Education is the most powerful weapon which you can use to change the world.

—Nelson Mandela, Nobel Peace Prize winner,
former President of South Africa

Behold the turtle. He makes progress only when he sticks his neck out.

—James Bryant Conant, chemist,
former President of Harvard University

One must view the world through the eye in one's heart rather than just trust the eyes in one's head.

—Mary Crow Dog, Native
American writer and activist

History has determined our lives, and we must work hard for what we believe to be the right thing . . . life is something we borrow and must give back richer when the time comes.

—Carlos Bulosan, Filipino American novelist

Every job is a self-portrait of the person who did it. Autograph your work with excellence.

—Anonymous

To become visible is to see ourselves and each other in a different mirror of history.

—Ronald Takaki, historian

Mistakes are their own instructors.

—Horace Mann, American education reformer

A cynical young person is almost the saddest sight to see because it means that he or she has gone from knowing nothing to believing in nothing.

—Maya Angelou, American poet and novelist

The revolution begins at home.

—Gloria Anzaldua, Mexican
American author and activist

We are not makers of history. We are made of history.

—Martin Luther King, Jr.

IDENTIFYING COMMUNITY ISSUES

Purpose

To learn what students think are important real-life issues in their community, to gather data for community-oriented, problem-solving lessons. This could be used in middle school humanities and high school history classes. Modify the concept by asking math students to generate community issues web related to increases in any of the following: population, increases in unemployment, crime, homes for sale, high school graduates. Place any of these words in the center of the web, and ask students to generate related information. Similar adaptations can be created for other subjects.

Materials

- Graphic organizer
- Chart paper

Time

Approximately 20 minutes

Introduction

- Ask students, "How long have you lived in this community? Please stand if you have lived here: your whole life, more than 10 years, 5 to 10 years, 1 to 4 years, less than a year."
- Ask students to turn to the person next to them and share three things they like about living here. Invite some responses.
- Tell students, "No community is without problems and issues. As community members, we can identify issues that concern us. Throughout the year, we can tie our studies into participation in our community."

Activity

- Have the students team up in pairs to generate a list of issues, concerns, or problems in the community and discuss how those issues impact them. Direct student partners to use the graphic organizer (Figure 4.16) to record what they believe are community issues in the boxes, noting possible impacts resulting from the issues on the lines beneath each.
- Elicit ideas from the whole class based on partner discussions. Record several ideas on the board or chart paper.
- Ask students to select three of their four issues based on ideas from the whole class.
- Ask two sets of partners to come together and come to consensus on one top priority issue. Discuss this question: What would it take to address or solve this problem or issue?
- Remind students about equity of participation in the discussion.
- Ask each group to share which issue they chose and one idea generated during their discussion.

Closure

Close by letting the class know that, as a teacher, your role is to prepare them to participate in a democratic society. Democracy depends on citizens participating in decision making about things that affect their lives. Throughout the year, you'll continue to explore how to make a difference in the community.

| Figure 4.16 | Identifying Community Issues |

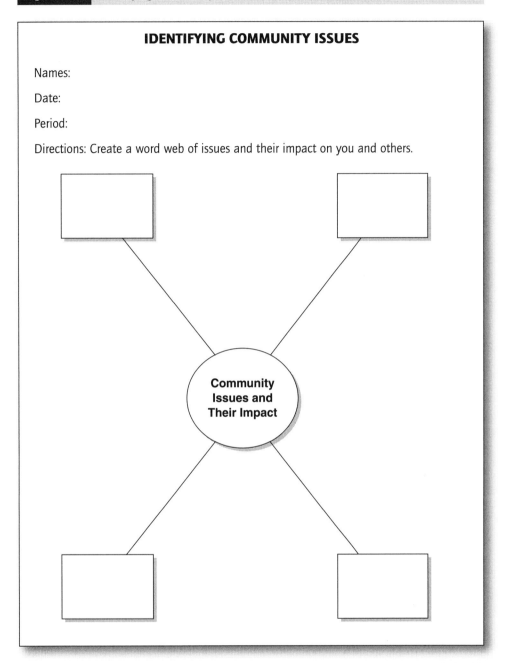

IDENTIFYING COMMUNITY ISSUES

Names:

Date:

Period:

Directions: Create a word web of issues and their impact on you and others.

5

Big-Picture Guide to Standards-Based Curriculum and Instruction

There's so much for students to learn about this subject; how do I determine exactly what and when to teach it all?

If a teaching year were akin to building a lovely, custom new home, teachers would be both the architect and the carpenter. The curriculum provides the architect's blueprint, design, and artistic vision. The content standards provide an explicit code about how each aspect of the house must be built. Lesson plans provide the carpenter's daily how-to guide to laying the foundation; setting structure; and building each room, door, and window. Books, visuals, equipment, strategies, and our content knowledge provide the actual tools for making it happen. In this sense, textbooks, even good ones, are not the curriculum. They are simply tools to help build the house. And as all architects and carpenters know, although the plan is a guide, it is constantly revisited as unexpected obstacles are encountered.

This chapter and Chapters 6, 7, and 8 provide you with three different layers of planning to help you teach. This chapter gives you guidelines for creating a blueprint for the house, the yearlong plan. Chapter 6 gives you specific direction in structure and strategy to help you teach effectively each day. Chapter 7 presents two different exemplary teacher's model plans for the first two weeks of school.

The good news is that it is possible to teach to your highest vision and that many of your creative ideas will work. However, in the beginning, all teachers find themselves constantly revising, reinventing, adding, or taking away. Despite your best efforts, sometimes, you will find yourself scrambling day to day, far from your original intent.

The art of planning brings together creativity, vision, and organization. Like many parts of teaching, once the planning process becomes internalized, it requires less effort and time. Planning in collaboration with others can also be invaluable in setting high standards while figuring out the day-to-day plan, or "what do I do next?"

Much attention has been focused on content standards and standardized tests as planning guides. We believe it is equally important to consider a bigger picture when deciding what to teach. In teaching your subject, you are always moving among the three interrelated modes of curriculum (what you teach), instruction (how you teach it), and content standards (the level of proficiency you want your students to reach).

Curriculum development is not just a beginning teacher's challenge. Creating curriculum that is consistent with common standards while, at the same time, allowing for individual teacher's creativity is one of the most important educational challenges today. Most schools and districts find themselves on a path of creating some core curriculum that is common to all.

The *American Heritage Dictionary* defines curriculum as "the courses of study offered by an educational institution to deliver essential concepts and skills." (The Latin meaning is "the course" or "path of the race.") In the absence of explicit curriculum models, what are the most important elements for you to consider when you are deciding what exactly to teach? In this chapter, we invite you to keep these elements of comprehensive curriculum in mind as we guide you through the process of creating a curriculum blueprint for the school year. In the first section of the chapter, we explain how to envision a big-picture, semester-long plan. We then move on to pose questions designed to help you with planning specific units. In the final section, we offer key suggestions to get you started with creating your syllabus.

STEPS TO STANDARDS-LINKED, BIG-PICTURE PLANNING

The following steps will get you started as you begin to conceptualize your plan for the school year. Although we feel that these steps capture the key imperatives for the planning process, keep in mind that your plans will always change and evolve. The Semester Planning Guide (Figure 5.1) that appears after these steps is meant to provide you with a template to use as you record and modify your plans for your first semester. The items listed in the Semester Planning Guide correlate with the steps below so that you have an easy way of organizing your notes.

Step 1: Gather Key Professional Resources

Along with your lesson plan book and/or template you've generated or downloaded from the Web, you will need to reference the following:

- State content standards for your subject
- Site-adopted curriculum and site course description
- Copy of the textbook you plan to use
- Copy of a sample syllabus developed by someone from your site or district
- A site calendar that indicates vacation days and dates for quarter grades, progress reports, finals, and state testing

Ask your department chair for help in tracking down any of these resources as needed.

Step 2: Determine the Essential Learning Objectives, Topics, Skills, and Thematic Links to Engage Students

Examine all of the resources listed above to determine the essential concepts and skills you will need to teach. Your district or department may already have identified which content standards are essential for each grade level. Some standards are chosen because they represent the heart and soul of the content area. Others may be emphasized by your district or school to address poor performance in a previous year linked to certain concepts and skills assessed by standardized tests. Standards may also be emphasized by a district to ensure progress in English Language Learners' academic language development.

Step 3: Coordinate Timing Factors and Dates

After studying the calendar, identify the continuous instructional days available. Ask yourself questions such as, "How many weeks of instruction are there for the first quarter (typically 9 to 10 weeks)?" "If this time is not interrupted by any standardized testing breaks or extended holidays, can I break this time into three 3-week units? Or two 5-week units?" "In the first quarter, how do I allow additional days to accommodate more community building with students?"

If you plan for a quarter with more instructional breaks, such as winter quarter with holidays and finals, factor in shorter units of study. *Post important site-wide dates and events in your plan book.*

Step 4: Identify Types of Cumulative (Summative) Assessments

Begin with the end in mind. Students should know from the start of a unit what they can expect to learn and how they will demonstrate new knowledge.

To plan unit lessons, we suggest that you consider the skills and content your students will need to know and how they will demonstrate knowledge for the final assessments. Chapter or unit exams are traditional ways to measure student achievement. You can also get ideas about projects, longer writing assignments, or criterion-based presentations from your textbook, state frameworks, content standards guides, and veteran teachers.

Step 5: Identify and Organize Materials and Resources for Students

Anticipate what you will need to put your unit plans into action. If you need to share textbooks, lab materials, or PE equipment, find out when these resources are available. You may need to coordinate shared materials through the textbook technician, department chair, or agreements with colleagues. Your planning may be impacted by the availability of materials. For example, anticipate in an upcoming unit of study if you want your entire class to use the library or computer lab.

Step 6: Begin Planning an Instructional Sequence

By now, you have the biggest picture to guide the design of specific units throughout the semester. Be sure to pace the units in terms of time needed for the following:

- For you to introduce concepts and offer differentiated groupings
- For students to engage in reading material, complete activities, and prepare for cumulative assessments or projects

Semesters usually include four to six smaller units of study, themes, types of literature, sets of essential standards, or other skill sets.

Step 7: Consider Topics and Themes That Elicit Students' Prior Knowledge or Life Experiences

Students learn more effectively when allowed to consider what they already know about the content, make connections to their life experiences, and reflect on the impact of their learning with others. Unit and individual lesson plans that allow for linking prior knowledge as objectives are introduced, engage student interest, promote critical thinking, and result in higher student achievement. (See Chapter 7, "The First Two Weeks of Math Class," for specific ideas about introductory activities.)

SOME GUIDING QUESTIONS FOR CURRICULUM UNIT PLANNING

Now that we've considered what goes into planning for the semester, let's look more closely at what's involved in curriculum unit planning. A helpful starting point for planning any unit involves asking, "In what way are my topics and facts linked to unifying themes?" In other words, why am I teaching a particular unit? What does this content tell us about people, societies, life? Table 5.1 on page 88 lists some examples of topics that might be explored in various courses along with the unifying themes that might pull those topics together into a unit.

Figure 5.1 Semester Planning Guide for _____

Semester Planning Guide for _____

(course name)

Planning Steps/Components	Notes
1. **Key professional resources** (State content standards, curriculum outline, framework, district and site guidelines, adopted texts, and the like)	
2. **Essential curriculum objectives, standards, concepts** (topics, skills, themes, genre, elements)	
3. **Timing factors** (shared materials, key site dates, calendar breaks, testing, due dates)	
4. **Types of cumulative or end-of-unit assessments** (exams, projects, writing assignments)	
5. **Basic materials and resources** (text, supplementary resources, technology; include those for English learner support and accelerated learning)	
6. **Sequence and pacing of major units** (skill sets, concepts, essential standards-based outcomes)	
7. **Topics or universal themes to elicit students' prior knowledge**	

Table 5.1 Topic Examples

Subject	Topics/Titles	Unifying Themes (Unit)
English	*To Kill a Mockingbird* *Romeo and Juliet*	Societies in conflict
Social studies	WW2 Japanese internment Rise of Nazism	Causes of war
Science	Marine mammals Marine invertebrates	Biodiversity

Here are some additional key questions to consider as you begin to create your units for the year:

- How will I introduce the learning objectives connected to this unit?
- How will I elicit from students what they already know about the topic?
- How will I build background knowledge?
- How will I develop students' academic language skills related to the content?
- What resources are available to support my plans?
- How will I provide differentiated activities and materials to support second-language learners? Accelerated students? Special education students?

The following templates, Planning and Designing Curriculum: Standards-Linked Unit (Part I and Part II), are provided to help you organize some of the complex questions we ask ourselves as teachers when deciding on a unit of study for our class. Part I (Figure 5.2) provides you with a space for brainstorming the essential concepts that will be covered in your class and determining the texts and resources you'll use to teach those concepts. Part II (Figure 5.3) can be used as a working document as you come up with ideas about the sequencing of essential topics and then consider those alongside plans for teaching academic language and formulating differentiated activities to support all learners.

Figure 5.2 Planning and Designing Curriculum: Standards-Based Unit, Part I

Planning and Designing Curriculum
Standards-Based Unit - Part I

Standard/Concept _____ Unit Length: _____week(s)

CONTENT: What are the three or four essential concepts and/or skills (enduring understandings, key themes, central questions) of this unit? *Students will learn...*

PREREQUISITE KNOWLEDGE: What are examples of subject-specific *prerequisite* knowledge and skills that students are expected to know and do that are foundational to these concepts? *Students should know...*

STUDENTS' DIMENSIONS: What do or should I know about students' current strengths and challenges related to learning unit concepts and skills? (Examples: Current reading or ELD levels, socio-cultural experiences, level of exposure to, and interest in related unit topics)

ASSESSMENTS:

- How will I assess what students are learning throughout the course of the unit? (Types of formative assessment tasks)

- How will I assess what students have learned about these concepts at the end of the unit? (Type of summative assessment)

Figure 5.3 Planning and Designing Curriculum: Standards-Based Unit, Part II

Planning and Designing Curriculum
Standards-Based Unit - Part II

Standard/Concept _____ Unit Length: _____week(s)

RESOURCES: (novel, supplemental articles, core text chapters, Web-based resources, videos, PowerPoint presentations, demonstrations, models, charts, primary source documents, worksheets)

SITUATIONAL/AUTHENTIC INTERESTS, i.e. FOSTERING STUDENT CONNECTIONS TO KEY CONCEPTS: What related topics, prompts, or resources are more immediately connected to students' socio-cultural dimensions or current interests?

INSTRUCTIONAL SEQUENCE (order of concepts, activities, resources, assessment tasks)

1.	6.
2.	7.
3.	8
4.	9.
5.	10.

CONTENT-SPECIFIC LITERACIES and/or ENGLISH LANGUAGE DEVELOPMENT SKILLS TO ADDRESS: (e.g. *how to* analyze word problems, sonnets, graphs; *how to* write persuasive essays; Clarifying cultural references embedded in resources, key words with multiple meanings)

CONSIDERATIONS FOR DIFFERENTIATED INSTRUCTION (alternative texts, grouping by mixed or like interests/proficiencies; extended research assignments, tasks or assessments linked to students' multiple intelligence strengths, learning styles, or gaps in prerequisite knowledge.)

CREATING YOUR COURSE SYLLABUS

Ideally, your department chairperson will be able to provide you with a sample course syllabus for each of your assigned classes. If you also belong to a particular interdisciplinary or career pathway team, team leaders will likely have some ideas for aligning certain subject matter concepts with the team's shared learning outcomes or themes. Typically, the district's Web site and/or that of your state's department of education will have links to documents or PowerPoint presentations featuring essential content standards, assessments, curriculum guidelines, and sample course descriptions. Use these resources and a sample of one developed by a site colleague to design your syllabus. Most high school and some middle school teachers present students with a course syllabus in the first week of school. Some schools require that class syllabi be posted on the school's Web site. The actual form may also have a section for parents and students to sign and return as confirmation that they have been informed of your expectations for the class. You may want to outline your grading policy, including expectations for homework on a separate sheet. When you create your syllabus, consider the following components:

- Course title (e.g., Algebra I, U.S. history, computer literacy)
- Course description (In addition to a description of your curriculum, you may want to include whether this satisfies graduation or university admissions requirements.)
- Course outcomes and/or essential content standards addressed
- Description of typical instructional methods or approaches
- Grading policy (What percentage of students' quarter grades are linked to homework, in-class participation, extra credit, tests, projects, and daily assignments? Some teachers cite their expectations for student behavior in this section.)
- Homework policy (How much homework is assigned weekly? What are expectations in relation to the quality, time spent, and due dates?)
- Absences and late assignments (What should students do or expect if they are absent or have late assignments?)
- Makeup options (Will you have makeup options for missed assignments or tests?)
- Progress reports (List the date when progress reports are submitted.)
- Teacher contact (How can parents reach you? Are there special conference days or minimum days for this purpose? When is the best time to reach you? Include school phone and your extension and/or your school e-mail address.)

6

Strategies for Daily Lesson Planning and Student Engagement

What can I do day to day to authentically engage my students in learning challenging concepts?

All of your students are capable of understanding key subject matter concepts. We also know students' multidimensional strengths and challenges impact how they learn. It is no longer a mystery why secondary teachers cannot come in and expect to dazzle students with a well-prepared lecture or assume that all students will take careful notes, read the text thoughtfully for homework, and demonstrate all they learned from these experiences.

Giving lectures and assigning independent reading tasks are valid as instructional practices. However, these will not work as the only methods of instruction for students who are not auditory learners or are not yet proficient readers and writers. Nor will these methods alone work for students who seem to come alive when concepts are also presented visually or through demonstrations. Social or interpersonal students usually benefit from discussion and group work. Those who *learn by doing* also benefit from working on projects.

Nearing adulthood, most adolescents appreciate a choice of projects involving authentic problems or applications that require them to consider, research, and present information linked to academic concepts in a variety of ways. Passive learning from lectures or independent reading also presents a particular challenge for students currently in one of the earlier stages of learning English as a second language or any student with limited proficiencies in the use of academic language or background knowledge linked to a grade-level concept you are planning to teach.

You can increase the probability that more students will engage and persist in learning advanced concepts when you use a variety of teaching methods, many featured throughout this book. Teaching methods should also reflect a consideration of the range of students' learning styles, multiple intelligences, and sociocultural linguistic experiences. Strive to also include materials that match resources (books, videos, music, magazines, and information sources accessed through the Internet) available to and preferred by students. Indeed, there are many things to consider. It takes practice to plan daily lessons that reflect an integration of students' dimensions as learners, varied and equitable assessments of students' learning, and methods that engage students to interact with one another as well as the content. Over time, you will internalize how to consider these variables as part of designing lessons that will transfer new knowledge to all of your students. The rewards are many, as you will see more and more students engage in the learning process and achieve academic success.

In planning and preparing for each day's lessons, we come to the heart of teaching. Some cultures are more advanced in honoring the planning process, such as in some Japanese schools, where public school teachers are given hours of daily planning and collaborating time as part of their paid workday. This refined planning process is sometimes referred to as "polishing the stone."

In United States, public school teachers are more likely to be polishing their stones by the seat of their pants. However, making time at the beginning to consider the essential elements of planning will come back a thousand fold in increasing your effectiveness as a teacher. As with many things in the first year of teaching, what seem like awkward steps gradually become internalized over time, allowing us to work smarter, not longer. As you begin to plan your lessons, we recommend that you keep the following essential questions in mind:

- What is it that I want my students to ultimately know or be able to do?
- Who are my students, and what do they bring in relation to this content?
- How can I know what my students are learning?
- What are the more specific objectives of my lesson?
- What materials do I need to teach the lesson?
- How will I move students forward?

Any successful lesson plan must take all of these critical questions into account, but how exactly do you use these general questions to *build* your lesson? Well, the Lesson Plan Template (Figure 6.1) breaks the lesson planning process down into the following more specific components:

Figure 6.1 Lesson Plan Template

FORMATIVE ASSESSMENT TOOL

Lesson Plan B

Name: _____ Mentor: _____

Grade Level/Subject Area: _____ Date: _____

Lesson Topic: _____ Content Standard: _____

The *Essential Components of Differentiated Instruction* FAS Resource offers specific ideas for differentiating instructional strategies, content, products or assessments in new and varied ways.

Learning Outcomes	Key Concepts & Content	Connections to Students' Knowledge, Skills, Experience
	Teaching Strategies & Sequence Opening	
Evidence of Learning (Product or Assessment)	Instruction	
	Guided Practice	
	Extension Activities or Independent Practice	
Materials		

Learning Outcomes

- Key concepts and content (objectives) connections to student's knowledge, skills, and experience
- Teaching strategies and sequence
- Opening
- Instruction
- Guided practice
- Closure
- Extension activities or independent practice

Materials

In Chapters 7 and 8, we offer two models of the first two weeks of school, with daily lesson plans organized with this planning template. The sample plans are in math and language arts; however, the activities are general enough that most content area teachers will be able to adapt the basic structure. In rest of this chapter, we provide a rationale and examples for each of the suggested planning elements.

LEARNING OUTCOMES: WHAT IS IT THAT I WANT MY STUDENTS TO KNOW OR BE ABLE TO DO?

This is the first question you need to ask before choosing a good novel, dazzling lab experiment, or captivating PowerPoint presentation. What do I want my students to know, and how will the teaching activity or strategy I'm considering get them there? To hold out high standards and expectations for success, classroom activities must follow from intended learning outcomes. Although it is always valid to want to make lessons fun and inviting, you also need to be prepared to justify *why* you are teaching what you are, on any given day.

Where do learning outcomes come from? They come from your content area teaching standards. Each content area has many standards, and it is still up to you to choose where to begin and which standards to prioritize. It can be helpful to meet with a new-teacher mentor, department chair, or friendly colleague to set priorities and chart a course through the many standards. It is also valuable to let your areas of passion guide you in choosing which standards allow you to start with greater possibilities of student engagement.

You need to make each of your learning outcomes explicit and clear to the students. The more clear students are about what you are teaching and why, the more they will comprehend, retain, and apply what you are teaching. Figure 6.2 provides examples of learning outcomes in two content areas. It also includes examples of corresponding "evidence" to be considered alongside each outcome—a practice that will be introduced in the next section of this chapter. In addition, Chapter 12 on assessment includes a chart providing sample outcomes and evidence from each of the content areas. The sample lesson plans in Chapters 7 and 8 also present learning outcomes in a variety of domains.

Figure 6.2 Learning Outcomes in Math and Language

Content Area	Outcomes *What do you want students to know or be able to do?*	Evidence *What product or assessment will show you what students know?*
Math	Solve equations and inequalities involving absolute values	Problem of the week, quizzes, cooperative group poster, create own equations, summary paragraph on process
Language (English, world language, English-language development)	Compare and contrast the presentation of a similar theme or topic across genres	Venn diagram, comparative essay, dramatization, poster presentation, dramatic presentation, literature log

Evidence of learning:

CONNECTIONS TO STUDENTS' KNOWLEDGE, SKILLS, AND EXPERIENCE: WHO ARE MY STUDENTS, AND WHAT DO THEY BRING IN RELATION TO THIS CONTENT?

This is probably the most critical question you will ask in the effort to make your lessons comprehensible and meaningful to students. Regardless of the importance of the concepts you want students to learn or your enthusiasm for wanting to use what you believe are interesting resources or activities, *if your students are not able to connect their experiences or prior knowledge to some aspect of new concepts, they will not make sufficient meaning out of what you teach.*

In much of the United States, a growing majority of students are from diverse economic, cultural, racial, and linguistic backgrounds. However, for the most part, school texts, the language of instruction, teacher–student interactions, and examples we tend to provide students to contextualize new ideas still presume that all students come from the same, predominantly white, middle-class backgrounds. All of our students come with a rich historical and cultural tradition of their own, as well as oral and written literacies. Your students provide you with a tremendous opportunity to widen your world, as you learn more about the histories, knowledge, stories, and traditions they bring. Your students are eager for you to recognize and build on their strengths, as well as their academic needs.

For example, students may not know details about U.S. history, yet they know a lot about societal issues that lead to immigration, conflict, economic changes, or war. Students may not have specific math vocabulary or practice, yet they know a lot about budgeting, mathematical problem solving, and dividing a small amount of money among many. Activities that help you learn more about your students early on will help you to plan lessons in a way that engages interest and makes sense (see Chapters 4 , 7, and 8 about community building activities that help teachers and students better know one another's background). So as you continue with your lesson planning, look beyond the outcomes, evidence, and key concepts you've already established to take into account what your students may already bring to the table and how you might tap into that prior knowledge.

What follows is a list of sample activities that can work across disciplines to help students bridge prior knowledge to the lesson of the day:

- *Freewriting.* Ask students to write to a specific prompt regarding what they know about the topic at hand. The prompt often works best when it is geared toward a larger concept rather than specific facts. For example, what do you know about conflicts among groups of people (social studies) or about how animals or plants adapt to environmental conditions (science)? When freewriting, students write continuously for amount of set time, such as three to five minutes to allow for more in-depth thinking and discovery. For English learners or others who may have vocabulary gaps, it can help to discuss the prompt with a partner before or after writing.

- *Quotes as writing prompts.* This activity is also a freewrite, based on a quote from current events, literature, or popular culture. Students can share responses with a partner as you circulate and monitor their writing. Encourage a few students to volunteer to read their responses aloud to the group.

- *Visuals as prompts.* As the lesson begins, display an everyday item, photograph, or drawing related to the concepts presented today. You can get as technical as a PowerPoint graphic or as simple as a sketch on the board. This activity can be done individually or with a partner and then shared. Direct students to describe the following:
  - What they see
  - Something they have experienced related to the visual
  - What they think is contained in the item or what they believe the item is used for
  - Three or four questions they have about the item or visual
  - Other responses

- *Word cards.* Prepare 3 × 5 index cards for the total number of students in your class. On each card, list words familiar to students that are synonymous or related to words they will encounter today. Duplicate cards are fine. Distribute cards and ask students to walk around, taking turns with another student to read and explain the word as they understand it. (*English learner modification:* Follow the same procedure from earlier, including the definition of the word on the back of the card.)

- *Quote cards.* Preview any text, procedural steps, or descriptions used for today's lesson using same procedure as in *word cards*. Copy and paste essential quotes or passages from text onto the cards. Ask students to read the passages aloud to another student, paraphrase or give their interpretation, and move on.

- *Word web or word splash.* Identify several concepts or words from the lesson that are thematically related. Write the words on an overhead transparency, whiteboard, or poster paper in a *splash* fashion, namely, not in a column or linear sequence. Direct students to spend five minutes writing sentences using no more than two of the words or word forms in each sentence. When finished, all students read their sentences aloud to a partner. Volunteers may read to the class. Record sentences on the board or overhead. Note how students have prior knowledge of concepts or vocabulary.

- *Find someone who.* Create a list of 10 to 12 items or concepts related to your content that has some practical implication, impact, or connection to students' lives. For example, in math related to estimation, find someone who can estimate (1) the number of miles traveled from his or her house to school round-trip in a week, (2) the number of times he or she made dinner for the family in the past month, and (3) the difference between his or her weight and a sibling's. Students circulate around the room. When they *find someone who* can, they list their name in the corresponding space. After a few minutes, ask students to share their responses.

- *Gallery walk.* Write a quote or other high-interest prompt at the top of a piece of chart paper. Additional prompts for science, math, or applied arts, such as pictures, problems, or models, can be placed at the top of this sheet. Create five to six different sheets and post them around the room. Divide the class into five or six groups. Provide each group with one marker of a different color. Each group gathers and reads or examines the item at the top of each poster. Teams have three minutes to brainstorm and record ideas, questions, and solutions related to the quote or visual. After three minutes, the teacher signals students to move to the next poster where they continue to record input. The process continues until they return to their beginning poster. Students quietly review everything that has been recorded. Ask groups to choose someone to report to the class about trends or patterns they observe.

- *Think-pair-share.* Think of a prompt connected to the lesson that you know to have some connection to students' prior life or academic experience. Choose something that students can talk about easily. (For example, in a history lesson on rights and responsibilities, "What school rules or policies are fair or unfair in your opinion?") Students pair up and take turns discussing the prompt for two to five minutes. Each speaks uninterrupted while the other listens. To close, the first student is directed to take 30 seconds to make a final statement or question about the topic. The second student responds similarly.

ASSESSMENT: HOW CAN I KNOW WHAT MY STUDENTS ARE LEARNING?

So you want your students to understand the causes of the two world wars—how will you know what your students have already successfully learned? Will you teach, hold your breath, and then wait until the final exam? Ideally, each of your lessons includes some form of built-in assessment that gives immediate feedback about what students comprehend or what else they need to know to make meaning out of your lesson.

Products that give you a sense of what students are learning as they go are often referred to as *formative assessments*. Some of the products described in Figure 6.2 are examples of evidence that speaks to assessment. It is important that the assessment provide you with data over whole range of the students in the class—those that typically have an easy time making meaning and applying new information as well as those who have a difficult time.

KEY CONCEPTS AND CONTENT: WHAT ARE THE SPECIFIC OBJECTIVES OF MY LESSON?

Now that you've determined your overall learning outcomes and the types of evidence you might use to gauge student progress, it's time to consider the more-specific *objectives* that will make up your lesson. When contemplating the objectives for your lesson, you are revisiting the essential question, "What do I want my students to know or be able to do?"

The specific objectives you come up with will be key concepts and content that come from the learning outcomes of the day, and they may be simply stated as *fractals* or *photosynthesis*. From the language example in Figure 6.2, if the learning outcome is compare and contrast the presentation of a similar theme or topic across genres, the key concept or objective in a day's lesson may be to identify themes presented in Poe's *The Telltale Heart* as an example of the genre horror.

MATERIALS: WHAT DO I NEED TO TEACH THIS LESSON?

What materials will you need to teach this lesson and where will you be able to find them? Who can help you find more materials or share with you in the department? Is there a budget for you to buy what you need and a process for being reimbursed?

TEACHING STRATEGIES AND SEQUENCE: HOW WILL I MOVE STUDENTS FORWARD?

In this section, we guide you through the actual teaching of a lesson.

Opening

The *opening* is where the lesson is introduced and *objectives* and *outcomes* are clearly stated. Outcomes should also be listed on a posted agenda on the board or overhead transparency. You can ask students to note the learning objective at the top of their binder papers or a graphic organizer you've provided.

This is your best opportunity to link the day's lesson to student's *prior knowledge*, by connecting the day's content to academic or life experiences that may relate to what is being taught. This is also the key time to harness creativity and hook the student's interest by any means you can!

Instruction

The *instruction* period is where new ideas, concepts, and information are presented. Instruction includes content, directions, and the teaching of any specific language, plus learning processes or procedures needed for participation in the lesson.

Many of us who are now teachers were successful students in a traditional high school and college setting where instruction consisted of listening to detailed lectures and taking notes, reading and completing assignments at home, and demonstrating what we had learned from these sources on a final exam. Although this form of instruction continues in many secondary schools, unfortunately it is working for smaller and smaller groups of students.

As we mentioned earlier, large numbers of students in our schools now speak English as a second language, and even larger numbers of students who were born in the United States are not proficient enough in academic English to be able to respond effectively to a lecture or to read and write at grade-level proficiency. Additionally, many students with no apparent language issues struggle with literacy because of a variety of social and academic factors that have led to general disengagement with the printed world. More and more students are turning up with both diagnosed and undiagnosed learning disabilities that require our attention to different learning styles and modalities.

The solution to this problem is complex and challenges new and veteran teachers alike. It involves compiling a large toolbox of teaching strategies that make direct instruction accessible to students with a wide variety of learning needs. The path requires that you listen to students, analyze their written work, and let them tell you what they need to engage with and master the content you teach. The following strategies and structures can help you to begin (see Chapter 9 for more detail on assisting students with reading comprehension):

- *Front load academic language and vocabulary.* Highlight and explain to students new academic terms, idiomatic phrases, and familiar words used in new contexts. Model any tasks you would have students complete as well as reviewing whether students are versed in the academic functions (summarizing, predicting, comparing) that you will have them do later in the lesson or unit (see Chapter 8 for a detailed description of vocabulary-building activities).

- *Modeling.* Demonstrate for students any new procedures, use of resources, or organizers. It is important to demonstrate or think aloud about the task while using the same graphic organizer or format students will use. *After modeling, check for students' understanding of the upcoming tasks.*

- *Guided note taking (graphic organizer).* Provide a graphic organizer labeled with essential concepts and vocabulary for students to record information presented in the lecture. You can also draw a graphic model for students to follow as they listen to the lecture. Labels or descriptors can match headings found on the topic in their textbook. Provide an overhead transparency of the graphic organizer as a reference as you deliver information. Draw a model of how you want students to organize their papers that students can reproduce and use as they listen to input (i.e., Venn diagram, traditional outline format, semantic web, matrix).

- *Video with guided note taking (graphic organizer).* Label the organizer with essential elements, themes, and questions that will be addressed in the video. Video input should be kept to a maximum of 10 to 15 minutes. Students take notes on the organizer as they watch the video. You may choose to stop the video intermittently to give students a chance to fill in their organizer.

Guided Practice

Guided practice provides a time for students to work individually or in groups to learn the concepts you have introduced that day. Practice time needs to include students' demonstrating or producing something to let you know what they have learned.

The time will be shorter at the beginning of the unit, longer if students have been given several lessons including content input and guided practice. Increase this time accordingly for block periods. Remember that even with input and guided practice, students need breaks during periods of independent work longer than 20 minutes for intermittent checks for understanding, peer feedback, process problem solving, or opportunities for sharing individual progress

Time may be spent completing a lab, drafting an essay, or creating a group presentation. Students can actively practice skills with one another or with the teacher in small-group instruction. They may use texts, graphic organizers, or a great variety of tools and resources to better understand key concepts. Sample guided practice activities follow:

- *Guided reading with graphic organizer.* Students read text to find information featured on the graphic organizer. The organizer should be explained before students proceed. Elements featured on this organizer include the essential concepts you want students to understand and will differ from traditional end-of-chapter questions. Organizers should help students locate, categorize, and analyze information.

- *Timed problem solving, practice, and application.* Students in math, science, applied arts, and technology classes follow task procedures and solve problems. These tasks or operations should have already been modeled by the teacher as an example of an essential concept or skill. Students can interact with peers, use teacher-provided references, and access the teacher's support during these activities.

- *Ongoing projects.* After unit objectives and essential input have been presented, students may work on an ongoing project such as research projects, poster presentations, or group problem solving. For the first two or three days, students can access resources and clarify ideas with the teacher and peers as they begin their project. Later, projects can be completed during independent work time or as homework.
- *Dialectical journals.* Dialectal journals are graphic organizers that provide alternate means of analyzing and interpreting text.
- *Lab or learning stations or centers.* If space and resources are available, learning centers or stations provide students with the opportunity for a more hands-on approach to learning. A traditional element of learning for all lab sciences, stations provide students with more opportunity for interaction and kinesthetic learning as they study essential concepts. The following are sample ideas for stations or centers:
  - o Provide folders with high-interest articles on themes or topics related to key concepts. Include graphic organizers and descriptions of student tasks related to the articles. Groups of four to six students can work with these resources.
  - o Stock file bins with realia, art materials, manipulatives, and authentic examples related to key concepts. Provide descriptions, directions, or visual representations of items that students can reproduce (art forms, design patterns, small poster representation of concepts in science, history, literature, foreign language, or math). Include a task related to the items and procedures for completing the task.

The following are projects that help identify evidence of learning in guided practice:

- *Problem solving.* In math or applied arts, direct students to solve a set of problems related to a lesson or procedure. In language-focused classes (English, English-language development, world languages), students can be directed to correct passages for grammar and sentence order.
- *Summary paragraphs.* Direct students to write summary paragraphs related to key concepts from the day's lesson. Students can summarize reading passages or information noted on graphic organizer during lectures or labs. The cognitive tasks involved in summarizing information are (1) deleting trivial or redundant information, (2) substituting detailed information by grouping ideas and then restating a trend, and (3) keeping key information. Remind students to include key vocabulary in their summaries, demonstrating their understanding of the terms.
- *End of chapter questions and problems.* Direct students to answer questions or solve problems provided at the end of a chapter or section.

- *Ongoing projects.* After students are introduced to foundational concepts and have been given opportunities for guided practice, more time can be provided for ongoing, individual projects. Projects allow students a measure of choice and an opportunity to independently apply content knowledge and skills.
- *Applying comprehension strategies.* Direct students to demonstrate their comprehension of material via prompts that require them to do the following:
  - *Describe or interpret* a character's action, author's intention, art form, events in history, steps for solving a math problem, or observations related to an experiment.
  - *Compare and contrast* events in history; examples of science-related systems in physical science, biology, or chemistry; and possible solutions to problems.
  - *Analyze* a complex problem, a character's actions, a quote, events in history, or lab observations.
  - *Predict* outcomes of character development, historical patterns, or current events issues.
  - *Generate questions* related to text, process, or other input. Students should generate two to three questions per reading section as well as possible answers.
  - *Classify or attribute* different aspects of science-related content, literary elements, mathematical problems, fine arts or applied arts concepts, and grammar via an appropriate graphic organizer.

Closure

Checking for understanding is key. When you help students to refocus their attention on the outcomes of the class, they will retain more of what you have taught them. Even a simple restatement or reference to the outcomes for the lessons as listed on a daily agenda will make a difference. The following are a few strategies you can use to check for understanding:

- *Teacher think alouds regarding student progress.* As you circulate through the class monitoring students during guided practice, make note of trends in student work. Identify evidence of progress and understanding as well as indications of challenges with the content or task. Then, as you close the lesson, do the following:
  - Simply restate (aloud) the lesson's targeted outcome or ask students to restate the outcome.
  - Record on an overhead transparency, poster paper, or board your general observations, including student successes and challenges regarding today's work. Keep observations general, using stems like, "I noticed that a number of you . . ." or "Some of you appear to have some questions about . . ." or "It might be helpful if we remember to . . ."

- *Student questions.* During the introductory days of a unit, use part of guided-practice time to allow students to generate a question about the content or process. Provide them with a 3 × 5 card on which to write the question. During closure, answer key questions generated by students.

- *Sharing student work.* While affirming student work individually during guided practice, you can also ask on-target students or group representatives to share their responses during closure. If you use this method on a regular basis, take care to be equitable in your sharing of student models. Make sure all students will eventually have an opportunity to be noted for their successes. *Variation:* Share the work of a student from another period related to the same assignment (without sharing the name of the student).

- *Anecdote, quote, sharing an alternative model.* To close a lesson, it supports students to hear or see another model or alternative solution related to their task. Note the relationship between what you share at this part of the lesson and the outcomes previewed at the start of the lesson.

7

Planning for the First Two Weeks of Math Class

Sample Lesson Plans

What exactly should those first weeks look like?

You may have already developed several lessons and units as part of your preservice coursework and student teaching experience. Other lessons you've downloaded from various teacher Web sites look promising. The priorities in the first two weeks of instruction include not only beginning the first instructional unit but also establishing routines and procedures, building a learning community, and starting to assess students. It is challenging to pull all these things together. To get you started, we have provided you with sample outlines and lessons for the first two weeks of school.

We have asked exemplary secondary math and English teachers to give you a step-by-step view of how they establish necessary components of a successful classroom in the first two weeks. Lesson plans for the first two weeks of math instruction are featured in this chapter, and lessons for humanities (English, social studies) instruction are featured in Chapter 8. Even if you are not a math or English teacher, we believe the information, approaches, and sequence of activities and lessons provided can be modified for your subject and grade level. What do exemplary teachers keep in mind while planning to make sure that students are engaged with content and experiencing academic success? Feel free to borrow or photocopy everything these teachers have done, and then gradually make it your own.

This is also the time of year to begin to assess and learn about your students. How do you find out what content knowledge and skills your students bring? How do you find out their language skills and needs, their goals and interests, their cultures and worldviews? All of this information will help you to be much more effective as their teacher (see Chapter 6 for suggestions on gathering this information).

The first two weeks are a unique time of the year. You should plan additional time for community building, assessment, and the establishment of clear routines and procedures. However, while timing may vary, the structure of your day will stay consistent throughout the year. The Elements of Daily Lesson Planning (Figure 7.1a) will help you plan the structure of your day, and it is designed to be used alongside the Lesson Plan Template (Figure 6.1) provided in the previous chapter (and repeated here in Figure 7.1b). These documents will help to provide you with structure not only for the first two weeks but also throughout the year.

The first of our two lesson plan models represents the first two weeks in a 9th- and 10th-grade algebra class. Both this teacher and the one whose instructional designs are featured in Chapter 8 have utilized a similar template for organization but brought his or her unique flavor and approach to teaching. Remember that the first two weeks set the stage, and you cannot overplan. The more smoothly your classroom runs, the more room there is for creativity. Be prepared to work hard and, above all, to enjoy your students.

Figure 7.1a   Elements of Daily Lesson Planning

Learning Outcomes
   What will students know or be able to do?

Connection to Students' Knowledge, Skills, and Experience
   What do students already know that will help them to learn?

Evidence of Learning
   Which product or assessment will show you what students understand?

Key Concepts and Content
   What is the focus of today's lesson? Which content standards will be addressed in this lesson?

Materials
   What do you need to teach this lesson?

Teaching Strategies and Sequence
   Opening
   - *First two weeks*
     o *Establish routines and procedures*
     o *Community builders*
   - *Throughout the year*
     o *Independent warm-up*
     o *Teacher may conference with individuals*
     o *Community builders*

   Instruction
   - *Review homework or previous study*
   - *Bridge prior knowledge and experience*
   - *Highlight essential concepts*
   - *Introduce new key vocabulary*
   - *Model, explain, and demonstrate new content*

   Guided Practice
   - *Teacher structures timing and procedures*
   - *Students interact with and practice subject matter content*
   - *Students work as individuals or in small groups*
   - *Students demonstrate evidence of learning*

   Closure
   - *Extension activities or independent practice*

Figure 7.1b Lesson Plan Template

FORMATIVE ASSESSMENT TOOL

Lesson Plan B

Name: _____   Mentor: _____

Grade Level/Subject Area: _____   Date: _____

Lesson Topic: _____   Content Standard: _____

The *Essential Components of Differentiated Instruction* FAS Resource offers specific ideas for differentiating instructional strategies, content, products or assessments in new and varied ways.

Learning Outcomes	Key Concepts & Content	Connections to Students' Knowledge, Skills, Experience
	Teaching Strategies & Sequence Opening	
Evidence of Learning (Product or Assessment)	Instruction	
	Guided Practice	
	Extension Activities or Independent Practice	
Materials		

LESSON PLANS FOR MATHEMATICS

9th- and 10th-Grade Mathematics

First two weeks of school

Day 0: Things to do before the first day of school

Materials and Resources

Find out the following:

- Where can you get chalk, pens, paper, poster paper, staples, rulers, protractors, and an industrial-strength three-hole punch?
- Where can you pick up textbooks (if applicable)?
- What are the school rules or policies for absences and checking back in after absences?
- Where is the staff bathroom, the copy room, computers for word processing and e-mail?
- Who is the custodian or groundskeeper? Who do you ask if you need extra desks or the like?
- What will you teach?
- Who is your department chairperson?
- What math courses does your department offer? What is the sequence? Type it or write it neatly on a transparency for students to see on Day 1.
- What, where, and how to use math manipulatives?

Think about and prepare the following:

- Rules and procedures
- Course expectations
- Syllabi for each course
- Assignment sheets
- A calendar for the first month of school
- An attention signal (bell or chime)

Get copies of examples from fellow teachers. It's okay to emulate what they do! In fact, if possible, find a veteran teaching partner to help you with pacing of your courses, curriculum development, and assessment.

Your Room

If you have your own room, stand by the door and imagine what your room will look like with 30-plus kids in it. Create an optimal arrangement consistent with the suggestions given in Chapter 2 of this book. Modify and experiment. If possible, create two easily interchangeable layouts—one for individual or pair work and one for group work. In particular, think about how students can transition from individual work (such as working in rows) to group work (such as working in clusters of four). Maximize your ability to use proximity—make sure every student seat is easily and quickly accessible. Think about putting your desk toward the back of the classroom. Create transparencies of your seating arrangement or arrangements so that you can put them on the overhead when you want your students to straighten up the room. If different groups of people use your classroom (other teachers or night school for example), tape a version of your classroom layout on the wall by the exit. This might help minimize the likelihood of finding your room a disaster zone when you enter it.

Create these items:

- A grade book with insides for five (or so) classes
- A calendar with all important school dates notated, such as finals, back-to-school night, and the like. Get your *district calendar* from your school office manager and copy over all the important dates.
- Folders for each class, with blank seating charts on the front (Hint: buy the kind that has two pockets or sleeves on the inside. Into the left pocket goes student work that you have to assess. Into the right pocket goes work to pass back.) Then, tape a transparency lengthwise across the bottom of the front cover of the folder to create a transparent pocket that can hold seating charts or other immediately important items (see Figure 7.2).

Figure 7.2	Preparation of Class Folder

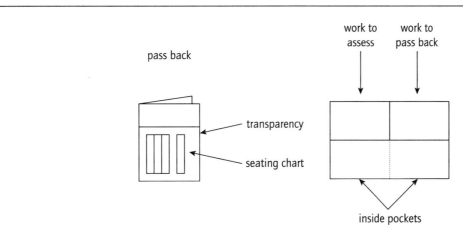

- Seating chart/room arrangements for both individual work and group work. Make many blank templates so you can change seating arrangements about once every two weeks. Also, copy many versions of the group sign-in sheet from Day 4. You should randomly change groups every two weeks or so.
- A folder filled with heavy-duty transparencies, a bin with lots of transparency pens, and a place in your classroom to clean transparencies. Bring in rags to wipe them clean and a spray-bottle of water. Cleaning transparencies is a dirty business and takes skill to do correctly. Ideally, you can train a student assistant to do it. If not, you'll either be washing your hands a lot or walking around with psychedelic hands!
- Will you use a grade-book program? Experiment with it beforehand. Create templates of classes and grading systems so you can more efficiently use it when school starts.

Copy

- Student information sheets
- Expectations, syllabi
- Assignment sheets
- Calendars for students for the first month or two

Hint: As you begin to write and/or accumulate these items, keep a fresh copy of each in a binder for next year! Do the same with worksheets, openers, quizzes, and the like over the next two weeks. Carry these good habits through the whole year, and Year 2 will be a whole lot easier!

Also, you will want to share some of these items with parents during back-to-school night.

A sample script for 9th- and 10th-grade math follows, beginning with the daily agendas shown in Figure 7.3. Use as much of the lesson plans as you feel comfortable doing. You may use only a couple of ideas, several lesson plans, or most of it. Adapt it, amend it, and make it your own. Be flexible. Incorporate ideas from your department chair, the teacher next door, training, texts, or your new-teacher support provider. *Note that sample assignments and activity forms follow each daily lesson plan.*

Oh—and did I say organize? It is time to get started!

Figure 7.3 Daily Agendas

Day 1	Day 2	Day 3	Day 4	Day 5

• Introductions
   o Teacher
   o Course
   o Students (think-pair-share)
   o Content standards
 • Assignment 1 (math autobiography)
 • Opener
 • Homework review (student-made transparencies)
 • Content standards (Cornell Notes)
 • Test/quiz procedures
 • Quiz
 • Assignment 6
	• New seating chart
	 • Review homework (pairs)
	 • Procedures
	 • Content standards
	 • (10 and 2)
	 • Assignment 2
	 • Opener
	 • Homework review (pairs)
	 • Content standards
	 • Quiz review
	 • Assignment 7
		• Opener
		 • Homework assessment
		 • Procedures
		 • Rubric
		 • Homework review
		 • Interview debrief
		 • Students at board
		 • Content standards
		 • Assignment 3
		 • (Groups of 4 today)
		 • Opener
		 • Homework review (student-made transparencies)
		 • Sentence strips
		 • Content standards
		 • Summary Booklets
		 • Assignment 8
		 • Test Tomorrow!
			(Groups of 4 today)
			 • Opener
			 • Group profile
			 • Group procedures
			 • Text quest
			 • Homework review (peer assess in groups)
			 • Content standards
			 • Cornell notes
			 • Assignment 4
			 • Homework review
			 • Unit 1 exam
			 • Assignment 9 (Cover letter for portfolio)
				(Groups of 4 today)
				 • Opener
				 • Homework review (transparencies)
				 • Procedures for presentations
				 • Presentations
				 • Content standards (Cornell notes plus number heads)
				 • Assignment 5
				 • Quiz Tomorrow!
				 • Opener
				 • 3-2-1
				 • Organize binders
				 • Anticipation guide for Unit 2
				 • Content standards
				 • Tests back
				 • Assignment 10

DAILY LESSON PLAN

9th- and 10th-Grade Mathematics

First two weeks of school

Day 1 (based on a 55-minute period)

Learning Outcomes

Outcome: Students will be able to identify key elements of course text and key components of syllabus. Students will understand course goals and expectations.

Evidence: Students will use colored markers to highlight key elements and components of course syllabus as they listen to teacher's overview of the syllabus. Students will respond to teacher's follow-up questions to confirm their understanding.

Outcome: Students will begin to build community in the class and set a positive tone for the study of math.

Evidence: Students will complete personal interview form, participate in partner and whole-group responses related to the interview.

Outcome: Students will begin to identify prior knowledge and application of the study of mathematics.

Evidence: Students will write their math autobiography.

Key Concepts and Content

Community Building:

This math course has clear expectations of students and is based studying a logical sequence of math concepts and themes. All students enter with some prior knowledge.

Materials and Resources

Before students arrive, have the day's agenda written in the place you will write it every day. Place the papers for the day on each student desk, so you won't have to waste time passing them out later. This would include your course syllabus, your assignment sheet, calendars, your expectations, and a student information sheet. As with all papers you pass out to your students, you should three-hole punch them beforehand. Write your name on the board or overhead and some simple instructions like, "Welcome to Algebra I. Please find a seat and fill out the student information sheet." As students arrive, greet them warmly at the door and prompt them to the instructions on the board.

Agenda I	Mr. Weil	09/04/08

Welcome to Algebra I! Please find a seat, and fill out a student information sheet.

- Introductions
  - Teacher
  - Course
  - Students (think-pair-share)
- Order of operations
- Assignment 1 (math autobiography)

Teaching Strategies and Sequence

Opening

Set a serious and professional tone. Introduce yourself to your students. Why did you choose to be a teacher? How long have you been teaching at the school? Where did you go to school? Briefly introduce your school's mathematical course sequence. For example, on an overhead, share a transparency that looks like this:

ABC High School Mathematics

Prealgebra

Algebra I Interactive Math Program (IMP)1
Geometry IMP

Algebra II IMP 3

Math Analysis IMP 4

Advanced Placement (AP) Calculus or AP Statistics

Describe the course you are teaching and where it fits in with this sequence. Describe the prerequisites (for example, this is an Algebra I class, so you expect that students have received a C or better in prealgebra). This is not a threat—you share it as an expectation. Also, tell them that you will spend some time reviewing some of the key concepts of the previous course.

Describe why you like math. When did it come alive for you? Do you like all kinds of math or just certain strands? Who played a positive role for you and why? What environments help you learn, and what hinders your learning?

After sharing about yourself, the math sequence at your school, and this course, let students know you would like to know a little about them and give them a chance to know a little about one another. This will help you begin to learn about your students, their life experiences, and interests—their prior knowledge that you will work to connect your lessons with. First, however, you would like them to finish the student information sheet.

Community Building Activity: Think-Pair-Share

Think: Prompt students to fill in student information sheet (Figure 7.4). Say, "Take a couple of minutes and finish filling in the student information sheet." Get around your classroom and answer individual questions.

Pair: Ask students to, "*Turn to a partner,* introduce yourself, and share some of your responses. For example, share what your hobbies are or careers that interest you. Let's take about five minutes." After about four minutes, prepare for the upcoming transition by saying, "Okay, take about one more minute."

Share: Ask the whole class, "What are some of the careers that interest you?" Write responses on butcher paper.

- Fill in the student information sheet
- Turn to a partner and share your responses
  ○ What are your hobbies?
  ○ What careers interest you?
- Whole-class share

Make an overhead with these prompts. *Always* try to give instructions both *verbally* and *in writing.*

Tell students to turn in the student information sheets because this is how you will take roll today. Transition now back to the course.

Note: If your department gives a placement exam to students, you should spend some time reviewing for it. This would be an appropriate time to do this. After a long break, students need some review. Also, placement tests should be used with other assessment data, such as teacher recommendations or grades to guide student placement.

Instruction

Usually, the first section in a math book or unit is a brief overview or quick review. Highlight what is important. If you do not have a textbook yet, or do not use a textbook, use this time to introduce your course or review key concepts from a previous course.

If your unit begins with a review of types of numbers (integers, rational, irrational, and real), you may tap your student's prior knowledge in a number of ways. Students already know how to categorize many types of items. For example, food can be categorized into fruits, vegetables, grains, and legumes. You can briefly demonstrate the categorizing process with food. Like food, or other items, numbers can be categorized in a number of ways.

Give some examples:

Discuss the attributes of each category.

Integers	Rational Numbers	Irrational Numbers	Real Numbers
2 5 −6	$\frac{1}{2}$ 1.5 0.33333…	3.1414927… $\sqrt{2}$	2 −5 $\frac{1}{2}$ $\sqrt{2}$ 0.5

Give some numbers and ask students to categorize them.

Connect the discussion explicitly with your text or other resources. What are the types of problems they will have to solve or exercises they will have to do? What are the instructions? Do some examples, clearly describing, writing, and demonstrating what they have to do. Let students hear it, see it, and then do it several times.

Guided Practice

Pass out Assignment 1: math autobiography (Figure 7.5). Students may begin in class. You may augment Assignment 1 with some problems from the textbook or first unit or other types of problems.

Nuts and Bolts: Teacher may choose to distribute and cover texts, sign schedules, make other site-based announcements, and so on.

Closure

Check for understanding on Assignment 1—it should be finished tomorrow when they enter the classroom.

After School

Read student questionnaires. Arrange them in alphabetic order, by first name. Write their names (first and last) on a seating-chart template, with names starting with an *A* more to the left and names starting with a *Z* more to the right. It doesn't have to be perfect. If you know some students and want to separate them early, do it. Notice unusual or difficult-to-pronounce names. Tomorrow, as you get around the class during homework review, privately check in with all students. Ask students how to pronounce their names and what they like to be called.

Put the seating chart in the transparent cover of a folder, which you will use to store student work to grade or hand back. If you have time, create an overhead of the seating chart so tomorrow, students can come in, see where they sit, and sit down.

Create packets of papers with all the handouts you passed out today. When you get new students over the next few days, simply hand them a packet.

In a three-ring binder, start collecting copies of all handouts. Today, insert a clean copy of your course syllabus, your assignment sheet, calendars, your expectations, a student information sheet, and anything else you may have passed back.

Think about tomorrow's lesson and script it. It helps to make a script of your lesson, complete with any definitions and examples, formatted as you expect you would format them on the board or overhead. Read over your script, or rehearse it aloud in the shower. Imagine the transitions from teacher-led instruction to individual or group work. What will it look like? What prompts or visuals will aid in your transitions? Like all of the work you use or create for each course, keep this organized in a three-ring binder for next year.

Figure 7.4 Student Information Sheet

Student Information Sheet

Algebra I

Name: _____Preferred Name: _____ Birth Date: _____

Parent/Guardian Name(s): _____

Parent/Guardian Phone Number(s): _____

Parent/Guardian E-mail: _____

Last Year's Math Class (es):_____ Teacher: _____ Grades: _____

Class Schedule:

Period	Teacher	Class

What is your favorite thing in the world to do?

What are some of your hobbies or interests?

What are some possible careers that interest you?

Do you own a calculator? If so, what kind?

Figure 7.5 Math Autobiography Part I

Math Autobiography Part I   Name: _____

Assignment 1

(From Ina Newberg, New Middle School)

I. Write your math autobiography

Write a one-page paper that addresses each of the four topics stated below. Reflect on the significant events in your mathematics education. Include important events that or people who shaped your mathematical background.

1) Your past experiences in math
   - What is it about math you enjoy?
   - What are you good at?
   - What do you find frustrating?

2) The kind of learner you are
   - What kinds of things help you to understand new ideas?
   - What is the best environment for you to learn in?
   - What types of learning styles/environment are challenging for you?

3) Your goals for math this year
   - What do you hope to accomplish?
   - What kind of grade do you plan to earn?
   - What do you plan to do to achieve your goals?

4) The role math plays in your life
   - Describe the role math currently plays in your life
   - How do you think it could affect your future?

This should be one page in length. It can be written in pen or typed on a computer.

Due Date:

DAILY LESSON PLAN

9th- and 10th-Grade Mathematics

First two weeks of school

Day 2 (based on a 55-minute period)

Learning Outcomes

Outcome: Students will be able to describe and demonstrate routines and procedures for quiet signals, homework, materials organization, and in-class work.

Evidence: All students are able to describe and demonstrate routines and procedures.

Outcome: Students will continue to build community and establish prior knowledge about math.

Evidence: Math autobiography is completed and shared with partner. Students begin parent math-history interview as homework assignment.

Outcome: Students will demonstrate understanding of the first new math concepts from curriculum sequence.

Evidence: Students correctly complete problem set in relation to new math concept.

Key Concepts and Content

All students are responsible to know and carry out classroom routines and procedures. All students have a personal math history.
  Math Content Standard: Functions

Materials and Resources

Write the agenda on the board. Have seating charts ready to go for all your classes today.

$$\boxed{\text{Teaching Strategies and Sequence}}$$

Opening

Put the seating chart on the overhead or somewhere where students can access it. Write on the board:

> Please find your assigned seat. If, because of vision or hearing difficulties, you need to change seats, please write me a short note and drop it on my desk.

Greet students at the door, and prompt them to take find their seats. Help them as necessary. Some might complain—just remind them that it's alphabetic by first name, and it will help you learn their names. Some will resist and want to sit by their friends. Today, and for the first two weeks, stick to the chart! Double-check to make sure students are in their correct seats. If a seat is empty, it signifies an absent student, so you can now quickly take roll. Preview the agenda.

$$\boxed{\text{Instruction}}$$

Math Autobiographies
(Community Building, Building Prior Knowledge)

Tell students, "Turn to a partner and share your autobiographies from your homework. Look for similarities and differences." Pass out graphic organizers (Figure 7.6) for them to record their thoughts. If you assigned some problems from the text, also prompt them to share any difficulties they had. After a few minutes, allow time for the whole-class to share. What were some of the similarities and differences that surfaced? Collect homework. They may have questions about how you will grade it, what if they don't have it, and so on, so this is a perfect time to begin covering procedures.

During this time, use proximity to check in with each student. Use your seating chart and use their names. If you are unsure how to pronounce a name, ask the student how.

Routines and Procedures

Use your quiet signal to quiet the class down. Discuss why transitions from group work to class work are important and what they should look like. Share how the quiet signal indicates that the class will be transitioning to another activity.

Discuss your procedures for checking or grading homework. What do you expect? How will you grade it? Broaden the discussion to your course syllabus and how you will compute their grades. Talk about the class rules. You can joke or smile most anytime except when talking about rules. Use a serious tone.

Will there be exams or quizzes? How much will they count when computing their final grades? How about homework, class work, and participation? For the autobiography, say that you will give all students who completed it full credit. On day three, you will work together to create a rubric that will guide you in assessing homework or assignments.

Math Content Standards: Functions

Prompt students to take out some paper for notes.

Cover section 1.2 in the textbook or unit. Usually, this is where the authors transition from basic definitions to some deeper concepts. Use a contextual *discovery* approach if possible in this early stage of the course. For example, if the topic is "word problems involving linear equations," do the following:

- Create a context. (e.g., write a table of values showing wages earned versus hours worked. Describe a worker or show a picture of someone working, like a Caltrans worker. Indicate the wage of this worker, for example, $21 per hour.)
- Make predictions. Record on the board. (How much will this worker earn for two hours or work? Three hours? Four and a half hours?)
- Move to the more abstract. Derive a linear function that models this situation.
- Connect back with previous example. (State wages as a function of time worked.)
- Demonstrate how to solve a complete problem, step by step. Explain, write, and show all the steps. The written part of your lesson should be clear and shown step by step. Leave this written model up for students to model their problems after.
- Give another example. Allow students time to apply what they learned from the first example.
- Teacher proximity—praise, prompt, leave. ("Good—I see you have completed the chart. Now, see if you can generalize." Then, don't forget to leave! In other words, don't get "hung up" on helping just one or two students. You need to get out and about. Your visuals will be helpful here.)
- Prompt them to turn to a partner and share approaches. Then share with the whole class.
- Use 10 and 2: After 10 minutes of teacher talk, give students a structured 2-minute prompt to debrief and make connections with a partner (or in some other small-group setting) then connect back to whole class.
- Repeat the 10 and 2 process with more content. (24 minutes total)

Introducing New Content: What Is a Function?

- Create context
- Discussion, predictions
- Definitions
- Example (Say it, write it, and model it. Leave the written example on board.)
- Second example—students do it. Teacher proximity.

- Say, "Turn to a partner and share. Did you use the same approaches or get the same answers?"
- After students have had a minute or two, ask volunteers to share answers or approaches. Respond and reinforce more elegant or appropriate strategies.

Guided Practice

To transition students into guided practice, ask them to find their assignment sheets from Day 1. Discuss how it works and how today you are on Assignment 2 (Figure 7.7). Model how to read the sheet and understand it. Then model how you (as a student) would start your homework.

"Get out some paper. On the top, write . . ."

Andrew Weil

Algebra I, 09/05/08

Assignment 2

Page 5, Problems 1–10, Parent/Guardian Interview

Preview the interview questions with them.

If you are also assigning math problems (recommended), model your expectations on the first few problems. For example, ask them to copy each problem down (they'll groan—but this is a fair and very worthwhile expectation!) and solve the problem step by step. Circle or highlight each answer. Actually, do the first several problems and model what you mean.

Continue Assignment 2 in class. They finish it at home.

Closure

Ask students to turn to a partner and briefly discuss the following:

- Three things they learned
- Two things they need to do
- One thing that is still unclear

Facilitate a brief discussion and assess how the class is progressing. Ask a student to verbalize what the homework is.

After School

Look over Assignment 2. What are some key concepts or ideas that students need to understand from it? Which problems or questions best illustrate these? Choose several.

Choose four to six problems that you will write on the board at the beginning of class for brave student volunteers to do tomorrow.

Choose two to three problems that you will randomly use to assess homework at the beginning of the class tomorrow. On a Post-it note, write the two to three problems and their answers. Stick this note on the front of your folder with the seating chart on it. You will use it tomorrow for a quick assessment of their homework.

Write an opening activity for tomorrow. On an overhead transparency, write three to seven problems arranged from easy to more difficult that will transition into the content standards you intend to cover. For example, if you are covering graphing functions, you can have some problems asking students to complete an in-out table and guess a rule. Include an interesting or more difficult problem at the end to challenge all students.

Figure 7.6	Math Autobiography Debrief

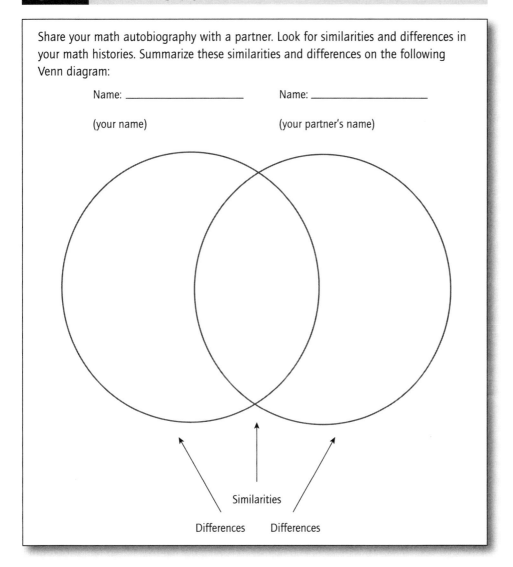

Share your math autobiography with a partner. Look for similarities and differences in your math histories. Summarize these similarities and differences on the following Venn diagram:

Name: _____   Name: _____

(your name)   (your partner's name)

Similarities

Differences   Differences

Figure 7.7   Parent/Guardian Interview

Assignment 2   Name: _____

Parent/Guardian Interview

Name of Parent/Guardian: _____

A. Find a parent or guardian to interview for this assignment.

B. Interview the parent or guardian about their math experiences, and record their responses.

Suggested Questions:

- What topics in mathematics did you like, and which did you dislike?
- Who were the people who played a positive role in your mathematical life and why?
- Who played a negative role and why?
- Describe your good mathematical experiences and the bad ones.
- In what environments do you learn the best?
- What environments hinder your learning?
- Where do you use math in your life today?

DAILY LESSON PLAN

9th- and 10th-Grade Mathematics

First two weeks of school

Day 3 (based on a 55-minute period)

Learning Outcomes

Outcome: Students will complete homework and in-class work based on a clearly defined standard identified by a rubric.

Evidence: Students are observed to be referencing the rubric while completing work. Homework and in-class work are completed to the highest level of the rubric.

Outcome: Students will continue to identify prior knowledge and home/school connection in math, based on parent autobiographies.

Evidence: Parent autobiographies are completed and shared with a partner.

Outcome: Students will demonstrate understanding of the building block math concept graphing standards.

Evidence: Problem sets on graphing standards are completed correctly.

Key Concepts and Content

Work in this class is expected to meet standards. We all come with prior knowledge on math.

Math Content Standards: Graphing

Materials and Resources

Create a visual instruction plan (VIP) for the content standard you will introduce today (VIPs are explained below). Write the agenda on the board. Write four to six problems from last night's homework on the board. Post or display your seating chart again for students who were absent, forgot, or who might start to *wander* toward greener pastures. Greet students warmly as they enter; let them know they'll need some paper to start the opening activity.

Remind students why you have created the seating chart (to help you learn their names).

You should be learning and using most names by now. Try to learn them all by the end of Day 5.

Teaching Strategies and Sequence

Opening

Seat work, problem sets. Introducing rubric and standards for completed work. Put three to five problems, from easy to more difficult, on the overhead that will connect students to the content standards you will cover today. For example, if you are covering graphing functions, you can have some problems asking students to complete some in-out tables or guess some rules. Include an interesting or more difficult problem at the end. While students are working on the opener, you can walk around and assess homework using this process.

On a Post-it note that is stuck to your seating-chart folder, write the two to three previously chosen problems you will check, with answers (choose typical or important problems, not the hardest ones). Walk around and check each student's work briefly, and comment on the problems you are checking. For example, you might see that they got two problems correct (mark them correct) and one wrong (circle the problem number). If you see why it's wrong (maybe they forgot a negative sign), say, "Good job on these two. I'd like you to check over your work on this problem—pay close attention to the rules for multiplying positives and negatives." Give credit in a way that is consistent with a rubric that you will share shortly with your students.

The key is to *praise, prompt, and leave.* To get around to your whole class in fewer than eight or ten minutes, you will have to hustle.

Write down on the Post-it only the names of those students who received less than full credit. At the end of the day, transfer scores to your grade book—everybody except students who were absent and students whose names are on the Post-it gets full credit. During the first and second week, try to collect no more than two or three assignments to assess more thoroughly during the week. During later weeks, try to collect no more than one or two assignments per week. If you collect more, you might burn out on grading. With practice, you can run a very efficient, fair, and worthwhile in-class homework-check assessment.

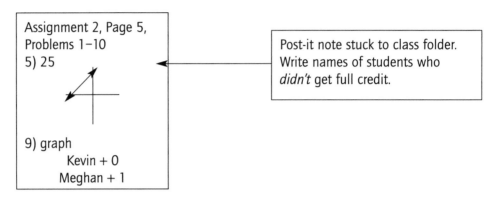

When you are finished, share your rubric with your students on the overhead or on poster paper. If you use a two-point rubric, your rubric might look something like Figure 7.8.

Figure 7.8   Sample Rubric

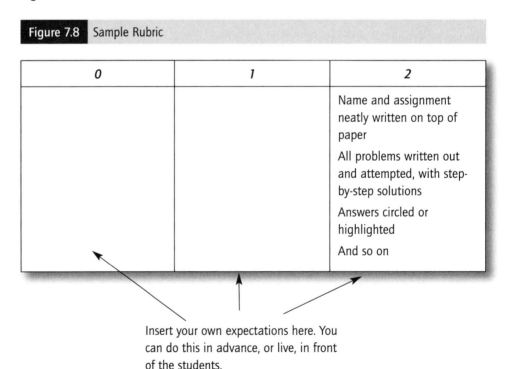

0	1	2
		Name and assignment neatly written on top of paper
		All problems written out and attempted, with step-by-step solutions
		Answers circled or highlighted
		And so on

Insert your own expectations here. You can do this in advance, or live, in front of the students.

Feel free to ask for and use input from students. Mold their suggestions into the expectations you have in mind. If you are not comfortable with this, feel free to create the rubric yourself. Finish the rubric. Keep a copy (either on poster paper or on a transparency) to refer back to frequently during the first few weeks of class.

Ask if there are any questions from the opener. Briefly answer them.

Instruction

Homework Review: Ask for four to six brave volunteers to write their solutions to the problems you have written on the board. Remind them what makes good solutions: A good solution is complete, step by step, and the answer is circled or otherwise indicated. Students may work simultaneously at the board. Wait until they are all finished.

Comment on the work to give students a chance to see how you react to student work. Say positive things about all the work on the board: "Nicely done. Maria showed her work neatly and went step by step. This one was done quite nicely, with only a minor error with the negative sign." Gesture to a less-than-perfect example. "Remember to show all the steps—we will be solving some pretty sophisticated problems before long, and solid problem-solving habits are a must." You may make comments about your expectations. Reinforce what you would like to see in their homework.

Wait Time

When addressing your class, it is useful to periodically think about your use of *wait time*. For many students, especially students whose first language is not English, a teacher's use of wait time is critical for including them in the course. Periodically ask yourself, "Are my students blurting their responses? When I ask questions, do I immediately call on the first volunteer? Do I typically wait for three to five seconds between giving an instruction and then prompting for an answer? Do I ever use equalizers to call on those who don't respond voluntarily?"

Autobiography review (prior knowledge, community building)

Ask your students to turn to a partner and share their interviews. After about two to three minutes, ask them to share where their parents/guardians use math (answer the last question). Record answers on poster paper.

Introducing Today's Math Content Standard:

Cover Section 1.3 in the textbook or unit.

The Visual Instruction Plan (VIP) (Adapted from Fred Jones)

Before the lesson, create a VIP that clearly illustrates each step of what students need to be able to do (see Figure 7.9). The VIP should be written neatly on butcher paper and displayed prominently in the classroom. Model how you use the VIP when going over some examples in class. The purpose of doing this is to help wean *helpless handraisers* who will want you to give them a private tutoring lesson during guided practice. Teachers who spend too much time reteaching material to individual students run the serious risk of losing control of the other half of the classroom.

Figure 7.9	Sample Visual Instruction Plan		

$2x + 6y = 18$	$2x + \blacksquare = 18$	$2x + 6y = 18$	$\blacksquare + 6y = 18$
Write the problem.	To find x-intercept, cover up the y term with your finger.	Divide 18 by 2. The x-intercept is 9.	To find y-intercept, cover up the x term with your finger.

Example: Graph $2x + 6y = 18$ by computing the x- and y-intercepts.

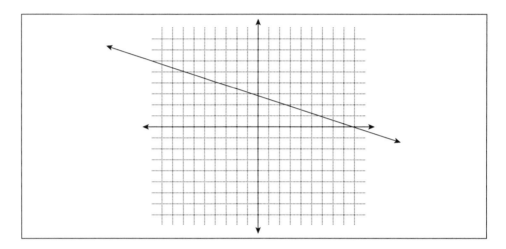

The VIP shows, step-by-step, what to do. You use it to help you solve problems. What you might write on the board?

Example 1: Graph $2x + 6y = 18$ by computing the x- and y-intercepts

$2x + 6y = 18$		
Let $y = 0$		Let $x = 0$
$2x = 18$		$6y = 18$
$x = 9$		$y = 3$

With all lessons, say it, write it, and model it—step by step. Leave your written work on the board as a visual cue for visual learners to reference during guided practice. VIPs are very effective tools to help visual learners learn the content.

Also, always use high-quality graphs in your demonstrations, and use a straight-edge when drawing straight lines. If you are sloppy, students will gladly sink to your level of expectations.

Guided Practice

Begin Assignment 3 in class. Do several problems with the whole class, using the VIP as a reference. As you use proximity, notice if students are using the VIP. If a student has a question, see what step they are on and use the VIP to prompt them to do the next step.

Closure

If you haven't done so, pass back their math autobiographies. Then, introduce the second part of the assignment (Figure 7.10), which involves students making a star with their math histories. This is an especially good assignment for younger students—if you are not comfortable doing this, it is okay. This activity is an excellent community builder and gives more visual students an outlet to share themselves.

After School

Enter homework grades from Post-it notes into your grade book.

Remind yourself what your classroom layout is for group work (if you created this before day one. Otherwise, determine one now).

Get a deck of cards and remove the nines through kings (for a class of 32). You will use these to randomly create groups of four students tomorrow.

Create and then photocopy a group-profile worksheet (See example at the end of Day 4).

Make sure you have decided on and created your *group procedures* (See example in Day 4).

Write your lesson for tomorrow.

Figure 7.10 Math Autobiography Part II

Math Autobiography Part II   Name: _____

Create a math star about yourself.

Using the four topics from the math autobiography, create a star that symbolizes your math autobiography. The middle square will be a picture of you. The pairs of points on each side of the square will each represent one of the four topics. You should decorate your star in a style that best represents you. Be creative!

Here is an outline for how to plan your star:

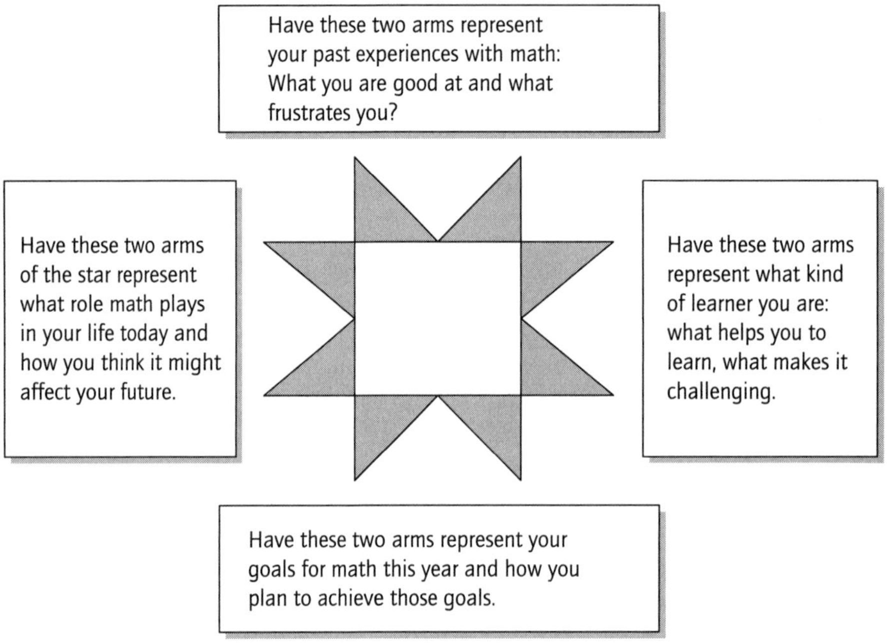

Have these two arms represent your past experiences with math: What you are good at and what frustrates you?

Have these two arms of the star represent what role math plays in your life today and how you think it might affect your future.

Have these two arms represent what kind of learner you are: what helps you to learn, what makes it challenging.

Have these two arms represent your goals for math this year and how you plan to achieve those goals.

This assignment is an opportunity for you to really shine! Bring in a small picture of yourself tomorrow for the middle of the star. We will laminate the finished stars and post them arranged as a quilt on the wall of the classroom. Have fun!

DAILY LESSON PLAN

9th- and 10th-Grade Mathematics

First two weeks of school

Day 4 (based on a 55-minute period)

Learning Outcomes

Outcome: Students will begin to work in groups and utilized group norms and procedures for team-building and academic work.

Evidence: Students work respectfully and efficiently according to group norms. Students complete group profile.

Outcome: Students will review and identify math book text features during group work.

Evidence: Each group member participates to correctly complete text quest form (Figure 7.13).

Outcome: Students self-assess completion of homework based on the teacher rubric.

Evidence: Homework is completed to the highest standard of the rubric.

Outcome: Students will utilize Cornell notes as a form of note taking from lectures.

Evidence: Students begin to take notes utilizing the Cornell notes form.

Outcome: Students will demonstrate understanding of the third building block concept from math standards.

Evidence: Students correctly complete problem set for math content standard.

Key Concepts and Content

There are class standards and norms for completing a group task or project together. The math book has explicit text features that will help to further math understandings. Students as well as teachers can assess homework to meet the qualities in the standard. Cornell notes can help process new math information.

Math Content Standard: Sequence

Materials and Resources

Write the agenda on the board.

Arrange your desks in groups of four.

Label each cluster of four desks as aces, twos, threes, all the way to eights (for a class of 32) (Hint: Use folded index cards or, for a more permanent and less obtrusive solution, hang table numbers from the ceiling).

Separate the aces through eights from a deck of cards, and shuffle them. As students enter the classroom, greet them and give them a card. Direct them to sit at the appropriate table. Let them know that you like to periodically shake things up and have them work in groups of four. These are randomly chosen groups that you will change every two weeks or so. Ask them to sign in on the group list (Figure 7.11). Preview the agenda.

Teaching Strategies and Sequence

Opening

Group Work: Establish norms and procedures for groups, team building (group profile).

Give groups some structured time to get to know one another by sharing their math stars and then filling out the group profile sheet (Figure 7.12)

Talk about group procedures. Here are some suggestions:
(Using overheads of room layouts help.)

Group Procedures

1. **Help** to form and disband groups quickly

2. Use **group** voices—keep conversations in your group

3. Listen to your group mates; learn and use their names

4. Follow instructions, both as an individual and as a group

5. Invite others to participate

6. Talk, question, listen, share, and learn

Instruction

Group Work, Studying Textbook Features (Textbook Quest)

Pass out the textbook quest form (Figure 7.13), and let students work in their groups on this activity. Use proximity and help as needed.

Whole-class share: Choose some of the problems to discuss.

Homework Review

> *Ask* students to *self-assess* their homework using the rubric we created yesterday. Refer back to your copy so they remember how the rubric works.

Next, ask students to *peer-assess*. Do self-assessment scores match up with peer-assessment scores? Why or why not? This is a good opportunity to discuss strengths of rubric assessment (flexible, holistic, formative) versus weaknesses (open to interpretation). Collect homework.

Transition

- Have students change the room back to rows. Having an overhead with the classroom layout helps speed things along. It may be noisy and seem slow, but with the map on the overhead, they will get there.

- Collect the math stars, the group profile (Figure 7.12), and the text quests. Remind students to make sure they put their names on them.
- *Math Content Standard:* Cover section 1.4 today. Remember 10 and 2 and VIPs, if appropriate.
- Introduce new content using Cornell notes, a powerful and structured note-taking method (see template [Figure 7.14] at the end of this lesson).

Guided Practice

Begin Assignment 4 in class. Do several problems with the whole class; then let them work on the problems.

Checking for Understanding

After giving instructions, it can be useful to check for understanding. A comment, such as, "So what are we going to do now?" or "Oh, I like the way Jenna is using her straightedge to neatly copy down the diagram," can be very helpful to make clear your expectations in transition times.

Closure

Have students straighten up, and ask a student to remind the class what the homework is.

After School

More thoroughly assess homework using your rubric. Choose two key problems to spot-check as well. Make your expectations clear. For example, if you require your students to copy each problem, show their work step by step, and circle or highlight their answer, indicate your expectations *in writing* to students who are not doing it yet.

When you are finished, enter grades into your grade book, and put the stack of papers into the right-hand side of your class folder to be handed back tomorrow.

Photocopy and post the group sign-in lists (Figure 7.11) for all classes for students who will forget their groups. Write the names of absent students into the groups with only three members.

Get eight overheads (which you will clean and reuse) and write a problem from the homework on each. Write an indicator of the problem—for example, Page 27, Problem 10. The students will write on these overheads and work through the problems when you instruct them to do so tomorrow.

When you have time, neatly arrange the math stars on the wall in your room. If possible, laminate them first. This builds community in your classroom. Parents will also enjoy seeing this at back-to-school night.

Be flexible if your room is used by other teachers or for night classes. Respect their expectations that the room arrangement will be consistent for them over time.

Note: Facilitating group work can be exhausting! Research shows that using groups can be an especially effective and equitable structure to include in your repertoire of teaching styles. Yet, it is also one of the most difficult structures to implement effectively in your classroom. Stick with it. Over time, you and your students will get better at it.

Figure 7.11 Group Sign-In Sheet

A ♠ _____   5 ♠ _____

A ♥ _____   5 ♥ _____

A ♣ _____   5 ♣ _____

A ♦ _____   5 ♦ _____

2 ♠ _____   6 ♠ _____

2 ♥ _____   6 ♥ _____

2 ♣ _____   6 ♣ _____

2 ♦ _____   6 ♦ _____

3 ♠ _____   7 ♠ _____

3 ♥ _____   7 ♥ _____

3 ♣ _____   7 ♣ _____

3 ♦ _____   7 ♦ _____

4 ♠ _____   8 ♠ _____

4 ♥ _____   8 ♥ _____

4 ♣ _____   8 ♣ _____

4 ♦ _____   8 ♦ _____

Figure 7.12 Group Profile

Names: _____ Date: _____

Group Profile

Group members' names:				
Favorite color				
Favorite music group				
Favorite television show				
Favorite movie				
Favorite food				
Favorite hobby/activity				
One interesting and unique talent				

What does this group have in common?

What are some differences between group members?

What have you learned about your group?

Figure 7.13   Textbook Quest

Algebra I   Name: _____
Textbook Quest!

Work in your groups to complete this quest.

1. What is the **title** of Chapter 1?

2. What page does the **glossary** start on?

3. What is an expression? (Hint: Use your glossary)

4. What is the **picture** of on Page 250? Why do you think the author included a photo like this one?

5. What is written in the **blue box** on Page 383?

6. What type of information do you think the author of this book puts in blue boxes?

7. The **table of contents** is at the beginning of the book. What is the title of the second section in Chapter 5, or **5.2**?

8. How many **example problems** are there in Section 9.4?

9. What is an **example problem** used for?

10. What starts on Page 633?

11. What is the answer to Problem 13 in Exercise 1.4?

12. Find the **index**. What page number would tell me something about a *prime factor*?

13. Find the foreword to the student. Do you agree with the statement the author makes in the second paragraph in the second column on that page? Why or why not?

14. Find the beginning of Chapter 5. Complete this sentence: "This section is meant for you to . . ."

15. Define the word *equation*.

Figure 7.14	Cornell Note-Taking System

Recall clues and questions   Class: Date:

Notes: The Cornell note-taking system

Preparing the system

1. Use standard three-hole paper.

2. Use only one side of paper.

3. In math, use a pencil (a mechanical pencil is best).

4. Draw a line one-third from the left side of the paper

5. Write ideas and facts on the right side of the line.

6. Skip lines between major ideas.

7. Record notes simply.

8. Write key phrases, not entire sentences.

9. Don't make an elaborate outline.

10. Write down all key terms and definitions.

Using the system

11. Include all relevant examples.

12. Use an abbreviation system.

13. Write as neatly as possible.

14. Leave blank space when you miss an idea. You can add information later after talking to classmates or your teacher.

15. Read your notes as soon as possible after the lecture or reading.

16. Rewrite illegible or abbreviated words that you may forget.

17. Check the spelling of any uncertain words.

After the lecture or reading

18. Improve the organization of notes by numbering, highlighting, and bulleting items.

19. Write key words or questions in the recall column that prompt the information in the note-taking column.

20. Cover the right side of your notes with a piece of paper.

21. Using the questions or key words in the recall column, recite aloud the facts and ideas of the lecture or reading in your own words.

Review method

22. Slide the paper down and check that portion of your notes to see if you remembered all of the critical information.

23. Check off questions in the recall column that you should continue to review more seriously

DAILY LESSON PLAN

9th- and 10th-Grade Mathematics

First two weeks of school

Day 5 (based on a 55-minute period)

Learning Outcomes

Outcome: Students will demonstrate understanding of basic math concepts and standards presented in Week 1.

Evidence: Students will take a math quiz related to Week 1 concepts and standards.

Outcome: Students will learn and demonstrate clear standards for classroom presentations.

Evidence: Students observing and giving presentations will demonstrate clear procedures and standards.

Outcome: Students will practice participation protocols through a cooperative strategy *numbered heads together.*

Evidence: All students can be observed to be participating effectively in the activity.

Materials and Resources

Write the agenda on the board. Let them know that there will be a quiz tomorrow on sections 1.1 through 1.4. (Of course, this is flexible. Give a quiz when it is natural to do so. It is best not to wait too long, however.) Arrange room in groups of four. Post or put on the overhead the groups formed on Day 4 to remind students which group they are in. Also, write a message on the board, such as, "Welcome—please join your group and start the opener."

Teaching Strategies and Sequence

Opening

Again, three to seven problems relating to the content standards you are going to teach today, arranged from easy to more difficult. Students may work on the problems in their groups as you assess homework using the rubric you created on Day 3.

After you go around and assess last night's homework, drop off a transparency and two overhead pens to each group and ask them to agree on and write a solution to the problem. Give them about five minutes to write the solution.

Pass back homework.

Page 17, Problem 10

Instruction

Transparency

Homework Review: Groups presenting solutions

Before you ask them to share their solutions, talk about two things: procedures for classroom presentations and tips for effective classroom presentations.

Procedures for Classroom Presentations

- Be courteous—no backs to the presenter(s).
- Raise your hand to ask a question or make a comment.
- Sidebar conversations annoy the presenter and fellow listeners.
- Direct your attention and questions to the presenter, not the teacher.

Write this on poster paper and post. Periodically, review it.

Tips for Effective Student Presentations

- Face forward; use eye contact when possible.
- The use of good visuals, such as transparencies, posters, chalkboard, handouts, and the like, helps your audience (and keeps some of the focus off you!).
- Visuals should stick to the point. Distracting art annoys your audience.
- For longer presentations, creating and sharing an agenda helps.
- Balance participation between group mates.

Write on transparency and share. Periodically, post transparency and revisit these important tips.

Group Presentations

Ask each group to make a very brief presentation on the solution to their problem. Students may address questions to the presenters. The teacher can respond to student work but should refrain from being the focus of this review process. Look for teachable moments. Reinforce elegant or appropriate approaches and strategies.

Math Content Standards

Combine *Cornell notes* with *numbered heads together* when presenting today's content standards. Remember to give the students about 2 minutes of processing time (numbered heads) for every 10 minutes of teacher talk (Cornell notes).

Guided Practice

Begin Assignment 5 in class. Do several problems with the whole class, then let them work on the problems. Focus on teacher proximity to get around the room and check in with the groups. Prompt them to move forward when necessary.

After School

Write opener for tomorrow.

Clean transparencies. (Hint: Bring in rags from home. Create a place in your classroom where you keep a water bottle and rags. This should be on a dark-colored table; it will get messy!) Learn to quickly and completely clean transparencies. It is an art form to do it correctly. Your life will be greatly enhanced if you have an aide that can learn this skill.

Write two versions of the quiz. How long should it be? Plan for 20 to 30 minutes. Be aware. How long did you expect it to take? How long did it take? How will you adjust?

Figure 7.15   Numbered Heads Together

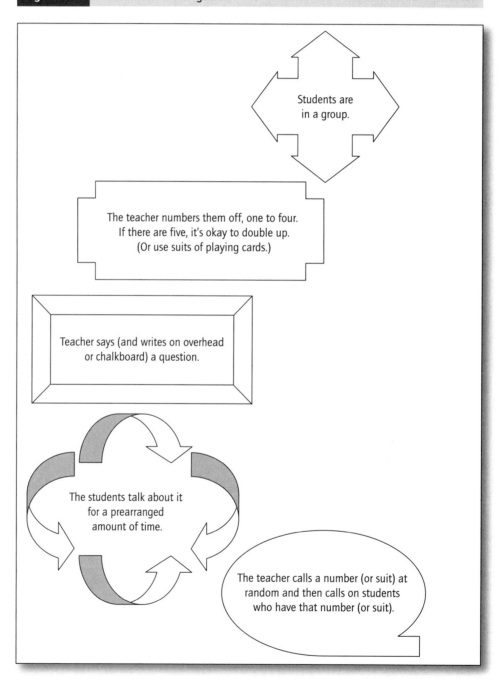

DAILY LESSON PLAN

9th- and 10th-Grade Mathematics

First two weeks of school

Day 6 (based on a 55-minute period)

Learning Outcomes

Outcome: All students will be accountable for concepts that are unclear to them by participating in the homework review.

Evidence: Students successfully record questions.

Outcome: All students have a clear understanding of procedures and protocols for quiz and test taking.

Evidence: Students demonstrate protocols when taking the quiz.

Getting Ready

Write the agenda on the board. Arrange the classroom for individual work. Warmly greet the students as they enter the room. Remind them where the seating charts are posted in case they forgot where they sit. Prepare an opener.

Teaching Strategies and Sequence

Opening

Use your own opener.
Assess homework during opener.

Homework Review

Teach them this highly efficient method to share their homework questions.

When students come in, if they have a question, pick up an overhead transparency and a pen from the place where you normally keep them (near the overhead is good). Neatly write the page and problem number, and write the whole problem. Also, include sketches, ideas, or partial solutions. Put the transparencies with the problems by the overhead. They should then indicate on the board which problem they wrote so another student doesn't write it up as well.

The teacher can either address and answer the questions on the overhead or redistribute them back to groups or clusters of students. Today, choose several questions and answer them on the overhead. If you don't address all the questions, indicate why ("I think you'll find that Number 7 was a lot like Number 13—try using Number 13 as an example and give Number 7 another shot").

Instruction

Use Cornell notes today.

Quiz

Make at least two versions of the quiz. Stagger them into a single pile before class starts. When passing them out, try to use a checkerboard pattern. This will help to ensure that neighbors have different versions. Don't dwell too hard on making your checkerboard perfect. Always go over your quiz/test procedures before giving a quiz or test. It doesn't hurt to talk about why you want it silent after they are finished (not everybody is finished, and everybody is entitled to the same nondisruptive environment). Sit in the back of the classroom during the quiz.

Test/Quiz Procedures

1. Work silently.

2. If you have a question, raise your hand.

3. Finished? Turn in your test or quiz, and *silently* begin the homework.
   Homework: worksheet, Page xxx Problems x, y, z

Guided Practice

Follow previous procedures—students will silently begin their Assignment 6 after completing the quiz.

After School

Grade quizzes. Look for patterns. Are there common errors or especially nice solutions? You should share your thoughts tomorrow.

Enter quiz grades and homework grades into your grade book.

Makeup Quizzes

What will you do for students who are absent on quiz or test days? One approach is to let them make them up during the half-hour before or after school. You can let them complete parts of it if a half-hour is not enough time. Avoid letting them makeup quizzes and tests during class, as they will then miss the lesson and fall behind. If you write your own quizzes on computer, you can easily modify the problems for the makeup tests. Many publishers create several versions of tests and quizzes, so if you use these, it is easy to create alternatives. Try to use different versions for makeups.

DAILY LESSON PLAN

9th- and 10th-Grade Mathematics

First two weeks of school

Day 7 (based on a 55-minute period)

Learning Outcomes

Outcome: Students will demonstrate problem-solving skills through the completion of a *discovery lesson.*

Evidence: Students will complete discovery lesson and participate in a group discussion about the lesson.

Outcome: Students will understand and be able to apply procedures for makeup tests.

Evidence: Students can describe procedure and sign up for makeup if needed.

Getting Ready

Write the agenda on the board. Have an opener ready to go on the overhead when they enter.

Teaching Strategies and Sequence

Opening

Again, three to seven problems relating to the content standards you are going to teach today, arranged from easy to more difficult. Assess homework.

Homework Review

Say, "Turn to a partner. Share one shortcut you discovered and one question you have. Brainstorm solutions." (Remember to write it too, for example, on the overhead.)

Use proximity and assess common problems. Praise, prompt, and leave so you can get around. Respond to common problems to entire class.

Instruction

A nice discovery lesson fits well here. (See Day 2)

Quiz Review

Pass back quizes. Post answers (overheads are especially efficient). Go over commonly missed problems. Remind them how quiz scores fit in with your grading scheme.

What are your procedures for makeup quizzes? Share them now.

Guided Practice

Begin Assignment 7 in class. Do several problems with the whole class, and then let them work on the problems. Use proximity to keep them moving forward. Check in with individual students concerning their quiz grades.

After School

Cut construction paper for tomorrow's *sentence-strip* activity (2 inches by 12 or more inches is fine). Locate pieces of poster-size butcher paper and masking tape.

DAILY LESSON PLAN

9th- and 10th- Grade Mathematics

First two weeks of school

Day 8 (based on a 55-minute period)

Learning Outcomes

Outcome: Students will utilize vocabulary and academic language related to math to summarize concepts learned in the first unit.

Evidence: Each student will create a sentence strip with the support of his or her cooperative group.

Outcome: Students will present a summary of each unit concept using words, symbols, and images.

Evidence: Students successfully complete chapter summary booklet.

Getting Ready

Write the agenda on the board. Set up their groups of four today. Have an opener ready to go on the overhead when they enter, and remind them where the group sheets are posted.

Teaching Strategies and Sequence

Opening

Use three to five questions very similar to tomorrow's test questions (same directions, same format, same level of difficulty). Assess homework. Remember to praise, prompt, and leave.

Homework Review

Student-made transparencies (see Day 5)

Sentence Strips

Ask students in their groups to brainstorm and come up with two or three topics they learned during the unit or chapter. Students write these topics on brightly colored strips of construction paper that were prepared yesterday (see the example in Figure 7.16). Stress that they should try to be unique and descriptive in their responses (for example, on a unit of probability, they write things like "combinations and permutations" instead of just writing "probability"). Students stick their strips to masking tape stretched across butcher paper. Leave these up. They will serve as writing prompts for the cover letters.

Figure 7.16 Sentence Strips

Types of numbers: integers, rational numbers, irrationals, and real
Properties of numbers
Opposites, reciprocals, roots
Closure property Integers closed under addition $5 + 3 = 8$ Integers not closed under division $3 / 5 = 0.6$
Commutative, associative, distributive properties
Absolute value
(Continue)

Instruction

Review for test.

Students will create a three-dimensional chapter summary booklet (see the instructions in Figure 7.17).

Think about how the unit breaks up into organized chunks. Each panel of their booklet can contain equations, definitions, sketches, graphs, and example problems. Model how you would create one or two of the panels as a review of some of the concepts. Give students some time to work on theirs.

Figure 7.17 | Construction of Summary Booklet

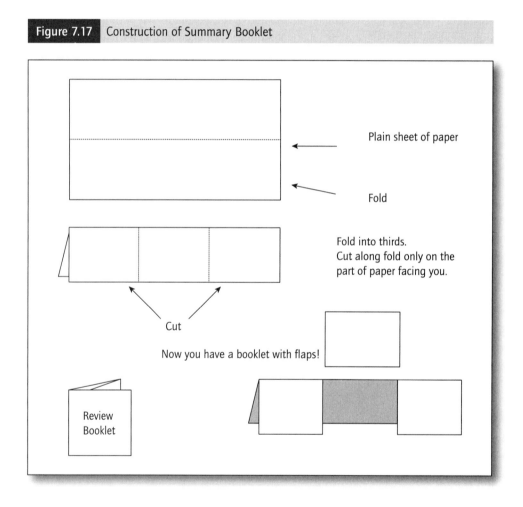

Guided Practice

Begin Assignment 8 in class. Part of the assignment should be to finish the booklet and part should be to do some problems similar to those that will be on their test. Do several problems with the whole class, and model how you can use and modify your booklet to help you remember the concepts.

After School

Write two versions of the exam. Stagger them like you staggered the quizzes on Day 6.

Clean transparencies. Try to wash all the blue and psychedelic stuff off your hands before you go home.

DAILY LESSON PLAN

9th- and 10th-Grade Mathematics

First two weeks of school

Day 9 (based on a 55-minute period)

Learning Outcomes

Outcome: Students will demonstrate comprehension of mathematical concepts from first unit (summative assessment).

Evidence: Students will complete first unit test.

Outcome: Students will self-assess progress and set goals for the class thus far.

Evidence: Students will describe their self-assessed progress and goals for the class in a math cover letter.

Getting Ready

Write the agenda on the board.

Teaching Strategies and Sequence

Opening

Review Assignment

Selects problems to review. Choose problems that are similar to those on the test.

Say, "Turn to a partner and take five minutes to share your chapter summary booklets." This time will allow for some review.

Collect homework.

Unit 1 Exam

Post quiz/test procedures. While students take exam, sit in the back. Assess homework and enter grades.

Instruction

Write a cover letter for the unit. Please write a cover letter to put in your binder for this unit. Include the following in your cover letter:

- A brief description of what the unit was about
- What mathematical topics you studied
- What you learned
- How you feel you progressed in the areas of
  ○ Working together with others
  ○ Presenting to the class
  ○ Writing about and describing your thought processes
- What you feel that you need to work on
  ○ Mathematical topics
  ○ Other classroom processes
- Any other thoughts you might like to share with a reader of your binder

After School

Grade tests. Look for trends that you will share tomorrow. Write an anticipation guide for Unit 2 (see the example [Figure 7.19] at the end of Day 10).

DAILY LESSON PLAN

9th- and 10th-Grade Mathematics

First two weeks of school

Day 10 (based on a 55-minute period)

Learning Outcomes

Outcome: Students are able to self-assess their progress.

Evidence: Students complete 3-2-1 self-assessment protocol in partners.

Outcome: Students are able to clearly organize materials and paperwork for maximum accessibility.

Evidence: Students demonstrate a clearly filled-out *binder checklist,* as well as a clearly organized binder.

Outcome: Students begin to demonstrate prior knowledge for upcoming unit.

Evidence: Students will complete anticipation guide survey designed for this unit.

Getting Ready

Write the agenda on the board.

Teaching Strategies and Sequence

Opening

3-2-1 Protocol

Say, "Turn to a partner. Read your cover letter to your partner. Then, your partner will briefly interview you with these three questions."

3-2-1

- What are the *three* most important topics you learned?
- What *two* questions do you still have?
- How might you use *one* topic in your life?

    Partners switch.

    Allow the whole-class to share.

Organize Binders

Imagine the very best binder a student could make in your class. What does it look like? What does it include? Make a check-off list of these items. Allow students to organize, then self- and peer-assess one another's binders. A sample binder check-off sheet is provided at the end of this lesson (Figure 7.18).

Building Prior Knowledge: Anticipation Guide for Unit 2

Pass out anticipation guide (Figure 7.19) to pairs. Pairs work together.

Instruction

Begin teaching the content in Chapter 2 or Unit 2. Remember 10 and 2.

Pass back tests. Post answers and review key concepts.

Guided Practice

Students begin Assignment 10 in class.

Figure 7.18 Binder Check

	Week 1	Week 2	Week 3	Week 4	Week 5	Week 6	Week 7	Week 8	Week 9
Assignment sheets, calendars, and guidelines are present									
Notes are Cornell notes									
Notes and assignments are in order									
Problems written out, solved, and clearly indicated									
Neat									
Cover letter									
Complete									
Total									

Figure 7.19 Anticipation Guide

Prealgebra   Name: _____

Anticipation Guide

Fractions

1. Read the items.

2. Decide whether you agree or disagree.

3. Share your responses with a partner.

4. Put your anticipation guide away.

1. Fractions describe relationships.   1) _____

2. Fractions are useful in real life.   2) _____

3. Fractions can be used to find percentages.   3) _____

4. Fraction problems can be figured out by drawing pictures.   4) _____

5. Fractions express ratios.   5) _____

6. Fractions can be expressed in only one way.   6) _____

7. Adding fractions is easier than multiplying them.   7) _____

8. Any number can be described as a fraction.   8) _____

9. A fraction is always less than one.   9) _____

10. I could probably find a fraction in a newspaper.   10) _____

DAILY LESSON PLAN

9th- and 10th-Grade Mathematics

First two weeks of school

Days 11 and beyond (based on a 55-minute period)

Where do you go from here? For the next several weeks, keep this in mind: Many secondary mathematics teachers will want to do these important things in their classrooms: opening activity, review homework, teach content, guided practice, and closure. It is important that as you settle into routines, you do not favor one type of information delivery system (such as lecture only or only group discovery). Try to employ a variety of teaching and learning modes in your classroom. This script has incorporated several different grouping and learning strategies. Elsewhere, this book describes other strategies you can try to use. Tap the teaching knowledge of your colleagues. Search for and utilize opportunities to develop professionally. Try what you learn. Share success stories. Bring examples of student work to a meeting and share with a partner.

Keep binders of everything you do. Copy especially good examples of student work to show your students next year. Many students who *see* what you expect will strive to do better.

Good luck this year!

Planning for the First Two Weeks of English and Social Studies Class

Sample Lesson Plans

What exactly should those first weeks look like?

If you turned to this chapter before reading Chapter 7, you may want to skim the first few pages of the previous chapter. Building on Chapters 4, 5, and 6, Chapters 7 and 8 feature specific lesson plans for the first two weeks of school that were developed by two exemplary secondary teachers. Regardless of whether you teach the same subject and grade levels featured in either chapter, you will find that the lessons, their sequence, and related resources are quite adaptable for the specific classes you teach. You will need to modify some activities and templates referencing subject-specific examples and skills. You might enhance a lesson with articles, quotes, prompts, examples, and other resources that increase the concepts or activities' cultural relevance to your students. You may want to include interactive video resources from the Web or supplementary computer-based programs associated with your literature anthology.

Consistent with the math lessons, you will notice that this chapter's lessons for the beginning of school build in additional activities for community building, assessment, and establishment of clear routines and procedures. Although the timing for certain activities varies, the basic structure of a day's lesson established during these first weeks should stay consistent throughout the year. For block schedule classes, you might modify these interactive lessons by integrating two lessons into one block schedule period. Review the objectives for both days. Determine which objectives and activities could be comfortably grouped given the time needed for instruction, student engagement, and progress toward completing tasks.

Figure 8.1a   Elements of Daily Lesson Planning

Learning Outcomes

What will students know or be able to do?

Connection to Students' Knowledge, Skills, and Experience

What do students already know that will help them to learn?

Evidence of Learning

Which product or assessment will show you what students understand?

Key Concepts and Content

What is the focus of today's lesson? Which content standards will be addressed in this lesson?

Materials

What do you need to teach this lesson?

Teaching Strategies and Sequence

Opening

- *First two weeks*
  Establish routines and procedures
  Community builders

- *Throughout the year*
  Independent warm-up
  Teacher may conference with individuals
  Community builders

Instruction

- *Review homework or previous study*
- *Bridge prior knowledge and experience*
- *Highlight essential concepts*
- *Introduce new key vocabulary*
- *Model, explain, and demonstrate new content*

Guided Practice

- *Teacher structures timing and procedures*
- *Students interact with and practice subject matter content*
- *Students work as individuals or in small groups*
- *Students demonstrate evidence of learning*

Closure

Extension Activities or Independent Practice

LESSON PLANS FOR ENGLISH AND SOCIAL STUDIES CORE

Seventh-Grade English and Social Studies Core

First two weeks of school

Day 0

Materials and Resources

Before the first day, gather materials and supplies.

Essential Materials Needed for Humanities Classroom

1. Overhead projector

2. Overhead pens

3. Blank transparencies for overhead

4. 11 × 18 white art paper

5. Color marking pens—sets for eight groups

6. Rulers—enough for 30 students

7. Class set of textbooks—history, anthologies (if appropriate)

8. Chart pad for daily agenda

9. Access to book room for novels (if appropriate)

10. Extra photocopying budget for handouts and the like

11. Bookshelves—at least one

12. Basic art supplies—glue, scissors, markers, and colored pencils

13. Wall map—especially of areas/time periods to be studied throughout the year

14. Dictionaries/thesauri—at least one for every two students (about 15 of each)

Once you've gathered these essential materials, it's time to begin planning your daily agendas. The daily agendas presented in Figure 8.1b can be used as a guide to help you through the process.

Figure 8.1b Daily Agendas

Day 1	Day 2	Day 3	Day 4	Day 5
• Agenda—copy • Introductions • Name tag share • *Get up and gather* (community builder) • Standards for listening • Student information sheets • Materials list **Closure** – Homework check – Key point for today (KFT) – Room cleanup – Ticket out **Homework** 1. Gather materials 2. Highlighter for Wednesday 3. Finish name tag	• Agenda—copy • Name tag share • *Find someone who* (community builder) • Quote work • *Standards for learning*—lecture and graphic organizer **Closure** – Homework check – KFT – Room cleanup – Ticket out **Homework** 1. Gather materials/note 2. Bring highlighter! 3. Finish *standards* handout and signature 4. Parent question	• Agenda/homework check • Name tag share • Quote work—define and rewrite • Syllabus—highlight main ideas • *I have/I need* materials organizer • *Group genius:* prior knowledge about world history **Closure** – Homework check – KFT – Room cleanup – Ticket out **Homework** 1. Materials packed and ready for class 2. Parent signature on syllabus 3. Interview parents for cultural history and historic time periods (*Group Genius*)	• Agenda/homework check • Name tag share • Quote work—learning actions and materials • Materials check—get them out! • Syllabus/*Standards* group quiz • *Personal learning history: Thinking back* • Study buddy numbers • Binder organization **Closure** – Homework check – Key point for today – Room cleanup – Ticket out **Homework** 1. *Learning history,* Part I 2. Call study buddy 3. Finish name tag	• Agenda/ homework check • Turn in name tag—teacher test! • Quote work—organize packet and quick quote quiz (QQQ) • *Learning history, Part II: Symbolic memory* • Preassessment: *Reading survey* **Closure** Quick write for Week 1 **Homework** Only if not completed from the week: 1. Materials? 2. Call study Buddy? 3. Finish *Learning history,* Parts I and II? 4. Quote work?
Day 6	Day 7	Day 8	Day 9	Day 10
• Welcome • Agenda • Roll call: Best part of your weekend—student response (5 min.) • Seating chart—explain and move (10 min.)	• Welcome/roll call • Agenda • Quote work • *Personal learning history*—gallery walk • Silent sustained reading – guidelines and reading chart	• Welcome/roll call • Agenda • Quote work • Silent sustained reading and journal entry • *Personal learning history*—write reflections	• Welcome/roll call • Agenda • Quote work • Silent sustained reading • *Hero biography* project: library visit (set up previous week)	• Welcome/roll call • Agenda • Quote work • Silent sustained reading • *Hero biography* project: create reading program plan • Prereading: *hero reading journal*

Day 6	Day 7	Day 8	Day 9	Day 10

• Quote work (15 min.)
• *Learning history: graphing*
 	
Closure
  – Homework check
  – KFT
  – Room cleanup
  – Ticket out
 	
Homework
  1. Complete quote work
  2. *Learning history*—final draft
	• Begin *hero biography: prior knowledge brainstorm*
	
	Closure
	  – Homework check
	  – KFT
	  – Room cleanup
	  – Ticket out
	
	Homework
	  1. Complete quote work
	  2. Silent sustain reading time at home and journal entry
		Closure:
		  – Homework check
		  – Key point for today
		  – Room cleanup
		  – Ticket out
		
		Homework
		  1. Complete quote work
		  2. Finish *learning history* reflections
			Closure
			  – Homework check
			  – KFT
			  – Room cleanup
			  – Ticket out
			
			Homework
			  1. Silent sustained reading time at home and journal entry
				• *Daily reading journal* —model selecting key events and response
				• *Guided practice—* daily reading journal
				
				Closure
				  – Homework check
				  – KFT
				  – Room cleanup
				  – Ticket out
				
				Homework
				  1. Free weekend from homework

DAILY LESSON PLAN

Seventh-Grade English and Social Studies Core

First two weeks of school

Day 1 (based on a 55-minute period)

Learning Outcomes

Outcome: Students will begin to build community and establish a classroom environment based on trust and respect.

Evidence: Teacher and students know one another's names.

Students have formed teams with clear norms and expectations.

Students can demonstrate standards for effective speaking and listening.

Outcome: Students will learn basic classroom routines and procedures.

Evidence: Students can describe and demonstrate procedures for the following:

- Bell work
- Copying and filing daily information
- Identifying *key point for the day*
- Copying and organizing homework assignments
- Cleaning and leaving room

Teaching Strategies and Sequence

On the board, write a welcome message as well as the name of the class, room number, teacher's name, and course title. Write the agenda for the day and any directions students may need to get started (see Figure 8.2).

Figure 8.2	Day 1 Board Text

Welcome!
Ms. Wolfe
English 1, Room 32

Please find a seat and have ready the following:
- Schedules
- Pen or pencil
- Piece of paper

Agenda 09/04/08
Copy agenda
Introductions
Name tag handout
Get Up and Gather
Info sheets—handout
Materials list—handout
Closure
  - Homework check
  - Key point for today
  - Room cleanup
  - Ticket out

Prepare the following:

- Tagboard strips, markers, and pens for name tags
- Materials list (Translated if necessary for parents)
- Information sheet

Opening

Greet at Door

As students walk in, be sure to welcome them personally and turn their attention to the overhead or board. On the first day, let students sit where they choose. Inform them at roll call that you are assessing their seat selection. How they choose to behave and learn will determine their permanent seat later this week when you create a seating chart. Have students take out their schedules and walk by to check them by the time the bell rings.

Roll Call

After the bell rings, welcome students. Introduce yourself and refer to the agenda on the board. Today will be the only day they won't be working when you are checking attendance because you want to make sure everyone is in the correct room and that you pronounce everyone's name correctly. As you call names, be careful to get the correct name/pronunciation and nickname noted, if appropriate. *This is especially important for students whose name is new to you or originates in a language other than English.* Let students know that they need to listen carefully not only to their own names but to others' as well.

Agenda

Explain to students that every day they will copy the agenda. Time management and knowing what they will learn each day are two strategies for success. Note any handouts, minilectures, or other important learning on the agenda. When students are absent, it is their responsibility to copy the agenda from others and ask for handouts or information they missed. Be sure to focus on the homework that is due tomorrow.

Explain that you will collect agendas at the end of each class.

Teacher Introduction

This is an important five minutes. Tell students about yourself: your education, your adventures this summer, your family, anything that makes you human. You can create a model name tag and use that as part of your introduction as well. A great connection is to describe how you were when you were in middle school (specifically the grade level now in your room). Be geekier and goofier than you really were . . . that will give a giggle and connection right away.

Instruction

Name Tags

Explain to students that it is important to you that you know their names as soon as possible. You have more than a hundred names to learn and need to think of each student in a significantly unique way. Name tags will be displayed on their desks to help you remember their names in a week. Show your name tag as a model and use the sample overhead to guide students (see Figure 8.3).

Figure 8.3 Name Tag Sample

Personal name:	Nickname:
Icon:	
FULL NAME	
(First, Middle, Last)	
Favorite childhood book:	Birth month:

Name Tag Share and Standards for Listening

Explain to students that they will share their full names and their personal icons or symbols. Before people share, it's important to teach how to be an effective speaker and listener, as outlined below.

Standards for Effective Speaking and Listening

1. Effective speakers use a *public voice*. They speak louder than they would in a normal conversation.

2. Effective speakers look at the audience. Be sure to look around the room and not at the teacher.

3. Effective listeners look at the speaker.

4. Effective listeners are silent when others are talking. Side conversations interrupt others' attention and don't honor what is being said by the speaker.

As students share their names and icons, notice how the class is listening. Give feedback by providing evidence of speakers who are using effective public voices.

Have students place their name tags on the desk facing you. Students will be responsible for bringing name tags every day for a week, at which point you will collect them.

Get Up and Gather

Get up and Gather is a community-building activity and an opportunity for the teacher and students to learn more about one another. This activity requires clear behavior standards before you begin.

Describe a category that has several choices. Students are to find others in the room that fit the same category. Some students will find that they are unique; that's great!

Provide an example. "If I said to find people who share your favorite season of the year—how many of you would stand with people who love summer? (Students raise their hands.) Love winter? Love spring? Love fall?" The following are possible categories:

1. Birth month—Find people born in the same month as you. Do we have any "twins"? **Stop**—have students record their birthdates and first and last names on a 4 × 6 card. Be sure they record their month as well. This will be a great piece of info for you to display on a calendar or poster.

2. Favorite sport

3. Favorite subject in school

4. Birth order (Oldest? Youngest? Middle?)

5. How do you best learn something new? Exploration? Reading? Hands on? Listening?

6. Toothpaste they used this morning.

Thank students for participating and listening well, and provide examples of what good participation looked like. Ask them to walk back *silently* to their desks and have a pencil ready to use.

Information Sheet

Pass out the information sheet (Figure 8.4) to students and explain that you will use this information to contact their parents for good and difficult things. Don't be surprised if some kids don't know all their addresses/numbers. Some move, some have just divided households, and so on. Use the sample at the end of the class lesson as an overhead to help students answer this information correctly.

Materials List

Explain to students that two indicators of success for all students are homework return and proper materials. Humanities class has specific materials that are needed to understand reading, support research projects, and write well. Read the list and explain what they will be doing with the supplies.

If there is any problem with getting materials, parents need to contact you before the due date. This is a key point for success. If students can't have an assignment turned in on time, they must tell you *before* the due date, not when you're collecting papers.

At the same time, be prepared that some parents may not speak English or may be intimidated about revealing a financial need. Whenever possible, make sure that important notes home are translated by school personnel who hold this responsibility. If no translator is available, ask students with parents who do not speak English to translate. Provide a check-off box that indicates a need for assistance with materials or other practical matters.

Closure

Homework Check

Students will need a highlighter in two days. If they can't bring one, tomorrow is the best time to tell you. If name tags were not completed in class, they must be completed tonight for homework.

Key Point for Today (KFT)

Students review the agenda and record one sentence about a key learning they had today. Some days the KFT might be informational while on other days it might be organizational or skill based. They will be graded on the quality and thoughtfulness of their responses. Have students record a sentence and ask for reading volunteers (remind them of public voice).

Note: Using acronyms is a great way to model shorthand for taking notes. During the first week, it's important to have students write out the word completely and slowly move into the acronym (e.g., OH = overhead). It can be helpful to have shorthand acronyms posted somewhere near your agenda.

Acronyms		
OH = Overhead	ML = Minilecture	QQQ = Quick quote quiz
H/O = Handout	KFT = Key point for today	

Room Cleanup

Ask students to look carefully around their desks and pick up any papers, bits, and pieces. This is our community space and must be kept neat. Have students stand and push in their chairs. They should also line up the desks as they were when they entered. The best cleanup job makes one think that a class didn't exist here during this time. This step is done when students are standing silently behind their chairs.

Ticket Out

Call sections of the room that are quiet and clean. Have them turn in their complete agendas (with names) to you as they walk out the door. Say good-bye with as much enthusiasm and contact as you greeted them with. Try to use their names as they leave or ask what they are one more time. Be sure to keep these agendas. You will turn them back to them when binders are organized.

Figure 8.4   Student Information Sheet

Student Information Sheet

Name: _____ Class Period: _____

Birthdate: _____ Age: _____

Parents'/Guardians' Names: _____
*If you live with one parent, please list his or her name

Mailing Address: _____

_____

*Phone Numbers:

Mother's Daytime Number: _____

Father's Daytime Number:_____

Mother's Evening Number: _____

Father's Evening Number: _____

Cell Phone Numbers: _____

Parent's e-mail (if they have it) _____
* If there are any restrictions on these numbers, please let me know!

Best way I learn: _____

Best place for me to sit: _____

Last year's teacher(s): _____

_____

An important thing to know about me is: _____

_____

DAILY LESSON PLAN

Seventh-Grade English and Social Studies Core

First two weeks of school

Day 2 (based on a 55-minute period)

Learning Outcomes

Outcome: Students will identify and understand basic principles and standards behind class rules.

Evidence: Students will complete Frayer model graphic organizer on standards.

Outcome: Students will be able to define and apply qualities for successful students.

Evidence: Students will complete quote work making a personal application on qualities of success.

Outcome: Students will learn a standard format for identifying new vocabulary and be able to provide literal and inferential interpretations of quotes.

Evidence: Students will complete binder section on quote work.

Outcome: Students will create a clear and consistent system for organizing binders.

Evidence: Students will have clearly organized binders.

Before Class

Copy the agenda on the board for the students.

Make a note on the overhead that reminds students of opening standards:

When the bell rings, please

- Put your name tag on your desk
- Copy the agenda

Prepare quote of the day.

Prepare minilecture on standards and handout for graphic organizer.

Prepare handout for "Find someone who."

Teaching Strategies and Sequence

Opening

Greeting

Greet students at the door and remind them to check the overhead for bell work. Describe the behavior of students who get right to work.

Agenda

Go through the day's agenda, explaining all acronyms.

Name Tag Share/Roll Call

Be sure to set standards again for listening and public voice before you call names.

Have students share their favorite childhood book title as you call their name today. As students finish copying the agenda, they can listen for common titles shared by classmates.

"Find Someone Who"

This activity builds community by helping students learn more about one another. It also gets students up and moving. Explain that students are to ask people in the class for information, record the information in the box, and have the person sign his or her name.

Encourage conversation as student's sign one another's chart. Stop students after four minutes of this activity. Check in on progress; acknowledge quiet tones and good work; realign any behavior you notice that needs to stop. Be sure that you participate with a chart that students can sign as well.

When a few students have finished, freeze the class, and have them go back to their seats silently. Debrief this activity by asking, "How many have read three books this summer?" Ask individuals to describe interesting facts they discovered about their classmates.

Students can turn this assignment in for credit (you don't have to grade them, just collect them, and see what students did).

Figure 8.5 Find Someone Who

Shares your birth month	Has two opposite attributes	Read at least three books this summer	Speaks another language	Knows the names of eight people in the room
Can name all seven continents	Has been to another country	Knows where materials are kept for students in the classroom	Has met someone famous	Has an incredible talent
Can spell the teacher's name	Has moved more than three times	Can name five world history leaders	Brought all required materials to school	Is artistic
Remembers his or her first lost tooth	Can name every teacher he or she's had	Uses a library card regularly	Uses the Internet for research	Has a pen pal
Eats something unusual for snack	Can explain how to open a combination lock	Would rather be outside than inside	Finds that math comes very easily to him or her	Keeps his or her room organized and clean every day

Instruction

Quote Work

This can be a regular activity that integrates language arts skills, history, and literary themes. Quote work is a powerful way to teach analysis, summary, evaluation, and other higher-level thinking skills. By using literary and historical quotes, students also expand their repertoire of names, places, and events essential to their grade level's standards. Quotes can provide many opportunities for word study and students can create learning packets based on vocabulary from quotes.

Note: Some quotes present particular challenges to English Language Learners if they contain complex vocabulary, are from old English dialects, are written in academic

English, or refer to people or events unique to the United States. Be sure to consider the needs of English Language Learners, and prepare to present key vocabulary and make bridges to prior knowledge before beginning this activity.

The following example is a quote that might be used at the beginning of the year (for additional quotes, see Chapter 4, Quote Discussion). Over time, students can be encouraged to look for and contribute powerful quotes to the activity.

> Whether you think you can or think you can't—you are right.
>
> —Henry Ford

Quote Discussion

- Ask students to copy the quote and check the spelling of new words.
- In partners, discuss what the quote might mean (3 minutes). Continue as group discussion.
- Ask students to record any new vocabulary words along with a brief definition, based on the information you have provided and dictionary work if appropriate. As a further challenge, students can synthesize the definition down to four words.
- Ask students to rewrite the quote in their own words, making sure that each word in the revised quote makes sense.
- Students can share their new quotes with a partner and compare content. Then have the class share. Have the students share their partners' writing rather than their own. This gives the students who are comfortable sharing in class a chance to talk and the more reluctant students a chance to have their words heard by the group.

Instruction

Standards for Learning or Rules

Note: There are many ways of describing standards and rules for any given class. The key points to note in our sample are the ways the teacher provides a clear rationale for each standard and resulting rule. She also outlines clear behaviors that she expects as evidence of meeting the class standard.

Yesterday, you told students that being prepared with materials and homework is an indicator of success. Applying *standards for learning* will also create success for students during the year. Successful people know what is expected of them and how to behave according to expectations. Pass out the graphic organizer for standards as you give this brief introduction. Students should have a pen or pencil ready to use.

Minilecture

"There are five standards for learning in this class. As I give them to you, please record them on your graphic organizer. We will use these standards for the entire year. When we all agree to behave and act according to the same standards, our class will run smoothly, and we will make good use of our time together. There are consequences for those who chose not to follow the standards and cause us to lose valuable learning time."

Standard 1: Truth—Why is truth important for our success? (*Have students brainstorm.*) Truth creates a climate in a classroom that allows us to trust one another when we are struggling to achieve. I will tell you the truth when you ask me questions about your achievement or why we do things. I expect you to tell the truth by stating your needs rather than complaining or being invisible, by being clear and honest when you blow it on an assignment, or when something is damaged in the room.

Standard 2: Trust—Why does trust make for a more successful classroom? (*Students respond.*) Without trust, we won't take risks to work harder than we've ever worked before. Without trust, people won't share their ideas or disagreements in discussions. Without trust, we can't know that our materials and work are safe. Trust takes time to develop; it won't come quickly. We will work on trust throughout the year. I would like you to trust me when I ask you to do something you don't think is possible. Trust is a cornerstone to our learning; success is impossible without it.

Standard 3: Respect—When we work together to be truthful and trust one another in the class, we can respect one another. I expect myself and this class to respect our time together, our materials, and one another. What are ways that people demonstrate respect for themselves and others? (*Students respond.*) How do you know when you're not respected by teachers? By students?

Standard 4: Active Listening—This is a different type of listening. Active listening means that you are fully engaged in what the speaker is saying. You are thinking about his or her ideas, rather then how quickly you can raise your hand and give a different answer. Active listening means you ask questions if you don't understand . . . and keep asking questions until you do. I promise that I will fully and actively listen when you want to speak to me, and I expect that you will listen to what I say and to what your classmates say. You'll know it's time to actively listen when I say, "All eyes this way." That's our class clue that it's time to put your pencil down, turn fully toward the speaker, and hear what is being said. I will wait until I see all these behaviors occurring before I speak.

Standard 5: Positive and Constructive Conversation—To establish and maintain trust, truth, and respect, we have to maintain respectful conversation in this room. Put-downs and other kinds of negative talk will not be tolerated here. Sometimes people use put-downs to be funny, but there are other ways to get laughs. We will maintain a positive learning environment by making sure our words are constructive, intelligent, and positive.

Guided Practice

Students record the standards for learning on the graphic organizer as they are described. After the minilecture, they complete the organizer. This particular organizer includes the labels *model* and *nonexamples* to emphasize for students the differences between behaviors that match model behavior and those that don't.

It is important to *model* completion of one or two sections of the organizer with the students before turning them loose. As with any graphic organizer, after using it several times, its use will become second nature to most students.

If students do not finish it in class, the homework will be to complete the organizer, as well as getting their parents to sign the standards. By signing the assignment themselves, students are saying that they understand what the standards for behavior are and agree to work in this structure.

Closure

Homework Check

Materials are to be gathered and ready to check in on Day 4. If students can't bring materials, they will need a parent note that lets you know of their need. Highlighters are necessary for tomorrow. Finish standards sheet and have parents sign to show they have reviewed the assignment with students.

KFT

Students review today's agenda, record their names, and reflect on the key point they learned today. Guide them to the standards for learning and the quote. A good prompt for KFT is "One thing I'll remember from today is . . ." or "I hadn't really thought about . . . before." Have students read their entries to a partner, stand up, and push in their chairs.

Room Cleanup

Students should put name tags, standard sheets, and materials lists in a safe and accessible place in their binders. When their backpacks are zipped up and on the desk, have them check around their desks and pick up anything on the floor. Students should also realign desks and be ready to turn in their tickets at the door to you.

Ticket Out

When the bell rings, have students dismissed in sections. As they stand quietly in a clean area, they can come to the door and hand you their agendas/KFTs.

DAILY LESSON PLAN

Seventh-Grade English and Social Studies Core

First two weeks of school

Day 3 (based on a 55-minute period)

Learning Outcomes

Outcomes: Students will understand standards of behavior for successful students (by using quote work and class discussion).

Evidence: Students completed quote work. All students will participate in partner work and class discussion on behavior standards.

Outcome: Students will become familiar with the plan and expectations for the year by use of the syllabus.

Evidence: Students accurately highlight main ideas on the syllabus.

Outcome: Students will begin to establish prior knowledge for course content on world history.

Evidence: Students will successfully complete group genius graphic organizer.

Materials and Resources

Before Class

Have the agenda prepared and in an easy-to-read location for all students. Be ready to greet students at the door and use as many of their names as you can.
Prepare handouts for the following:

Find Someone Who

I Have, I Need

Organizers for Group Genius

Syllabus

Teaching Strategies and Sequence

Opening

Bell work

Students should have their name tags out on their desks and be copying today's agenda when the bell rings. Be sure to let students know that they will receive a tardy if they are not actively copying the agenda by the bell. Check your school's consequences to know what steps you should take for tardies. State the outcomes for today and go through the agenda as the student's copy it. Note that they are to have their highlighters today and that you will be starting a new project about their history as learners.

Name Tag Share/Roll Call

State the standards for listening and speaking. Today's name tag information is their birth month. As you call names, students can share their birth month and date.

Instruction

Quote Work and Standards of Behavior

Today's quote is

> Learning is not attained by chance; it must be sought for with ardor and attended to with diligence.
>
> —Abigail Adams, wife of President John Adams

Before reading the quote aloud, preview vocabulary that might be new to English Language Learners and other students as well (ardor, diligence, sought).

Read the quote aloud, and ask volunteers to paraphrase it in their own words, to clarify the literal meaning.

Ask students to interpret the quote. What does it look like to "seek with ardor" and "attend to with diligence" in school? What makes a student successful?

Ask students to discuss with partners their understanding of the quote and what it might mean to them as students. Share ideas. Returning to their partners, ask students to do the following:

1. List five behaviors that increase learning.

2. List five materials that help increase learning.

3. List eight behaviors that inhibit learning or success in school.

Have students share their ideas, and record them on an overhead or chart paper. What behaviors might increase their learning and success? What materials and resources?

This quote assignment will tie into tomorrow's material check. This is a good opportunity to remind students that they need to have their class materials ready, especially their binders and dividers, for successful organization of their learning materials.

Instruction

Syllabus for the Year and Highlighting Main Ideas

In passing out the syllabus, there are several goals:

- To show students the plan for what they will be learning over the year
- To introduce highlighting main ideas and key points
- To prepare students to explain syllabus highlights to parents

Before you pass out the syllabus, you will need to explain the procedures for using a highlighter. Many students just highlight everything without understanding why. Explain that using highlighters helps our memories capture and home in on the author's most important words and phrases. *What we highlight depends on why we're reading.*

Highlighting the syllabus will be an all-class activity. Read the syllabus one paragraph at a time and ask students what they think should be highlighted. At the end, have students highlight where parents are to sign.

Students can turn the syllabus over and summarize the three most important points that parents and students should know about the year. This can be an individual or partner assignment.

| Guided Practice |

As an introduction to the year's content in history, explain to students that you want to know what they already know about times, places, people, and events in world history. This will help you assess the student's starting point and better plan the curriculum.

In forming groups, you can have students count off by fours (random grouping), or you can ask students to form groups of four of their own choosing. Be aware of reluctant participants. Move throughout the room and orchestrate movement and grouping. Be sensitive to outsiders who may not assert themselves; bring them into groups graciously and gently. Watch how students work together to assess who they are as community members; this information will help you determine seating charts, cooperative groupings, class energy, and leadership.

Group Genius—Bridge to Prior Knowledge About Historical Periods

Pass out the graphic organizer Group Genius Brainstorm (Figure 8.6) to the groups and give them the titles you want them to brainstorm and record. (For example, seventh grade will have Fall of Rome, Middle Ages, Medieval China, Medieval Japan, African Empires, Aztecs, Mayans and Incas, Islam, Renaissance, and Reformation.) Each group should select a first recorder—the pencil will switch hands as groups move through each historical period.

Be prepared that students from different cultural and language backgrounds will have very different bases of prior knowledge. Try to give a brief introduction before each time period, helping students to draw on sources of knowledge they may not realize they have (movies, literature, comics, and folktales). Start with one historical period and let groups brainstorm for three or four minutes, writing down everything they know about that time and place. When you go on to another historical period, the groups can switch recorders.

After each historical period, take a few minutes to name a few key events or other facts that the groups know before moving on.

Figure 8.6 Group Genius Brainstorm

PEOPLE	PEOPLE	PEOPLE
PLACES	PLACES	PLACES
EVENTS	EVENTS	EVENTS
ARTIFACTS	ARTIFACTS	ARTIFACTS

Closure

Materials Check: I Have/I Need

As a reminder of materials needed, ask students to create a T-chart that looks like Figure 8.7.

| **Figure 8.7** | I Have/I Need |

I Have	I Need

Go through your materials list and have students assess what they have and what they need. State your standards for papers that are to be turned in so that students have a clear idea of your expectations. Then, collect the exercise from the students. Be sure to look through these sheets today before you leave. What do you need to gather for students, or what is your plan for having them borrow materials from others?

Homework Check

- Bring materials to class tomorrow
- Explain key points of the syllabus to parents and obtain their signature
- Interview parents on any information they may know about the historical time periods discussed. This is a follow-up activity to Group Genius to help bridge home and school. Many students come from families with less formal schooling who may not have studied these periods. In this case, students can prompt parents to describe the oldest history they *know* in the culture of their family. Interviews can be recorded in short phrases and do not have to be written out word for word.

KFT

What is the most important thing they learned today? Remind students of the agenda, since today's agenda included several key concepts and topics.

Room Cleanup

Name tags are put away. By today, you should have close to 90% of the names memorized. Complete the cleanup procedure that you have established, and clearly describe the actions and behaviors of those who are taking care of the classroom well.

Ticket Out

Peel off sections of students who are ready to go. Be sure they turn in their agendas with completed KFT sentences.

After Today

You should now be able to develop a seating chart for the class, ready for Day 5. Unclear names need to be a focus for tomorrow.

DAILY LESSON PLAN

Seventh-Grade English and Social Studies Core

First two weeks of school

Day 4 (based on a 55-minute period)

Learning Outcomes

Outcome: Students will understand behavior standards.

Evidence: Students will successfully complete group quiz with student-generated questions.

Outcome: Students will begin to establish a student learning history (preassessment) about experiences, strengths, and needs each student brings to their education.

Evidence: Students will successfully complete graphic organizer Learning History: Thinking Back.

Outcomes: Students will establish study buddies for support and accountability outside of class.

Evidence: Each student has a list of study buddies and phone numbers in a clearly accessible place.

Outcome: Students will be able to clearly organize and access all learning materials.

Evidence: All students have clearly organized binders.

Teaching Strategies and Sequence

Opening

Agenda

Students need to begin copying the agenda before the bell rings. As you greet students at the door, remind them that they must begin copying the agenda and have their name tags out to be considered on time.

Quote Work

Ask students to find their quote work packets and be ready to share their ideas from yesterday. Show today's quote on the overhead and read as a whole class.

> *Michael Jordan said, "You have to expect things of yourself before you can do them."*

Brainstorm ideas as a class about the meaning of the quote.

- How does this quote relate to learning with "ardor and diligence"?
- If you expect yourself to be successful, how will that impact your motivation to learn and succeed in school?

Ask students to write silently their reflections about the quote.

Explain that tomorrow there will be a quick quote quiz (QQQ). Students will be writing in response to a prompt that asks them to show their thinking about this quote. They will also turn in their quote work for the week, so it's important that they are organized and know where this packet is.

Materials Check

Ask students to get out the materials that were requested on Day 1. Have the list on the overhead as a reminder. Pass back the T-Graph I Have/I Need worksheets to students so they can create an action plan for getting any materials they still might need.

Instruction

Syllabus and Standards Group Quiz

Have students work with a new group of three or four. Students may use the information from the *standards* work or the syllabus to create three to five questions that will stump others.

Sample Questions

How will you know if someone is active listening?

Which historical period study will include a museum visit?

The information must come right from the text, and the question cannot ask students to quote words specifically. Give groups five to eight minutes to work on questions. Gather questions up and divide the class into two teams. You decide how to have answers given (Person in front? Group response? Written on the board? Help from group? No help?). This is a way to build community and remind the class of important information; remember to keep the standards strong and the atmosphere light.

Guided Practice

Personal Learning History: Thinking Back

Purpose: The purpose of this assignment is to understand a student's learning experience in strengths and needs they bring to their educational experience. This assignment will also allow students to develop the skills to create a complex project by breaking it down into sections. The final product can make a great display. However, it can also be an exercise in trust for those whose learning history has been difficult, so be sensitive to how the information is shared.

Introduction: History is the study of people and the events that shape them—or perhaps the study of events and the people who shape them, depending on your perspective. We all have our own history, and part of that history is our learning history. This assignment will have us behave as historians and think about the effects of events and people on our current lives and attitudes.

Step 1: Students will use the Learning History: Thinking Back graphic organizer, Figure 8.8, to record initial memories about their school experience. Some years they might not have many memories to record. That is fine. Students can talk to their parents and ask about their points of view on their school experience. It is a good idea to model your own learning history to inspire and clarify the project to your students.

Figure 8.8   Learning History: Thinking Back

Best Year	In	Most Difficult Year
	Learning	
	Friends	
	Achievement	
	Experiences	

Instruction

Study Buddy

Study buddies are fellow students in the class who a student can call when he or she is absent or doesn't understand an assignment. Tell the students, "Study buddies may or may not be your friends, but they should be students who are in class on time and prepared. Everyone needs to have at least two study buddies because two students may be absent on the same day!"

Students can record the names and numbers of study buddies on the inside of their binders. Some people write the numbers at home, as well, to avoid problems with lost materials. Give students three minutes to find partners and get numbers. Watch for students not interacting and find ways to gather numbers with them. Have students find out the times that work best to call, and record this information next to the number.

Tonight's homework involves calling study buddies. Review phone etiquette. How do you ask for people when they don't answer the phone? Model a call that qualifies for tonight's homework. ("Hi, this is _____. I'm _____'s study buddy at school. May I speak to him [or her]? Thank you.")

Binder Organization

This shouldn't take too long, but it's an important part of the students' success. Students were instructed to bring three or four tabs (based on your divisions). Have students get out the dividers for their binders, as well as the work they've done thus far:

- Agenda
- Quote work
- Learning history
- On the overhead, record the divider titles. One set of titles might be
- Calendar/agendas
- Quote work
- Learning logs (Work being done throughout a unit of study)
- Homework

Decide what divisions you will need and create a title list. As students record and create dividers, have them slip in the work they have done this week. You may want to hand back the agendas they did on Days 1 through 3, either today or at another time. Handing back work is a great way to memorize names.

When students are done dividing and organizing, they can hand their binders to a partner for a recheck. They should look carefully at agendas, quote work, and the learning log section: Is everything in order, easy to read, and complete? Are the quote work and learning history work correctly titled? Where is the study buddy information?

Closure

Homework Check

Finish quote work, learning history work, and name tag. Tomorrow all name tags will be collected. Success in school is all about organization and completion of homework—are students showing success by the work they've done this week?

KFT

Have students go to their agenda sections and record the KFT.

Room Cleanup

Have students stand and clean up around them.

Ticket Out

The material check sheet is their ticket out today. As you see clean sections, call the students and have them say good-bye with their ticket out in hand.

DAILY LESSON PLAN

Seventh-Grade English and Social Studies Core

First two weeks of school

Day 5 (based on a 55-minute period)

Learning Outcomes

Outcome: Students will demonstrate ability to interpret and analyze quotes.

Evidence: Each student will successfully complete the quote quiz.

Outcome: Students will continue to establish class learning history, student experiences, strengths, and needs by reporting through text and symbols.

Evidence: Students will complete graphic organizer Personal Learning History.

Outcome: Students will gather preassessment data on student reading engagement, skills, and interests.

Evidence: Each student will complete the reading survey.

Teaching Strategies and Sequence

Opening

Agenda

By today, students can be expected to go right to their seats, after they are greeted at the door, and begin to copy the agenda. Be sure students have their name tags out where you can see them. This is an important first assignment to assess responsibility and completion.

Roll Call

Today's your big day! Have students hide their name tags and see how many you remember. If there's time or a need for an energy outlet, turn around and have students switch seats. Turn back around and try to name as many students as you can. Collect name tags at the end.

Quote Work

Reread the quote; then, in a full-class discussion, ask for a few interpretations and applications to this year. Give any insights and inspirations you have about learning being active and sometimes difficult.

Students should have at least a minute to think and process the quiz prompt with a partner and then write their own response. Limit the time for this to about five minutes. Ask students to reread and revise anything that might not make sense. Collect the packets.

Quick Quote Quiz

- Collect the page(s) of quote work you did during the week. Staple a blank page on top. Be sure that you put your names, date, and class in the correct place on the page.
- **Quiz:** Can you think of something you've learned, either at home or in school, that took a lot of patience and hard work on your part? What were the consequences of this accomplishment? (Think about immediate and long-term consequences.)

This first writing sample is a great first assessment. What do you notice about content and thinking? What about writing skills (grammar, sentence structure, and spelling)? Note what trends are in this class's writing and begin planning direct instruction on the topics.

Instruction

Personal Learning History: Symbolic Memory

For each year of school, students will create a symbol that clarifies and explains the most memorable aspect of the year. Using the Personal Learning History worksheet (Figure 8.9) as a graphic organizer, the students will enter the following information for each year: their grade level and age, their teacher's name, learning/events, best memories, and low points. They'll also have space to create a symbol for each year. The students need to think about their audience: a symbol shouldn't be so personal that a viewer won't understand the meaning. This is still a rough draft, so students won't need to color their symbols.

Figure 8.9 Personal Learning History

Grade Level/Age	Teacher's Name	Learning/ Events	Best Memories	Low Points	Symbol

Instruction

Reading Preassessment

Explain to students that it's important to *preassess* to know different things about them so that you can ensure their success and growth this year. Students have given you information about their families (info sheet), their school history (learning history project), and their writing (quote work); now you want to know about their reading attitudes and abilities.

Distribute the reading survey (Figure 8.10) to the students. Review the assessment, set the standards for quiet, independent work, and be clear what they will do when they are finished. When they turn in this assessment, be sure to read their feedback. What do you know about the trends and individuals of this class? How will you begin reading instruction and form assignments?

Figure 8.10	Reading Survey

Name: _____ Class: _____ Date: _____

Thank you for taking this survey. I will use this information to plan assignments and lessons that are best for your interests, styles, needs, and strengths.

1. I read the following F = Frequently, S = Sometimes, N = Never

• Newspapers	F	S	N
• Magazines	F	S	N
• Novels	F	S	N
• Web sites	F	S	N
• Reference books	F	S	N
• Poems/song lyrics	F	S	N
• Textbook assignments	F	S	N
• Internet chat rooms	F	S	N
• Comics/graphic novels	F	S	N
• Autobiographies	F	S	N
• Biographies	F	S	N
• Plays	F	S	N
• Manuals	F	S	N

2. I would rate myself as a _____ on a scale of 1 to 10 as a reader. Why?

3. What are your favorite types of reading? List your top three:

4. Which types of reading listed in Number 1 are the most difficult for you? Explain.

5. I would describe myself as a _____ reader. Explain.

6. My favorite book of all time is _____. Why?

7. The best reader I know is _____. Describe what he or she does.

8. Reading is something you either can or cannot do well.   Agree   Disagree
(Circle one)

(Continued)

Figure 8.10   (Continued)

9. Check any of the following that help you to better understand what you read:
   - Reading it aloud to yourself
   - Having someone else read it aloud to you
   - Talking about what you read with others
   - Taking notes
   - Drawing or doing art in response to a question or inspiration from the reading
   - Reading silently to yourself during class time
   - Talking in groups about what you read
   - Talking as a class about what you read

10. Of the classes you're taking this year, which ones ask you to read the most?

11. Which class has the most difficult reading?

12. I expect the reading I do for school to be

   ___ Boring
   ___ Interesting
   ___ Difficult
   ___ Useful

13. If I could improve three things about myself as a reader, I would

   _____

   _____

   _____

14. Check all that describe what you do when you read your school assignments:
   - I eat and drink while I read.
   - I listen to music or have television on while I read.
   - I read at my desk with the computer on and connected to the Internet or a computer game.
   - I lay on my bed while I read.
   - I sit in a comfortable chair while I read.
   - I read in a room where the rest of my family is assembled while I read.
   - I reread directions for the assignment prior to doing the required reading.
   - I have a phone or pager on and in my study environment while I read.
   - I make sure that I have the necessary tools—paper, dictionary, highlighter—handy before I start reading.

15. When I am reading something and I get stuck, I try the following strategies: (Check all that apply)

   ___ I skip the difficult part.
   ___ I skip the difficult part and come back to it later.
   ___ I reread it.
   ___ I read it aloud.
   ___ I try to put it into my own words to help me understand it.
   ___ I look at other information on the pages (pictures, words in bold or italic, captions).
   ___ I try to draw it (or somehow see it—timeline, cluster, mind-map).
   ___ I ask someone else to read it aloud so I can hear it.

Closure

Homework Check

Homework should only be for students who didn't complete one of this week's assignments.

Week in Review

For a ticket out, have students write the best part of class this week and the toughest part of class. Be sure they write their names on it. This will give you insight about the makeup and attitudes of your students.

Room Cleanup

Have students pack up their things, stand up, and push in their chairs. They need to check around their desks for trash to pick up and wait for your dismissal.

Ticket Out

Call students off by birthday months and collect their tickets out.

DAILY LESSON PLAN

Week Two

Days 6–10

Continue each day with a predictable routines and procedures, including

Opening:	Instruction:	Closure:
Welcome	Key concepts and learning activities	Review the day
Agenda		Homework check
Quote work		KFT
Role call		Room cleanup
		Ticket out

Classroom Organization

Seating Chart (introduce by Day 6)

By this time, you have looked at student information sheets and know who has special needs and must sit in specific places. You have also observed and noticed who works well with whom.

These seating assignments are not negotiable unless there is something medical involved. *Stick to this!* Students might feel their life is over if they have to sit next to a certain boy or girl, but this is a point to show your clear expectations of a learning community. Have the chart ready on a poster and orient students to how it is laid out. Give students four minutes to get to their new seats and settle into work.

Learning Outcomes

Outcome: Students will continue to establish class learning history, experiences, strengths, and needs by using math modalities and graphing.

Evidence: The class will successfully complete learning history graphs.

Outcome: Students will examine one another's learning history graphs to compare and contrast data.

Evidence: Each student will complete a Gallery Walk summary sheet.

Outcome: Students will self-assess progress and reflect on learning history activities.

Evidence: Each student will complete a learning history reflection.

Outcome: Students will establish prior knowledge about heroes and qualities of heroes.

Evidence: Each student will participate in the think-pair-share activity and class brainstorm and will complete the heroes in history graphic organizer.

Outcome: Students will select an appropriate biography and establish prior knowledge and prereading questions.

Evidence: Students select biography appropriate to interest and reading level; students complete hero reading journal.

Outcome: Students will establish reading schedules and reads regularly, recording key points and reading response.

Evidence: Students complete daily reading journal and heroes in history organizer.

Instruction

Learning History Project

The following lessons will continue the learning history project over the course of the second week of school.

Graphing Memories

Rough Draft

Using a scale of 1 to 10, with 10 being the highest, student's rate each school year in value and impact, plotting the results on an X-Y graph (with time on the *x*-axis and the students' ratings on the *y*-axis).

Final Draft

Students will create a black-ink version of the graph they plotted previously. They should begin with the axes and then put the data point for each year in its place. Each year should be labeled with

- Grade level (or age)
- Key learning (in five words or less)
- Symbol

Students connect the data points with lines to create a continuous learning history graph.

Reflecting on Learning History

Using the graphs as a prompt, students will choose the most difficult and the best year in school and write a compare and contrast paragraph. The following graphic organizer will help them to put thoughts in order before writing the paragraph. The areas of comparison will help students think about the bigger picture of their learning history. They can add other big-picture areas that make both years notable in their own history.

Gallery Walk—Learning History Projects

As students set up their graph, have them place a piece of blank paper beside it. Explain to students that they will be walking around the room, observing one another's graphs, and using these blank sheets as a space to record their thoughts. Create a model graph on the overhead and have the class practice comments and observations. This practice provides an opportunity to model academic English as a frame for comments. Review the following standards and procedures with your students so that they know what is expected from them for this activity.

Standards and Procedures for a Gallery Walk

- A gallery is a place where people go to look at art. As people walk around, they may talk to a partner, but it's typically quiet. You will walk around our gallery with open eyes and quiet mouths. If you notice something interesting, you can show it to a friend nearby.
- It's important for everyone's work to be seen. Each learning history graph can be viewed by one person at a time. If someone is at a display, you must go to another desk until it's available.
- As you look at the graphs, look for something interesting or unusual or for something that you have in common with the creator. Record an observation and your name on their gallery sheet, next to their graph.
- You will need to look at five to nine graphs during our gallery opening. Each graph must have at least five observations. If you come to a graph that has six comments, look at it quickly and move on to another graph that needs your comments.

Closure for the Gallery Walk

Compliment students on how they proceeded through the gallery.

Note: If it isn't working, stop it. Don't let students abuse this opportunity to share their work. If students aren't ready to walk around and be independent, give them a similar experience by sharing their work in groups of four and getting feedback from their peers in a structured format.

Project Reflections

Have students organize all their papers that were part of this gallery walk process. On a separate sheet of paper, students need to look over the comments they received from their fellow students about their graphs and then reflect on how they have done so far this year in terms of deadlines, daily work commitment, completion, and quality. Ask them to write a brief response (one or two paragraphs) to each of the following questions:

- What did you do well on this project? How do you know?
- What did this project make you think about yourself as a learner?
- What did you have in common with other students in the class?
- What was unique about your school experience?
- What would you do differently next time (timelines, completion, quality, effort)?

When they are done with the self-assessment, they can attach it to their projects and turn them in. These are great displays for back-to-school night as well as an ongoing community builder for the class. The project also provides a lot of information about attitudes and experience that will enrich instruction and guide your approaches to many students.

Hero Biography Reading Project

Think-Pair-Share (Bridge from Prior Knowledge)

Ask students to write to the prompt

Who are your heroes?

What makes a hero?

Ask students to turn to a partner and share there responses.

Following the partner share, students can share with the whole class the results of their partner discussion. Make one chart titled *Heroes* and one chart titled *Qualities of Heroes.* Ask students to take notes from the charts in their own notebooks.

Quote Work

The following quote can be used for the quote work activity on the day that the hero biography project is introduced. Other quotes about the power of reading can also be used.

Books are the carriers of civilization. Without books, history is silent, literature dumb, science crippled, thought and speculation at a standstill. Without books, the development of civilization would have been impossible. They are the engines of change, windows on the world. . . . They are companions, teachers, magicians, bankers of the treasures of the mind. Books are humanity in print.

—Barbara W. Tuchman
American historian, writer

Instruction

All students will be reading a biography about a favorite hero. The teacher may want to gather books ahead of time as a resource or lead a visit to the school or local library to gather resources together.

Once students have their books, have individuals share with the class how they selected them. Remind students that they will be expected to have their book in class with them every day to have silent sustained reading (SSR) time in class and support their homework load. Remember, models are powerful! What book have you selected? Be sure that you go through exactly the same process so that you can share your reading behaviors as well.

Review the heroes in history handouts (Figures 8.11 and 8.12) to go over specific guidelines and expectations for the students' report.

Figure 8.11	Heroes in History

HEROES IN HISTORY

BIOGRAPHY/AUTOBIOGRAPHY READING

Name: _____ Date Project Is Assigned: _____

Due Date: _____

1. *Think* about people you've heard about or have read about in history that you consider heroic.

2. *Record* the names of five to eight of those people below:

3. *Brainstorm* 5 to 10 characteristics shown in these heroes. Put a * by the characteristics most of them have in common.

4. *Look* at the library's selection of biographies and autobiographies. Of the people you listed, who has a book written about/by them? Put a **B** next to the names of people represented in the library.

5. *Skim* at least five books you find. Which books look like they would not be *too* easy or too difficult to read? Which book looks the most interesting? You will be reading this book for two weeks (approximately 10 days). Which book will challenge you to complete it but is possible?

6. *Select the book* that you will use as your silent-sustained-reading (SSR) book for the next two weeks. *Write* the name and author of the book here.

(Continued)

Figure 8.11 (Continued)

7. In class, *create* a reading program for yourself. Take the number of pages and divide it by 10. *Record* your reading program below.

Date	Pages ___ to ___	Time Read	Initials

Each night, record how long your page amount took to read and initial it to demonstrate that you completed your reading assignment for the day. If you get behind, you will need to recreate your reading program so that you are able to finish the book in the two-week period. You have to read on the weekend. Plan ahead!

8. Reading Journal: Effective readers think about what they read and make connections between the book and their lives. This journal will ask you to take about 10 minutes after each reading and record thinking and connections you have made while reading. This will be due at the end of the two-week reading assignment

Figure 8.12 Hero Reading Journal

Before you read, answer the following questions.

1. What do you already know about this person? How do you know this information (books, conversations, TV, movies)?

2. What do you hope to learn about this hero? What do you hope you *don't* learn about him or her?

3. What does it take to be a hero? What qualities (use your worksheet), characteristics, actions, and background create a hero?

Figure 8.13	Daily Reading Journal

Date/pages read	Important event(s) in hero's life (include page numbers)	Ingredients or characteristics of a hero you observe (include a quote from the book)	Your thoughts or questions about this hero after today's reading

Note: Create your journal pages so that you have adequate space. Honor your hero by taking the time to record deep thinking and careful information.

9

Supporting Secondary Students to Read Subject Matter Text

I am not a reading specialist! What can a single-subject teacher realistically do to help all students read grade-level texts?

Teaching content-literacy skills *as a part of helping students to understand* subject matter concepts advances both their content knowledge and their reading skills. Consider this: the difficulty, density, specificity, and complexity of ideas described in today's middle school and high school texts are such that *all* students, including those who read at grade level, benefit tremendously when they learn exactly how to read about subject matter concepts. Students reading far, far below grade level may also need additional instruction from reading and/or second-language specialists to develop basic literacy proficiencies. A single-subject teacher, someone who is effective at *reading and thinking like a scientist* (or mathematician, historian) should teach all of his or her students the particular skills needed to *read to learn* about subject matter content.

If you are reading this chapter, it is probably because you have confirmed that many of your students struggle to read grade-level text. You may be concerned that without the various *scaffolds* you provide (including flat-out *telling* what the books says), some students cannot effectively read to learn new concepts on their own. As said in previous chapters, it is important to engage students in learning through projects and other types of hands-on learning. And to sustain their interest and ability to read to learn about concepts independently, students need specific instruction in the particular content-literacy skills presumed of anyone reading advanced subject matter texts. This chapter offers several teaching strategies and ideas about reading development to guide your thinking about this component of subject matter instruction. We begin with a quick review of concepts you may have examined in your preservice literacy courses.

When do reading skills begin to develop? Concepts about the phases of reading development provide the basis for identifying prerequisite skills adolescents should have. As one of their subject matter teachers, besides teaching grade-level concepts and literacy skills, you may need to reinforce and build on some of these prerequisite literacy skills, especially in the areas of vocabulary development and reading comprehension. (Remember that it is appropriate to seek *additional* instructional support from your school's reading and language development specialists for students who read many years below grade level or for some English Language Learners.) One of the initial phases, *learning to read*, takes place for most children ages preschool through second grade. This is when children are learning to accurately recognize and speak the combinations of letters and sounds that make up the written code of a language they (ideally) have heard since infancy. Using innate critical-thinking skills, they learn how to read books containing simple, familiar words and sentences and pictures about familiar topics. *Reading to learn* is the second phase, when typically students in the third through seventh grade are guided to read increasingly more difficult text, a chapter that describes a few new concepts, contexts, or academic skills. In this phase, highly proficient readers implicitly (and for some explicitly) learn and apply an array of reading comprehension skills. They actively *analyze* and *clarify* words they encounter. They *generate questions, summarize, interpret*, and *make predictions and inferences* about new ideas from multiple types of literature or informational texts. This is a very important phase. In theory, this is the period when readers, independently and/or with the help of instruction, develop several prerequisite reading skills essential for comprehending increasingly difficult middle school and high school texts.

What are key features of adolescent literacy? A lot has been learned in the last few years about the unique features of the ongoing reading development of proficient readers as it may progress during the period of adolescence. Highly proficient readers of any age make connections between what they read, their prior knowledge, and their interests. If proficient preadolescent and adolescent readers continue to read a lot, they get better and more sophisticated at effectively using specific types of background knowledge and reading comprehension strategies in ways that go beyond foundational reading-to-learn skills. As they continue to read to learn during this phase, they acquire more and more knowledge, deepen their understanding of language structures and vocabulary, and become more adept at flexibly using reading comprehension strategies specific to certain types of texts. As their knowledge grows, their initial interests continue to be enriched and even expanded to include other interests. With each passage they read, they increase their reading capacities to such an extent that they *persist* in reading challenging text, especially when the topic interests them and even when it doesn't.

Texts written at 9th- through 12th-grade reading levels are challenging for most readers of any age because of the increasing amount of subject-specific background knowledge needed to read and understand *multiple* concepts in multiple ways. The density of supporting ideas and specificity of details linked to each concept often presume knowledge of related concepts from other subjects as well (Heller & Greenleaf, 2007.) In this *multiple-viewpoints* phase of reading development (Chall, 1995), a proficient adolescent reader flexibly uses several comprehension skills to comprehend (i.e., interpret, infer, evaluate, compare, contrast, classify, summarize, synthesize, hypothesize, solve for, or prove) ideas contained in a chapter and sometimes in a passage as short as a set of directions or single phrase. During this phase, a reader may also develop *critical literacy* or the ability to reflect on the significance of multiple ideas, themes, concepts, events, variables, or interactions from multiple perspectives.

In this chapter, we give you a start on a few practices that will help advance your students toward adolescent literacy proficiency:

1. Teaching explicitly what good readers do

2. Using information from reading assessments

3. Engaging students in prereading

4. Developing students' reading comprehension strategies

5. Building vocabulary

6. Providing resources for content area reading

7. Motivating students to accelerate

We encourage you to view the strategies and approaches listed as elements to be integrated as a part of rather than added to teaching subject matter concepts. You will begin to see students' confidence in using reading skills develop and appreciate students' progress as they become independent readers and learners of your content!

TEACHING EXPLICITLY WHAT GOOD READERS DO

As proficient readers, we have long ago internalized the process of reading. Most of us could not explain the hundreds of processes occurring in our brains as we work our way through text. The great news is that research has confirmed that most of the habits and skills of proficient readers can be transferred to less proficient readers through skillful instruction (Stanovich, 1986). Research about what proficient readers do has provided educators with tremendously valuable information about the components of the reading process (Snow, Burns, & Griffin, 1998). Overall, students can learn effective reading skills, when provided with modeling and instruction from teachers who understand the basic components of proficient reading. Single-subject teachers can support adolescent readers by developing their general and subject-specific reading-to-learn skills and using instructional practices designed to engage students in learning and applying academic language.

Essentially, proficient readers monitor what they read as they interact with the text. As they read, they ask questions, create mental images, compare what they read to other information, and make predictions and inferences. Proficient readers reread and look for context clues when something doesn't make sense. (See Figure 9.1 for a summary of what proficient adolescent readers do.) Support your students to more effectively read about subject matter concepts by doing the following:

- Provide students with mini-lessons and guided practice in the subject-specific application of these literacy skills.
- Use a combination of required texts and related supplemental resources that are easier to read or more culturally relevant and interesting to your students
- Think aloud about the skills you use to read complex subject matter text
- Implement mini-lessons, supplemental texts, and think-alouds to explicitly clarify the particular knowledge and skills needed to read subject-specific materials

Figure 9.1   What Do Highly Proficient Adolescent Readers Do?

1. Read Strategically

During *pre*reading, they do the following:

- Scan the structural features of the particular text, (i.e., title, subtitles, prologue, table of contents, chapter questions, cover notes to novels, introductions, graphics, highlighted sections, vocabulary, parts of a word problem, and steps for a lab experiment) to make predictions about or determine a purpose for reading the text.

During and after reading, they do the following:

- Use an array of reading comprehension processes in flexible ways and monitoring the accuracy of their comprehension of passages being read. They stop intermittently to possibly
  - o *compare* and *contrast* ideas with other ideas they've read about or know from experience;
  - o *classify* or *categorize* different types of information;
  - o *summarize,* and then continue to *predict, clarify, infer, evaluate, interpret,* or *analyze* what they are reading.

After reading, they do the following:

- Make inferences, evaluate, hypothesize, and interpret what they have read
- Deliberate differences (i.e., compare, contrast and classify different points of view, perspectives, information contained in a passage, chapter, or set of directions)
- Analyze the author's purpose for writing about a certain chapter, excerpt, passage, or process

2. Use Background Knowledge and Prior Experiences

- Link new ideas encountered in prereading and during reading with prior knowledge of the text's topic and connections to the reader's interests and sociocultural dimensions
- Apply current literacy skills in their first or second language to clarify subject-specific uses of new words for known concepts, new words for new concepts, and new meanings of known words
- Interpret information by identifying and analyzing for different points of view and determining the importance of the information to their overall understanding

USING INFORMATION FROM READING ASSESSMENTS

How can you learn about your students' current reading levels? Reading tests usually assess the grade-level equivalent of students' word analysis skills (e.g., ability to identify the correct word for a passage based on spelling, word order, meaning, and/or context) and reading comprehension skills, (e.g., ability to correctly identify a passage's main idea, or supporting details). Your school has probably adopted a particular multiple-choice reading test that is quick to administer and score. At the middle school level, language arts or humanities teachers are usually responsible for testing incoming students' reading skills and interpreting test results. Teachers of other subjects usually meet with humanities teachers or site reading specialists at the beginning of the year to identify the range of their students' current reading proficiencies. In similar fashion, high school English teachers or teacher leaders of smaller learning communities may take responsibility for administering and sharing the results of these assessments. Many school district Web sites provide access to each individual school's "report card," which includes information about the average reading scores for students of a particular grade or subgroup. Results from some standardized state assessments including high school exit exams provide similar information about individual students. Many schools are now able to generate reports based on this state assessment data. Ask your school's data technician if it is possible to get information about the reading skills (i.e., grade-level equivalent) for students in each of your classes.

Why and how might you use this information? In a single class, you may have students who read above grade level, at grade level, below grade level, and far below grade level. (Note that most students reading far below grade level and/or students in the process of learning English as their second language may *also* need concurrent instruction from literacy specialists.) As part of teaching students to read about your content, it is helpful to know the gap between their current reading levels and the level at which your core text and other materials are written. Why is this helpful? Understanding these gaps will guide you in identifying the types of reading skills you'll need to help students develop as a part of teaching your subject matter. You will also get a better idea of the types and levels of supplemental materials that would support your students to simultaneously advance their literacy skills as well as their content knowledge.

If you don't have access to information about students' reading levels through the resources previously described, consider this quick process for assessing their reading skills. Although you may already have a good idea about your students' current literacy proficiencies, this process will help you to more specifically determine whether text your students will encounter is written at their *independent, instructional,* or *frustration* level.

1. From one class, identify three or four students, each of whom read similar to other students you consider as having high, average, and below-average reading skills. Select students you believe would be willing to quietly read a short passage to you, perhaps while the class is involved in a somewhat noisy group project.

2. Prepare by choosing an excerpt of exactly 100 words from your textbook or resources you typically ask students to read.

3. If possible, have a copy of that excerpt that you can highlight as a student reads.

4. As the student reads, highlight a word or part of a word that produces a *miscue* by the student. Miscue examples? The reader skips a word, mispronounces any part of the word, substitutes another word, and/or does not correct a miscue within three or four seconds. If the student (especially one with possibly far below skills) produces any of these miscues while reading the first couple of sentences, stop. Thank the student for helping you figure out how to help students understand the text better.

5. In reading a passage of 100 words
   - if a reader has five miscues or fewer out of 100 words, the text is written at his or her independent level. The reader can read and comprehend what is read with 90% to 95% accuracy.
   - if a reader has 6 to 10 miscues out of a 100 words, the text is written at his or her instructional level. The reader, supported with instruction, guided practice, interaction with other readers, or repeated readings, can read and comprehend text ideas with up to 70% to 85% accuracy.
   - if a reader has more than 10 miscues out of 100 words, the text is written at his or her frustration level. Even with support noted for the instructional reader, the reader can read and comprehend text ideas with less than 70% accuracy.

How can you use this information? As an example, if you discover that your text or an article you provide is written at the instructional level for approximately 50% of your students, you may need to help students to understand what they read by providing additional support. Examples of the kinds of support you can offer are described throughout the rest of this chapter.

Note: Proficient readers will also benefit from engaging in these content-literacy activities as well as reading other challenging materials linked to your current unit of study.

ENGAGING STUDENTS IN PREREADING

Developing prereading skills will increase students' interest and overall comprehension of text concepts. Supporting students to learn prereading skills primarily involves (1) modeling effective skills, (2) guiding students to identify and understand the purpose of each skill, and (3) engaging them in activities and resources (e.g., graphic organizers) that develop the accurate use of these skills.

Effective readers use the following prereading skills:

1. Scanning the structural features of the particular text
   a. For a novel, the cover pages and liner notes
   b. For a single chapter in a novel, the title, first and last lines of the chapter, and sample dialogue by a key character
   c. For informational texts, the book title, table of contents, prologue, chapter title, subtitles, chapter questions, introductory paragraphs, graphics, highlighted sections, and key vocabulary

2. Making connections about ideas and key vocabulary contained in these structural text features and readers' prior knowledge about the ideas and words

3. Determining the amount of time and concentration they'll need to effectively read the selected section of text

4. Predicting the focus of the text and purpose for reading it based on analysis of ideas contained in structural text features

Figure 9.2 is an example of a prereading guide using the types of features associated with history textbooks. Take some time to develop a similar type of *chapter prereading guide* for students to use with your main text. Include features that match the structural features of your textbook's chapters, a novel, or chapters of a novel. Once you've developed a generic form representing text features and taught students how to use it, you can duplicate it for students' prereading of continuing chapters. Reading to learn through this resource and activity will become a vital part of students' prereading routine as they begin to read about each new subject matter concept.

Figure 9.2   Sample: Chapter Prereading Guide

Chapter title: _____

Number of pages: _____   Number of graphics: _____

Number of key words highlighted in the introduction: _____

Quote one sentence from the introductory paragraph.

List the chapter subtitles.

Write a one-sentence description of the chapter picture or graphic that is most interesting to you.

List the highlighted vocabulary words or terms in two columns. Circle the words you have heard before, know a little bit about, or understand.

Review the questions at the end of the chapter. Write the question you think will be easiest to answer followed by the question you think will be the most difficult to answer.

What do you predict someone might learn by reading this chapter?

SEMANTIC WORD WEB

Purpose

1. To build background knowledge and subject-specific academic language

2. To guide students to key terms linked to essential concepts

Activity

1. The teacher preselects a key word related to a targeted concept. The teacher then draws a circle with three to five spokes radiating to other circles. A targeted concept or phrase should be written in the center of a circle. The concept or phrase could be from the core text or an alternative, more accessible book related to the concept. In the circles surrounding the keyword in the center, write three to five related words that help to explain, provide examples, or process steps related to the key word.

2. Ask students to individually or in pairs to write any words they know are connected to the words in the web. Ask them to label their individual ideas by putting their initials in parentheses by each word they list. You might ask student pairs to share the words they generated with another pair. Or you could ask volunteers to read their words. Follow up by writing down examples, details, or defining characteristics of the original terms you displayed.

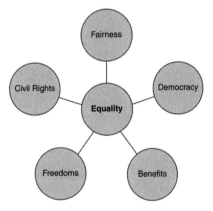

INSTRUCTIONAL READ ALOUD (GENERAL)

Purpose

1. To support students in comprehending the main concepts in assigned text

2. To build background knowledge about a topic

3. To model reading skills

Activity

1. The teacher reads aloud a key passage from the core text that exemplifies an essential concept or skill. He or she pauses periodically to think aloud with a prediction, a question for the text, or to analyze new or unfamiliar words or passages.

2. During an instructional read aloud, the teacher refers to a copy of the passage displayed on an overhead transparency. Students list what the teacher said or did during the thinking aloud, later sharing their notes with a partner. The teacher clarifies what he or she did, why this was done, and then repeats the process as students reference their copy of the passage.

MATH OR SCIENCE INSTRUCTIONAL READ ALOUD

Activity

1. Choose an excerpt that explains a key concept or application of a mathematical or scientific concept (such as steps for building a three-dimensional model).

2. Determine three or four stopping points to think aloud about the process.

3. Ask students to stop and *think-pair-share* to paraphrase, summarize, interpret, or provide examples for some aspect of what was read. (Remember to review and model the language to express summarizing, interpreting, or predicting prior to starting the *instructional read aloud*.)

4. Display your prompt on an overhead or on the board for the benefit of English Language Learners. Students who read below grade level or have limited background knowledge about the topic might benefit from first hearing you read about the same concept from a text with more real-life, socioculturally parallel scenarios.

LANGUAGE ARTS, HISTORY/SOCIAL SCIENCES INSTRUCTIONAL READ ALOUD

1. Choose an excerpt from the text, an alternative text or article, or related poem (two to three pages for literature concepts, one to one and a half pages for history). The excerpt for literature should be pivotal to the theme, character development, plot, style, or literary device that students are learning. For history, the excerpts or story should be linked to the period, context, universal theme, or event students are about to study. Continue to follow steps two through four described earlier.

DEVELOPING STUDENTS' READING COMPREHENSION STRATEGIES

Reading comprehension skills are developed over a lifetime. You can support adolescent readers to develop these skills by providing opportunities to read from texts written at grade level and at their independent reading level, along with instruction that

- clarifies the specific steps and components involved in a particular reading comprehension strategy like summarizing, comparing, or contrasting ideas;
- models and clarifies how to analyze the meaning of words to understand a phrase describing a subject matter concept;
- helps students to internalizing the question, "Does this make sense?";
- provides them with practice in generating questions about text ideas; and
- offers students resources and prompts to support them in linking their prior knowledge with the text.

You can teach students to apply comprehension strategies before, during, or after reading texts. Besides those mentioned earlier, students need support in *paraphrasing, classifying, evaluating, interpreting, describing, inferring from,* and *analyzing* information (see below for examples of activities for developing students' comprehension strategies).

MAIN IDEA MAP (NOTE-TAKING GUIDE)

Purpose

1. To utilize a graphic organizer to clarify and prioritize key concepts in lecture or chapter

2. To identify supporting detail, explanation, or evidence

Activity

1. The accompanying graphic organizer *(main idea map; Figure 9.3)* provides a framework that can guide you in presenting a short introductory lecture about key concepts linked to a new topic. At the same time, it serves as a guide for students to take notes. Stay true to the graphic! Remember that students are learning a comprehension frame as well as content. Present your information per the structural components of the map.

2. Once students have practiced with the main idea map as a note-taking guide, they can also use it to record ideas when reading text independently.

DOUBLE ENTRY OR DIALECTICAL JOURNAL (NOTE-TAKING GUIDE)

Purpose

1. To build background knowledge

2. To develop subject-specific academic English around being able to *interpret, compare, evaluate, or analyze* information

Activity

1. The accompanying graphic organizer *(double entry journal; Figure 9.4)* provides additional structure for students to home in on skills of summarizing, interpreting, analyzing, identifying inferences, or arguing a position. The teacher preselects three to five key quotes from a section of text linked to essential concepts, processes, or significant events. Students respond to the quote utilizing language from one of the academic structures the teacher has identified.

2. Before beginning the activity, it can be useful to identify and post visibly words and language structures that best support the task.

3. Based on Figure 9.4, you may choose to develop a full page double entry journal template, expanding the spaces for quotes #1–4, and student responses. For each assignment, you could type in the quotes in the column on the left. If you don't wish to do that for each assignment, you can develop a more generic form and ask students to copy selected quotes, signifying the pages and chapters where they can be located.

Figure 9.3 Main Idea Map

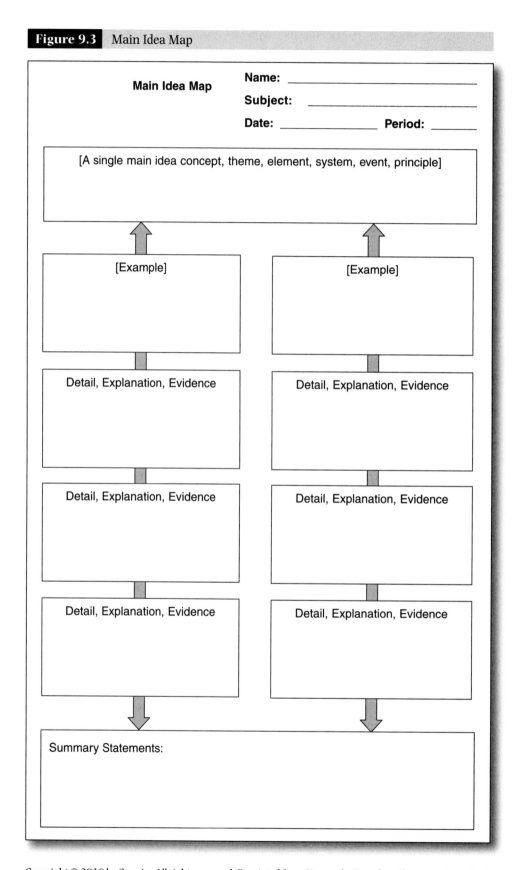

Figure 9.4 Double Entry Journal and Strategic Response

Topic:

Double Entry Journal	Strategic Response
• First, copy the four quotes the teacher has selected into the boxes below (in this column). Fill in the page and chapter numbers for each quote. • Think about what you may already know about any idea, phase, or word in the excerpt; underline these ideas. • Use a marker to highlight or a place a check next to the phrases that you think are the most important.	Circle teacher or student choice for today's lesson for responding to the quotes by either *summarizing, interpreting, analyzing, arguing* **(for or against it), or identifying inferences drawn from it.** • **Use the space in the boxes below (in this column) to respond to each quote.**
1. (From page(s) _____, Chapter _____)	
2. (From page(s) _____, Chapter _____)	
3. (From page(s) _____, Chapter _____)	
4. (From page(s) _____, Chapter _____)	

QUESTIONING THE AUTHOR

Purpose

1. To support students to understand literary devices and elements

2. To develop skills of analysis and interpretation by close reading of an author's intentions, decision making, perspective, or style

3. To give students practice and raise confidence in questioning the author (i.e., challenging, probing, and clarifying possible meanings, intentions, and writing skills)

Activity

1. Teacher selects three or four pivotal sections of an article, a chapter from a textbook, a novel, or a single poem. The section could be new or a reread.

2. Students read a selection silently.

3. Have students write their answers to the following questions or discuss them with a partner first and then write. Some questions are more geared toward narrative and some toward expository writing.

   • What is the author trying to tell you?
   • Why is the author telling you that?
   • How could the author have said things more clearly?
   • What would you say instead?
   • How did the author let you know something has changed in the characters mind?

- How did the author make you experience what was going on?
- How did the author resolve the challenge faced by the character?

4. Option: Create a template similar to the dialectical journal listing some of these queries on the left and the page number or the beginning sentence of a passage that you want students to refer at the top of each section on the right.

TIPS FOR SUBJECT-SPECIFIC TEACHING OF CRITICAL-THINKING SKILLS

Purpose

1. To teach the subject-specific components, steps, and uses of critical thinking skills

2. To scan the reading for specific types of information linked to the task

3. To read for a specific purpose and increase reader motivation

Activity

1. Outline the specific steps and components for interpreting or summarizing ideas that are particular to your subject matter. Choose a topic and materials that are accessible and/or familiar to students.

2. Think about the types of prior knowledge (topic-based or personal experience) a student needs to apply a certain critical-thinking process. To what degree would interpreting or analyzing an historical event require prior knowledge of topics not necessarily included in the assigned section of text?

3. Explicitly teach students the elements and specific steps involved in a critical-thinking process for prewriting one or multiple paragraphs. For example, after brainstorming several ideas, examples, and details from a chapter or chapter excerpt, a reader should do the following (i.e., the mental processes for summarizing text information).
   - Identify the main idea(s).
   - Delete or eliminate trivial or redundant information from your brainstorm that you probably won't include in a written or oral summary. Instead
     o Construct cohesive statements about examples or certain details that convey broad categories rather than a list of specific items, or events
     o Construct a concluding statement that ties together the other information included in the summary

   In the case of classes that don't use text, such as the arts or PE, teachers can still teach students the vocabulary or discourse language associated with each skill.
   For examples, (analysis) Think about what happens during a forced out, what should a player do if faced with this type of situation at second base? Or (interpretation and comparison) How might you compare Van Gogh's use of blue tones versus Monet's?

RECIPROCAL TEACHING

Purpose

1. To learn the habits of proficient readers to monitor understanding of text before, during, and after reading

2. To teach the reading habit of rereading

3. To develop persistence in digging deeper into text that isn't easily understood on the first pass

Activity

1. This process was developed by Palincsar and Brown (1984) to engage a group of students to cooperatively assume the four processes used by proficient readers to monitor comprehension. The teacher explicitly describes the aspects of each role (summarizing, clarifying, questioning, and predicting) prior to directing students to engage in reciprocally teaching the text.

2. The teacher selects several contiguous paragraphs about a single topic. In groups of four, one student assumes the role of summarizer, another clarifies a word or idea, another forms a question about the passage that he or she can answer, and another makes a possible prediction about what might be read next.

3. This cooperative reading strategy may be taught over a period of a few weeks. Model or think aloud to clarify the process as you begin. Take time for students to learn each of the processes individually before applying them as a set of tasks.

BUILDING VOCABULARY

Including vocabulary development instruction in each lesson will support all students, and especially struggling readers and English Language Learners to effectively comprehend subject matter text. When students are supported to actively and effectively use subject-specific vocabulary, they increase their reading proficiency as well as their understanding of essential concepts. Besides an increase in volume of what students read, explicit focus on developing subject matter vocabulary will increase reading comprehension for all students. Students benefit from explicit instruction in both new and essential subject-specific words, such as *mitosis, dénouement,* and *executive branch,* as well as the academic language that defines what students are supposed to do with what they read or hear (*analyze, differentiate, delineate*). To significantly improve student access to key concepts and text content, researchers in vocabulary development suggest 5 to 7 minutes of explicit vocabulary instruction daily in each 55-minute secondary class, with 8 to 10 new, essential words weekly. Of course, students can be encouraged or given assignments that will require them to learn words in addition to the essential words you will focus on. These other words may include words that are examples of or modify the essential academic words.

High-utility academic words (i.e., vocabulary found repeatedly in different contexts) should be taught through word analysis strategies or word studies. Using reading comprehension resources like *main idea maps* expose students to new meanings for words they know. *Concept webs* also help students to link words to prior knowledge and associate words with new academic concepts. Researchers recommend that exotic words that are rarely seen or used but referenced in an essential excerpt or passage should be defined upfront.

Should Nonproficient Readers Use Dictionaries?

Nonproficient readers, English Language Learners, and many other learners may encounter so many new words in a paragraph that it breaks up the flow of reading and stops comprehension to look them all up in the dictionary. In addition, dictionary definitions themselves may present a new set of vocabulary challenges for English Language Learners and struggling readers. Of course, a dictionary is an essential reference for all students. Besides encouraging its use as a quick reference, strategically modeling its use as part of building their academic vocabulary supports students to build their academic vocabularies. All students, regardless of their current reading proficiencies, benefit from learning multiple strategies to tackle new words they encounter. Learning word-analysis skills (see Dissect and Define on p. 205) supports all students to potentially rely less on using the dictionary to understand common, subject-specific, or rare words. As students intentionally learn common prefixes and suffixes (only 20 of each comprise 90% of English words that contain them) as well as frequently used root words (most of these are part of common English words), they gain strategies to tackle many of the new words they encounter. When dictionaries are used, some dictionaries and thesauri are more appropriate than others for secondary English Language Learners and struggling readers.

What Types of Words Need to Be Studied and Taught?

Consider the following quote from the cover of a standards-based 10th-grade world history textbook:

> If cultures and civilizations are the tectonic plates of world history, frontiers are the places where they scrape against each other and cause convulsive change.

Besides fluently reading the words for this sentence, students require both certain knowledge and skills to simply paraphrase this statement They need to know the following:

- Background information linked to social science and physical science concepts
- High-utility academic words and phrases, subject-specific vocabulary

They need to be able to do the following:

- Interpret the meaning of a phrase based on recognizing markers for hypothesis "If . . . (then) . . ."
- Recognize and interpret phrasal verbs—*scrape against, cause change*
- Interpret analogous relationships of phrases across different subject matter
- Interpret figurative language—metaphors
- Apply critical-thinking processes specific to the subject (considerations and language that expresses interpretation or analysis of information)

The teaching of content area vocabulary demands that teachers generate specific strategies for high-utility academic words and a focus on viewing texts from multiple viewpoints (Chall, 1995). Given time and appropriate resources, word study can easily become a fun and engaging time in your day (see the following pages for activities to help students build their vocabulary).

PROVIDING RESOURCES FOR CONTENT AREA READING

The following are descriptions of sample resources, conceptual frames, and activities that support students to more quickly access content area texts. The suggestions are organized into two major subject matter groupings. Students can be involved in creating and modifying these resources as topics change. All provide effective reading scaffolds for English Language Learners as well as nonproficient readers.

Math, Science, Applied and Fine Arts

Posters and Word Walls

Create or help students to create concept visuals for math, science, and applied and fine arts. Highlighting and posting a list of 9 to 15 vocabulary words

INDIVIDUAL VOCABULARY JOURNAL

Purpose

To provide a place to organize and retrieve large numbers of new words

To provide guided practice in word analysis

To develop background knowledge for subject-specific vocabulary

To develop comprehension strategies for new or unfamiliar vocabulary

Activity

Provide or ask students to bring a notebook that has at least 200 pages and one file pocket. One section of the binder will be for detailed word analysis of key words, and one is for simple definitions of general new words.

Select 7 to 10 essential vocabulary words associated with a theme or a single topic, concept, or chapter. Words should be *essential* for understanding a concept. Try to limit rare words or suggest that they be submitted as separate extra credit pages.

Provide a template of five to seven aspects related to the word that you want students to include in word analysis, for example, (a) a picture of the word/concept, (b) its etymological roots (e.g., Latin: *cognoscere*), (c) synonyms and antonyms, (d) derivations of the word, (e) how the word is used in your subject matter or a sentence from the text that includes the word, (f) a definition of the word, or (g) how the word or its derivative is used in other subjects. (See Figure 9.5 for the individual vocabulary journal.)

Guide students to complete at least one entry in class. Depending on the class, set a due date by which students will complete more vocabulary journal entries independently. You may decide to make several copies of this template for students to use or provide each student with a copy as a model for including and formatting the same information about a word directly in their journals.

DISSECT AND DEFINE

Purpose

To provide students with guided practice in word analysis including comparing words with multiple meanings depending on the subject matter
To develop students' background knowledge in subject-specific vocabulary

Activity

Identify a key word or concept from the upcoming reading that ideally contains a prefix or suffix, as well as a root or word stem that students will encounter in other academic words and contexts.

Provide each student with a prefix, root, suffix reference list (remember 20 words represent 90% of the most commonly-used prefixes). You may find quick lists on the web. Prentice-Hall has several versions of root or stem words in their various "(Subject) Teachers' Book of Lists". The *Reading Teachers' Book of Lists* has lists of commonly-used words by subject matter.

Pronounce the featured word for students; Write it on an overhead transparency, board, SMART Board, or chart paper.

Ask students, "What is the 'root' or main part of the word?" What word or part of a word do you see within this word: "Dissection" ('sect-section")?"

Direct students, by saying: "look up 'sect' in your root or base word reference page. What does it mean?" (to cut, or a cut) Use your overhead pen or marker to box or otherwise highlight the root, base or other parts they can identify using their own prior knowledge or reference page.

Ask, "What are the other parts of the word?" Highlight each word part that carries meaning (i.e. morpheme), and ask the students what each section means. See Dissect-Define example at the end of activity description.

Ask, "What do you think "dissect" means? ("cut" + 'separate". Dictionary: "To cut apart or separate" or to "dissolve into smallest units/components."

Variations:

Elicit predictions
Use a dictionary to confirm responses
after "dissecting and defining"
Brainstorm words that contain:
a) the same affix or root,
b) similar within-word segments, or synonyms,
c) different verb forms of the same word

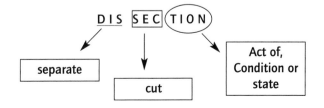

Figure 9.5   Vocabulary Journal Log

Individual	Name: _____ Date: ____
Vocabulary	Unit of Study/Key Concept:
Journal	_____

Essential Word: _____

A sentence quoted directly from a subject-related text, article or worksheet that includes this word

---

| *Definition:* Using the text glossary or dictionary, write a definition of the word that best matches its use in the sentence. | *Etymology:* Use a dictionary to identify the different parts and/or roots of the word as well as the word's language of origin. Represent the word parts and origin in this box. Underline the root or base of the word. |
| *Synonyms and Antonyms:* Use your prior knowledge, ideas from text, and/or a thesaurus to list two synonyms (or synonymous phrases) and two antonyms for the word. | *Word Derivations:* List four words with the same root or base as the essential word (e.g. signal, signature, signify) |

Representation: Draw a symbol or picture related to the meaning of this word linked that relates to the topic or unit of study. Use ideas from text pictures, graphics, or your own original ideas.

---

essential to the current unit of study printed in large letters serves as a consistent cue card for students about academic language. With your support, groups of students can create poster-size visuals labeled to highlight the following:

- The meaning of scientific, mathematical, technology-linked symbols; key vocabulary words or concepts; order of operations, procedures; cycles; physiological, geological, and environmental systems, principles (e.g., of design)
- Systems of the human body, sample solutions to typical word problems, concepts including real-life applications of academic concepts (e.g., how to balance a checkbook), lifelike representations or cross sections of science models, examples of types of art.
- Words that signal a certain type of action, procedural step, application, transition to a new or opposing idea, and a response to a question

Index Cards

Use index cards or half-page sheets that include simplified explanations or definitions of key concepts and/or related vocabulary words (one per card). Card information could include examples of the concept, a real-life application, and/or a visual. Use the cards to *introduce* a key concept *before* students read about it in the text.

- *Option 1:* Create several sets of cards or half-sheets that define, illustrate, or include examples related to one of 8 to 10 vocabulary words linked to an essential concept. For a class of 32 students, examining eight words, create four sets of cards. As a warm-up, distribute one card to each student. Direct students to read the information on the card to themselves then choose two things on the card that they will read or explain to another student. Students continue to share information with three other people.
- *Option 2:* Students can reference the cards when studying on their own or as a preview of words in an upcoming unit. Student pairs can sort word cards into categories and identify the relationship among words.

Bookmark Guides

Bookmark guides help students remember key chapter concepts, vocabulary words, or procedures for a particular unit, experiment, or concept. Create a column of information that lists key concepts, examples, evidence, vocabulary, problem solving, test taking, concept patterns, samples, or tips for order of operations. Format your lists so that several columns of the identical information will fit onto one sheet of paper. Print sheets of bookmarks (four to six to a page) and cut them into individual ones to distribute to students. Explicitly introduce the information on each new bookmark.

Web Sources

Online resources may provide similar comprehensible, jargon-free explanations, formats, and visuals of academic concepts and tips. Incorporate some Wikipedia sources into bookmarks, index cards, or posters for math, science, and applied and visual arts classes. Even if students have adequate access to computers elsewhere, it is helpful for students to be able to reference a classroom poster, bookmark, and/or their personal set of cards or notes while in class.

Literature and History

Posters and Word Walls

Create or help students create concept visuals for language arts, literature studies, and history. Post these handy references on the walls of your classroom. With your support, students can use posters to highlight the following:

- Key vocabulary words or concepts (e.g., literary devices, historical eras, systems of government)
- Real-life scenarios of literary themes, conflicts, characterizations, and personal dilemmas
- Present conditions resulting from historical events, legislation, impact of leadership, systems of government, and features of essay types or genres
- Words or phrases that signal transitions to or contrasts between events, beliefs, examples, opposing ideas, and a response to a question

Bookmark Guides

Bookmark guides help students remember key concepts, vocabulary words, or procedures for a particular unit or chapter. Format key concepts, words, strategic reading tips, questions, themes, or procedures in a column so that you can print and cut three to five bookmarks on one page. For history textbooks, create a new bookmark guide for each chapter or era noting key concepts, chronological events, important people, or types of cause and effect interactions. For teaching a difficult or lengthy novel, create a bookmark for each chapter or sections of the book that can be distinguished by a focus on a specific character, event, setting, or transition in the overall story. On the other side of these bookmarks, you could note the related content standard or samples of questions or tasks that might be included in a test about the content. Explicitly introduce the contents of each new bookmark and explain how the concepts support reading comprehension.

Main Character/Key Leaders Chart

These charts serve a similar purpose as the main idea map (see Figure 9.3). Display laminated, reusable, poster-size graphics to identify main versus subordinate characters in a novel or key leaders or groups involved in a historic event or era. These charts help students keep track of the relationships among and the importance of certain people and events. You might also provide students with a binder paper-size version of this graphic organizer.

Alternative Texts

Once you've identified the essential concepts, historical or literary themes, and specific elements about a novel, locate articles; picture books; sections of science, history, or geography reference books linked to the novel. Use these to widen the appeal and match the interests of students for whom the traditional text is not that compelling. Using themed or topic-related excerpts from books that parallel the sociocultural backgrounds of your students will also help to motivate students to sustain their interest in the text. Speak with your librarian to borrow a cart of books for a classroom library linked in some way to the novel. Gathering alternative texts and online or print media articles to increase background knowledge about leaders, historical, and current events is also recommended.

MOTIVATING STUDENTS TO ACCELERATE

Besides developing specific content-literacy skills, teachers of adolescents must provide students with resources and activities that will motivate them to read challenging texts. Motivating students to accelerate their reading proficiencies means planning lessons that simultaneously strengthen both academic literacy skills and student motivation.

Drawing on information about your students sociocultural and linguistic backgrounds and interests, use supplemental texts or resources that appropriately reflect socioculturally responsive themes, perspectives, or prompts to engage students in reading and critical thinking. You can support students to learn more about interesting topics by simultaneously providing instruction in the literacy skills they need to accomplish reading tasks. Students should have access to a wide variety of reading materials to engage in *wide reading.* Wide reading includes reading about a topic from multiple sources: textbook, magazine, and newspaper articles; short stories; poetry; appropriate online blogs; personal narratives; and fine arts by authors from a wide range of sociocultural perspectives. Prompting students to read after establishing authentic reasons or compelling purposes for reading is also critical. Despite their current skill level, older students have cognitive skills and life perspectives that are essential strengths for engaging readers in text concepts. These are elements to build on while developing reading skills.

Standard English Learners and former English Language Learners reading challenging academic materials may need additional instructional support based on the same motivational approaches to reading we've described andthose that develop academic language for English Language Learners. These practices are featured in Chapter 10. Standard English Learners are students who almost exclusively speak English associated with conventions of African American, Mexican American, Native American, and Hawaiian American language structures. Please remember that not all students who happen to come from these racial backgrounds are automatically considered Standard English Learners! A Standard English Learner is someone who is unable to effectively code-switch between his or her predominantly home or community language to academic English. Many white students and/or students from socioeconomically poor backgrounds may also lack sufficient exposure to and use of what is considered academic English, the predominant language of subject matter text. One could argue that these students should also be considered Standard English Learners as well. Proficient and nonproficient readers in the same class will benefit from reading a range of well-written materials written at students' independent and instructional levels reflecting perspectives that are socio-culturally relevant to students. Many students who have struggled with most school-based texts are often motivated to read about academic concepts that are conveyed, at least in part, through the socio-cultural references, contexts, and anecdotes included in these texts. No matter what your subject area is, it is important to respectfully frame questions and tasks. You can promote multiple perspectives by eliciting and reflecting the multiple perspectives of your students (Ladson-Billings, 1999; Obidah & Teel, 2000).

Flexibly grouping students to engage in a variety of reading and research tasks is one way to promote *situational interest*. Increased engagement in motivational tasks and resources increases students' practice of essential literacy skills. Practice fosters skill mastery, which, in turn, influences lifelong self-motivation. Motivation also builds when you offer students choices, as well as connect projects to students' interests and goals. Activities that promote student interaction are described earlier in this chapter and in the following chapter, which describes methods for teaching English Language Learners. Figure 9.6 describes the impact of and examples for culturally and personally relevant prompts and themes.

Figure 9.6 Culturally and Personally Relevant Themes and Prompts

1. By preassessing students' sociocultural backgrounds and interests, you can develop culturally responsive or universal themes that will frame core concepts. Learning theory tells us that knowledge transfer occurs when links are made between new ideas and a learner's prior knowledge, interest, or experience.

Examples of Culturally Universal Themes: Coming of age, conflict resolution, transitions, identity, use of personal power, identifying alternative solutions, principles of design (ideas, objects, social movements), identifying and creating patterns, (patterns in nature and human nature), borders or the gains and losses involved in territorialism, family dynamics, civil rights, human motivation, quality of life, personal freedom, principle of checks and balances in human interactions, and thinking processes (e.g., equality and inequality in algebra, government)

2. You can develop prompts and identify quotes, models, visuals, or related current events articles that introduce concepts and frame new subject matter in a perspective that is socioculturally relevant to students. Instruction that fosters situational or authentic interest provides the necessary springboard and motivation for students to persist in developing their background knowledge and engagement in learning to apply subject-specific reading strategies (Jetton & Alexander, 1984).

10

Teaching for English Language Learner Success

Key Ideas and Strategies for All Secondary Teachers

Are you looking for more ways to improve your English Language Learners' (ELL) literacy skills and content knowledge? Have you wondered why some ELLs make more progress than others in the same amount of time? You are not alone. In a study by the Center for the Future of Teaching and Learning (Gandara & Maxwell-Jolly, 2005), secondary single-subject teachers identified these professional development needs as equally important:

- Understanding how sociocultural and linguistic factors influence ELLs' academic achievement
- Learning how to apply practical strategies that develop ELLs' content knowledge and academic language skills

To help teachers understand and apply these concepts, this chapter features key ideas and specific instructional strategies for teaching subject matter content to ELLs. The chapter contents are organized into three sections as follows:

- **Conditions that promote language learning** features foundational principles that help to foster language development, that is, the conditions for learning language. These conditions are introduced by comparing scenarios from a nonschool context that parallel the challenges of teaching and learning language. A checklist of questions linked to each condition is provided to guide teacher reflection, lesson planning, and goal setting.

- **Preassessment of adolescent ELLs** emphasizes the importance of preassessing ELLs' unique sociocultural, linguistic backgrounds including their school and nonschool literacy and individual strengths. The section includes a one-page outline of language development stages. These aspects inform how to create differentiated assignments and assessments that equitably foster ELLs' academic progress.

- **Six key strategies that advance students' content knowledge and academic language skills** describes six key strategies and related activities developed by the New Teacher Center (a national professional development organization first established in Santa Cruz, California) that support all adolescent students to learn both subject matter concepts and the academic language associated with those concepts. Sample applications are included.

To guide your initial review of this chapter, we offer options based on your level of prior knowledge regarding ELL instruction:

1. *Emerging:* Have little or no ELL preservice coursework or related student-teaching experience
    a. Read the first section of the chapter thoroughly; reflect on the comparison between Scenarios 1 and 2.
    b. Consider the reflection questions for the first three or four *conditions* in Table 10.1 to adapt textbook materials and student tasks.

2. *Developing:* Have completed preservice coursework linked to ELL instruction
    a. Review the Rationale in the shaded column for each condition in Table 10.1.
    b. Read the second section of the chapter to confirm multiple types of information about your ELLs.
    c. Review and implement strategies from the third section and ideas from Chapter 9.

3. *Advancing:* Have extensive ELL preservice coursework and student teaching experience
    a. Review the second section of the chapter to confirm preassessment of your ELLs' current proficiencies.
    b. Review the third section and Chapter 9 strategies to inform adaptations for lessons.

CLASSROOM CONDITIONS THAT PROMOTE LANGUAGE LEARNING

This section clarifies key principles of ELL instruction, that is, the particular *conditions for learning* that promote language development. The following non-school scenarios are offered to *contextualize* (another language development strategy) these conditions. Compare these hypothetical scenarios as a way of *tapping* your *prior knowledge.*

Scenario 1

You are touring a country for the first time. You arrived at your hotel late yesterday evening. This morning you need to ask the hotel desk clerk for directions to the train station. The clerk does not speak your language, nor do you speak his. You are becoming increasingly frustrated and anxious as you notice that the hotel counters have no displays of highlighted brochures, fold-up maps, or a bilingual glossary of handy words for travelers unfamiliar with the region. The clerk has some idea that you want to get somewhere from your packed bags, gesturing, and the pleading tone that accompanies words he does not appear to understand ("Will you help me?"). His body language conveys that he is getting impatient with your futile attempt to communicate, as he sees other customers approach the desk. From the expression on his face, you believe that he is also frustrated with your situation, but you are not sure why.

As the clerk finally begins to speak to you, you stop your gesturing and utterance of single, transportation-related words so that you might hear him as he tells you something in phrases spoken so rapidly that they blur together. You believe he has told you how to get to the train station because you think you heard the word "tren" or something close to it. With no other person offering to help interpret for either of you, after 10 long, frustrating minutes, you still haven't learned how to get to where you want to go but dare not ask the man to repeat what he has said. You quickly pay your bill and leave.

Scenario 2

You walk down the street and enter a different hotel. On entering the lobby, you see a map of the town on the wall. All the hotels of the area are clearly labeled on this simple map, as are the locations of the bus and train stations. As you study the map and begin to place your finger on the train station symbol, the front desk clerk of this hotel steps up to greet you. He doesn't speak your language either. But from the corner of your eye, you noticed that he has been smiling, nodding his head, trying to observe and listen, as if assessing your needs, as you attempt to read the name of the train station and other landmarks on the map. His interest, body language, and general demeanor cause you to immediately relax, and regain the courage to ask *this* clerk how to reach your destination. He points to the train station on the map and with a phrase that raises like that of the end of a spoken question; you believe he is checking to be sure that that particular spot is your desired destination. For your benefit, he carefully articulates the words written on the map next to the train station symbol. He gestures, pointing to the name of his hotel on the map and to the train station to give you a sense of distance. He points to each street that you would cross to get from the hotel to the station, intermittently stopping to watch your face, checking to see if you were following along.

The clerk calls to an assistant in a nearby room, apparently asking him to get a copy of a smaller and much more detailed map before joining the two of you. His assistant uses his limited English to review the same directions given by the clerk. With such support, you are not deterred by this newer, more text-laden map listing different words and more unusual words to denote the train station. He immediately follows his use of a short phrase in what must be the equivalent of a phrase he knows in English to identify important information (i.e., "*This is [the name of the hotel.]* The name of *this* street is _____.") For each time he repeats the latter phrase, he holds up a finger, verbally filling in the blank with the name of each of the four streets you will cross before reaching the station.

Not only do the resources, friendly and repeated reassurances, and patient review of directions help you to confidently reach your destination (with a map to reference just in case), but in 10 short minutes, you've begun to build your background knowledge, in this case, words in another language equivalent to *one, two, three, four, hotel, street,* the location and names of four streets you'll need to know to reach your destination, plus the phrase the locals use when referring to the *train station.* Your enthusiasm and interest in the journey ahead are renewed!

Comparing Conditions for Language Learning

In both scenarios, traveler and local clerks alike had limited knowledge of one another's primary language. But the *conditions* present at the second hotel produced very different results than those of the first. At the second hotel, the traveler encountered helpful visuals and friendly, invitational interactions that allowed the traveler to speak to two people, one with some knowledge of the traveler's language. Additional strategies included *contextualizing* the directions (i.e., access to an expert's *thinking and reading aloud*), while pointing to a map, and explicitly clarifying the route the traveler should take step-by-step. Those particular activities were examples of strategies used to transfer critical information. These strategies were part of overall conditions that not only helped the traveler reach his destination but they also eased his anxiety enough to engage in learning new vocabulary, both general as well as topic specific. These are some of the same critical conditions students need to maintain a *low-affective filter* as part of learning a new language or the subject matter concepts conveyed through that new language.

These scenarios reflect many of the same conditions of learning foundational to several instructional approaches designed to promote second-language development (Chamot & O'Malley, 1996; Freeman, Freeman & Mercuri, 2002). In essence, conditions that foster learning a second language involve particular instructional strategies, resources, as well as teacher dispositions differentiated to develop students' knowledge and use of language as well as content. Teachers of students at the beginning to intermediate stages of English-language development (ELD) will benefit from embedding all of these *conditions for learning* in their thematic lessons. All other teachers of current and former ELLs will benefit from implementing, especially those linked to instructional, strategies that advance students' academic language. To increase the effectiveness of ideas you might apply, take some time to review the information about students' sociocultural and linguistic backgrounds. This will help to inform the amount and types of support, (i.e., language scaffolding) to provide your students (see Section II for preassessment ideas).

Using Table 10.1 and Figure 10.1

Reference the following graphics related to a few conditions for language learning featured to help you to (1) plan and establish class routines and select supplemental materials or (2) identify the type or level of support students may need to learn a new academic concept or apply subject-specific language. (See also the options explained earlier to guide your review of this chapter.) To use Table 10.1, follow these steps:

1. Read the *rationale* statements in the shaded column on the left for each of the conditions.

2. Choose two or three conditions that are most interesting to you or strike a chord regarding some aspect of your practice you would like to improve.

3. Review the questions listed in the reflections column and think about your responses. (ELD teachers might examine four or five conditions.)

4. If possible, share your thinking with another beginning teacher, an experienced teacher from your department or ELD team, a new-teacher mentor or coach, or others who might support you to identify one or two goals linked to these ideas.

Then using the graphic organizer in Figure 10.1, identify ways you currently apply or might like to apply the first three or four conditions listed in Table 10.1 in a unit or single lesson. Consider using this graphic format for reflecting on the other conditions.

Table 10.1	Conditions for Language Learning: Checklist of Reflective Questions

Rationale, Principles, Reflection, and Specific Applications for Secondary Teacher Practice	
Condition and Rationale	**Reflection**
• **Demonstration/Modeling** As English Language Learners (ELL) are beginning to learn a language, they cannot completely rely on current language proficiencies to understand academic concepts.	In practice, how do I do the following? • Demonstrate skills and concepts whenever possible; provide visuals, graphics, or actual models of concepts or related products that students are expected to replicate • Think aloud (i.e., model the types of thinking or reading processes I assign students to use for a particular task) • Promote a variety of interactions that will allow students to work with peers who are bilingual or who have more advanced language proficiencies, great interest in a subject, or more background knowledge
• **Engagement** Comprehension occurs when the learner is supported to actively engage in learning tasks. Effective teachers of ELLs provide resources that facilitate learning and motivate students to engage in the trial and error process of language learning.	In practice, how do I do the following? • Intentionally state and consistently uphold class norms that ensure that all students' voices will be respected as part of their right to learn? (Zero tolerance on put-downs!) • Plan lessons that are meaningful and interactive, providing students with additional resources (e.g., texts, visuals) that are culturally responsive and tasks that are varied and have authentic purpose) • Give students a variety of assignments based on preassessed literacy strengths (both school and nonschool) as well as what is indicated as part of standards-based instructional goals • Support students to develop their language skills in an environment with a low affective filter (i.e., invitational, respectful, and validating of cultural and individual differences; embarrassment free) • With humor and reflection, occasionally demonstrate my own trial and error process as a learner of content and language
• **Immersion** ELLs usually need more time and varied types of input to hear and read words to develop the level of language acquired by native speakers of the same age.	In practice, how do I do the following? • Design my classroom, project centers, or individual units so that students have ample amounts of high-quality *environmental print* (i.e., charts, word walls, and eye-catching, accurately labeled posters or graphics) • Provide resources for individual student use that are well labeled and have graphics that are meaningful or culturally responsive to students (i.e., that both the resources and the input I provide students clearly convey the focus, purpose of learning activities) • Provide students with access to a variety of alternative texts related to core content or key themes; provide materials of wide-ranging readability levels including bilingual dictionaries and other texts whenever possible

Condition and Rationale	Reflection
• **Application and Approximation** It is important to provide students with opportunities to actively use language (both social and academic) to advance their academic language proficiencies.	In practice, how do I do the following? • Provide multiple opportunities, ways in which they might interact with peers to examine a new academic concept and its parts, then complete tasks that require listening, speaking, reading, and writing about the concept • Promote subject-specific application of concept and academic language; *English-language development:* Review the structural features of the driver's license test booklet; *Literature/History:* Write a letter giving advice to a main character (or world leader.) *Math/Sciences:* Graph the life expectancy rates among women based on information from eight countries. Brainstorm with two other students some reasons why you think the rates differ
• **Response** Feedback is given appropriate to the specific language forms and concept the student is striving to learn.	In practice, how do I do the following? • Give feedback to students individually; base feedback according to the student's stage of language development • Base feedback on a rubric, guidelines, examples of student work that are clearly explained and understood allowing students to interact with their peers to offer feedback or share work before and after my feedback

Figure 10.1   Conditions for Language Learning: Note-Taking Guide

Subject Matter Concept:_____

Related *Academic Language Forms and Functions: _____

_____

(*High-utility and subject-specific vocabulary, language structures, skills linked to reading and writing processes including *how to* summarize, compare, predict, analyze, solve, write an essay, interpret a word problem, or follow listed procedures)

Condition	Application
Demonstrating/Modeling How will I and what will I use to do the following? • Demonstrate, highlight visuals, think aloud, or promote a variety of interactions that will allow my students to communicate with peers who can also model more language skills and encourage interaction through language experiences	

(Continued)

| Figure 10.1 | (Continued) |

Condition	Application
Engagement How will I and what will I use to do the following? • Ensure students feel comfortable using their developing content knowledge and language skills • Provide students with meaningful, interactive tasks and support from modeling, preteaching vocabulary, and culturally responsive themes and texts as a resource for engaging in academic work	
Immersion How will I and what will I use to do the following? • Surround students with varied and ample access to English text (wall charts, varied texts) • Ensure that the print materials they encounter are comprehensible, interesting, culturally responsive, and respectful; that materials extend their knowledge of English as well as subject-specific academic concepts	
Application and Approximation How will I and what will I use to do the following? • Provide students with opportunities to actively use language (both social and academic) to advance their academic language proficiencies	
Response How will I and what will I use to do the following? • Give students feedback that is appropriate considering the students' current language development level and language forms the student is currently learning • Distinguish and acknowledge students' progress in second-language development and learning specific academic concepts	

PREASSESSMENT OF ADOLESCENT ENGLISH LANGUAGE LEARNERS

Cultural and Linguistic Profiles

ELLs who enrolled in U.S. schools as adolescents must do *double the work* of adolescent peers who speak and read English as their first language (Short & Fitzsimmons, 2007). These ELLs must continue to develop two language structures; trying to use *but not confuse* all that they listen to and speak, read, and write about. As explained in the previous chapter, developing one's reading comprehension alone (an essential requirement for academic success) is dependent on applying the breadth of two overarching, interdependent elements of equal importance:

- Having and using sufficient *background knowledge* and *experience* about what one hears, speaks, reads, or writes about. This includes using the depth of one's *prior knowledge* (i.e., the life and language experiences, interests, and proficiencies a person brings to and from reading and other literacy experiences)
- Knowing how to apply a number of *thinking strategies* (e.g., summarizing, comparing, analyzing, evaluating, inferring, solving) for subject-specific listening, speaking, reading, and writing

To support students to effectively develop and use these fundamental elements of reading, it is appropriate to ask, "Who are my students, and what do they bring to reading and learning?" In doing so, you acknowledge that new knowledge transfers best when it's linked to the learner's previous experiences, contexts, and literacy patterns (i.e., which is already *known*). This approach, Vygotsky's classic *Zone of Proximal Development* (ZPD), knowledge plus one, suggests that teaching and learning experiences targeted to match a learner's current knowledge *plus one* added measure or level of rigor. We encourage you to preassess your students' subject-specific content knowledge and identify the related literacy applications student have already learned to use effectively (see Figure 10.2). Preassessing for other types of data, that is, aspects of your students' sociocultural and linguistic backgrounds, will also go a long way to explain the significant influence of culture and one's first-language experiences (those acquired from infancy through age 4) on literacy development overall. Preassessment is an important first step in informing how and to what degree you might need to help students understand and use subject matter concepts and the academic language of your discipline.

Figure 10.2   Preassessment Data and Suggested Methods for Assessment

Types of *Prior Knowledge* That Influence Literacy Development: *English Language Learners' (ELL) Sociocultural, Linguistic, Literacy, and Individual Qualities*	*Samples of Preassessment Methods, Activities, or Resources*
Student's educational history: Years of schooling plus student's pattern of regular or continuous attendance in native country and the United States	**Review students' individual records to identify the following:** • Patterns of attendance and years of schooling in native country and the United States • Past and present participation in school-based programs or special services • Grade point average; commendations and accomplishments

Figure 10.2 (Continued)

Types of *Prior Knowledge* That Influence Literacy Development: *English Language Learners' (ELL) Sociocultural, Linguistic, Literacy, and Individual Qualities*	Samples of Preassessment Methods, Activities, or Resources
Student's culture-specific traditions, beliefs, values: • Family based, linked to native country traditions or holidays, noting historical, cultural, or religious leaders and events • Traditional rituals, ceremonies, and celebrations • Community activities linked to culture and language • Language used at home, school, among family, and peers	**Prompt students to discuss, write responses to short essay questions, or prepare *choice*-based projects about the following:** • Universal themes, life experiences, strengths and challenges, individual interests, family or community traditions, future goals (optimal at the start of the year/semester) • Autobiographical incidents, opinions on world issues, common dilemmas ("In El Salvador, we . . ." or "In the Philippines, we . . .")
Student's individual learning styles and strengths: • Student's learning style preferences and multiple intelligences; student's interests, short- and long-term goals • Student's favorite classes in the United States and in native country • Student's perspective on native language, English, or effort to learn English	**Survey students to determine the following:** • Interests in school and outside of school (nonschool literacies) • Multiple intelligences or learning styles (many surveys for determining students' learning styles are available online); design flexible groups, authentically engaging tasks. • Native country experiences in learning math, science, reading, history, applied and fine arts, PE
Student's sense of efficacy (i.e., perception of self-worth) including perceived level of support inside and outside the school community	**Preassess using combinations of all the above *plus* the following:** • Student-partner interviews, writing samples, student–teacher and parent conferences
Sample features and structures of student's primary language, possible contrastive elements to consider relative to forms of standard (academic) English: • Alphabet versus ideographs, spelling, word order, word endings, and the sounds they make • Sentence structures, forms, and uses of figurative language, punctuation, pronunciation, meaning	**Analyze and interpret the following:** • Student's writing samples with English-language development resource personnel or others familiar with structure of student's first or predominant language
Current levels of literacy proficiency: • Primary language (L1) proficiencies • English (L2) language proficiencies; grade level equivalent of English reading • Predominant language use: types of social and academic language used by student (Higher levels of proficiency in one's native or predominant language facilitate effective transfer of another language.)	**Review data specific to an assessment of student's stage of English-language development:** • Standardized data available through language specialists, counselors, or site administrators • Verify using resources indicating characteristics of language development stage (e.g., Table 10.2)

Stages of Language Development

Adolescent ELLs who attended school in their native country on a regular basis usually enter U.S. schools with native language skills comparable to their U.S. school-age peers. Recent immigrants with limited or disrupted educational histories may be proficient in the social language but not in the academic forms and uses of their first language (L1). Because academic language proficiency in one's L1 impacts the degree to which second language (L2) skills will transfer, newly arrived students with limited academic literacy in their L1 might also need additional instruction and resources to develop first or *primary language* skills.

Although more skilled in literacy skills overall compared to students who immigrate to the United States at a much younger age, adolescent students are expected, in one to four years after starting to learn a new language, to learn complex subject matter concepts from high school textbooks written for native speakers reading at grade level. Studies, such as August & Hakuta's 1997 report, *Improving Schooling for Language-Minority Children: A Research Agenda,* indicate that it takes a person of any age with adequate literacy skills in their L1 (an ideal minimum of fifth-grade literacy skills) between five and seven years to learn the academic knowledge and forms of a new (or second) language. It is important for all teachers of current and former ELLs to keep all of the factors described in both parts of this chapter section in mind when designing instruction and analyzing an assessment of ELLs' work.

Table 10.2 provides a quick look at sample indicators for the *stages of language development,* adapted from the work of Jill Fitzgerald (1995). We recommend that you also consult online sources, including Web sites of professional organizations and states' departments of education, for more detailed descriptions of the stages (see the Resources at the end of the book). We include Table 10.2 as a tool for gauging your students' current level of English-language proficiency. It will help you determine how much you will need to differentiate or scaffold the tasks and texts you assign students based on various methods detailed in the other two sections of this chapter. Use the ELL Class Profile format, Figure 10.3, to organize your data linked to Figure 10.2 and Table 10.2.

Table 10.2 Stages of Language Development for English Language Learners

Stages of Language Development	Characteristics of Language Development L2 = Second language (i.e., English)
Beginning 1. *Preproduction* 2. *Early production* 3. *Early speech emergence*	**Becoming familiar with language** • Mostly listening to and seeing language (print) modeled • Eventually able to respond with one or two word sentences or phrases • Learning to communicate linked to basic needs: interpersonal, familiar social interactions, the language of school culture and environment (e.g., cafeteria, break, periods, library, attendance, grades, homeroom/advisory)

(Continued)

222 KEYS TO THE SECONDARY CLASSROOM

Table 10.2 (Continued)

Stages of Language Development	Characteristics of Language Development L2 = Second language (i.e., English)
Early Intermediate, _Late speech emergence_, Intermediate (independent English reading level equals approximately Grades 2.0 to 3.5+)	**Developing and using vocabulary and phrases linked to familiar concepts** • Understands contextualized information (e.g., visuals, modeled, guided, authentic, or familiar), has limited proficiency to communicate ideas in L2 (mostly, basic social interpersonal communication skills, BICS) • Reproduces familiar phrases; writes and speaks in simple, modeled sentences • Starts to recognize L2 grammar patterns (e.g., word order, punctuation, spelling); attempts English pronunciation **Developing and using language, recognizing simple L2 grammar patterns** • Demonstrates increased comprehension of contextualized information • Approximates recognizable simple English structures; learns and uses simple past tense forms; recognizes common English idioms; can interact socially with native speakers using short, common phrases (small talk) • Engages in conversation and produces narrative (retelling) linked to contextualized language (story, article, teacher modeling); uses many more high-frequency words and is able to learn and use some high-frequency English phrases (mostly BICS) • Reads and comprehends books highlighting familiar themes and visuals, written with simple, idiom-free English sentences; with modeling, responds to critical thinking tasks or reading processes (e.g., summarize, identify main ideas, predict, and classify) linked to familiar topics or themes (introduced to some high-frequency academic terms); understands and uses new vocabulary with some previous scaffolding or contextualizing of related concepts
Early Advanced (Independent English reading level equals approximately Grades 3.5 progressing up to 6.0)	**Developing and increasing accuracy of language use, academic vocabulary, and comprehension of written English with continued language scaffolding** • Communicates social and academic concepts well; continues to advance vocabulary to achieve in content classes _with_ continued support from instructional strategies for developing academic language, especially if given more time • Gives opinions and reasons; summarizes, draws comparisons, justifies views and behaviors using expanded subject-specific vocabulary linked to topics • Engages in conversations and produces sequential narrative

	• Demonstrates increased comprehension linked to academic concepts demonstrated through speaking, listening, reading, and writing with contextualized supports • Can effectively respond to feedback/correction related to subject-verb agreement
Advanced	**Approaching native-speaker proficiencies in all aspects of language; comprehending written English at par with some contextualizing** • Comprehends and generates discussions and presentations in social as well as academic settings • Reads, comprehends, and writes coherent responses to grade level, subject matter text, especially if given more time.

Source: Adapted from conceptual model developed by Krashen and Terrell, 1983.

Figure 10.3 English Language Learner Class Profile

Student Name 1. Grade level and age 2. Parent contact information 3. Teachers (ELD and subject matter)	Socialcultural and Educational Profile 1. Languages spoken in the students' home 2. Educational history (instruction in native country and United States) 3. Aspects of cultural traditions, family history, immigration experiences of student or family members; community involvement 4. Number of generations represented in household	Individual Qualities 1. Learning style preferences; self-reported challenges 2. Multiple intelligences 3. Current interests in and out of school 4. Future goals	Language Development Proficiencies 1. Current, assessed stage of English-language development (ELD) and English reading grade level 2. Reading level in first language
Name:			
Name:			
Name:			

SIX KEY STRATEGIES TO ADVANCE STUDENTS' CONTENT KNOWLEDGE AND ACADEMIC LANGUAGE

This section describes instructional practices and resources adapted from the New Teacher Center's *Six Key Strategies for Secondary Teachers of English Language Learners* (Bongolan, 2005). They represent a select range of strategies that are practical and specific enough that teachers new to language development instruction can easily use them to guide lesson planning. The strategies are not so much single, effective activities like *think-pair-share* or resources like *word walls,* but instead they represent overarching *categories* for activities and resources recommended in numerous studies of ELL best practices (August & Hakuta, 1997; Echevarria, Vogt, & Short, 2004; Garcia, 2003; Gersten & Baker, 2000; Wong-Fillmore & Snow, 2000).

A common misconception about ELL instruction is that its purpose is to only engage students in a series of activities that *avoid* or minimize contact with academic text; for example, filling in graphic organizers with a few academic phrases or participating in a series of vocabulary games. The *Six Key Strategies for Secondary Teachers of English Language Learners* (Bongolan, 2005) represent language *scaffolds* used to *introduce* and reinforce academic concepts and literacy skills. The (Bongolan) strategies further advance language skills built by conditions promoting initial engagement and development of students' basic interpersonal communication skills (BICS). They specifically develop students' cognitive academic language proficiency skills (CALPS). When secondary teachers use the *breadth* of these particular strategies, they will significantly advance students' knowledge of academic concepts *and* the language used to convey them. The *Six Key Strategies for Secondary Teachers of English Language Learners* include the following:

1. *Vocabulary and language development.* Through the first strategy, teachers introduce new concepts by discussing vocabulary words key to that concept. For example, exploring specific academic terms like *algorithm* and related student-accessible words starts a sequence of lessons on larger math concepts and builds the students' background knowledge.

2. *Guided interaction.* The second strategy allows teachers to draw out and build on students' prior knowledge of essential vocabulary or background knowledge. Teachers intermittently model and set expectations about academic language that guide how students will work together to understand concepts through listening, speaking, reading, and/or writing about them through productive group work.

3. *Metacognitive reading processes.* The third strategy combines teaching and then guiding students to use *metacognitive reading* processes. Rather than having students simply memorize or copy information, a teacher models and explicitly teaches thinking skills crucial to monitoring students' comprehension of concepts. Metacognitive reading skills (e.g., prereading structural features of text, stopping to clarify the meaning of words, making predictions about what the text will describe next) are critical skills for learning concepts in a second language. They are the same skills used by highly proficient readers of any language! Engaging students in metacognitive reading skills also helps students monitor their understanding of

concepts and application of a reading process. Given that ELLs may understand but not yet know how to express their understanding, students should be allowed to demonstrate what they know about concepts in multiple ways, including those that are not wholly reliant on advanced language skills.

4. *Explicit instruction.* The fourth strategy involves explicit teaching of reading comprehension skills needed to complete assigned tasks. After students read about a topic, you may ask them to "summarize the last part of the chapter." Engaging students to use metacognitive reading processes while they read does not ensure that they can effectively write about or effectively discuss key ideas (summaries) or their interpretation or comparison. Explicit instruction involves clarifying the subject-specific components and steps for summarizing or comparing and contrasting text-based information.

5. *Meaningful contextualization and universal themes.* The fifth strategy refers to presenting new ideas or language skills in a manner that is authentic, easily recognizable, or linked to some aspects of students' lives. Teachers introduce new information and skills through fluent reading of short excerpts linked to essential ideas; an initial focus on a pivotal word, single phrase, or quote; reflective prompts; short video clips; or visuals that connect students' life experiences to targeted concepts. These activities serve as springboards for learning targeted academic concepts and skills.

6. *Modeling, visuals, and graphic organizers.* The sixth strategy includes the use of modeling or demonstrating reading skills and how to complete tasks or show models of completed projects to increase students' comprehension of ideas and related applications. Using a variety of visual aids, including pictures, diagrams, and charts, helps all students, and especially ELLs, easily recognize essential information and its relationship to supporting ideas.

These strategies are explained further in Figure 10.4, which includes lists of sample activities, and Figures 10.5a and 10.5b, which provide sample applications across subject areas. At the end of the chapter, Figure 10.6 provides a graphic organizer for you to record specific applications to your units. Note that activities and resources for teaching reading included in Chapter 9 are effective for ELL instruction and are examples of applications of one or more of the six key strategies. Detailed descriptions of activities on the following charts can be found in Chapters 7, 8, and 9 and/or on teacher Web sites listed in the resources at the end of the book.

Figure 10.4 Six Key Strategies for Secondary Teachers of English Language Learners, With Sample Activities

1. Vocabulary and Language Development	2. Guided Interaction	3. Metacognitive Reading Processes
Preteach essential vocabulary, both subject-specific and high-utility academic terms **Preteach foundational English language forms** as needed appropriate to students'	**Facilitate multiple ways for productive group work** facilitating interactions based on choice, areas of interest, learning styles and strengths, and literacy development proficiencies	**Model and then facilitate students' engagement in specific metacognitive processes** used by highly proficient readers and writers

(Continued)

Figure 10.4 (Continued)

1. Vocabulary and Language Development	2. Guided Interaction	3. Metacognitive Reading Processes
English-language development stage (e.g., language applications, sentence structures, grammar, idioms, transitional, and other common phrases and vocabulary that are essential to the unit of study)	**Guide student interaction; state clear outcomes and provide models of academic vocabulary and language structures** for listening, speaking, reading, and/or writing about subject matter content	**Support students to monitor their understanding of key concepts and language forms** as they engage in and are introduced to subject matter concepts through their use of these metacognitive (i.e., reading-thinking processes)
Sample activities: List-group-label, word sorts, vocabulary journals or logs, (vocabulary) word bank, word or concept walls, use of sentence frames, close procedures, demonstration of word analysis skills (e.g., dissecting and defining words [prefix, root, suffix], LINK word	Sample activities: Think-pair-share, find someone who, carousel brainstorm, perspective or attitude line-up, Jeopardy; (group) I-search projects, web quests, talking chips partner interview, save the last word, jigsaw reading, newscasts (interview characters from novels; historical, scientific, fine arts leaders, innovators)	Sample activities: Instructional read aloud, questioning the author, reciprocal teaching-plus, question-answer-relationship, think aloud, what you know-what you want to know-what you learned (K-W-L), interactive writing, text or chapter walk; Processes for word analysis, prewriting and note-taking: Cornell notes, double entry journals, completing main idea map
How I (would) apply this strategy/activity:	**How I (would) apply this strategy/activity:**	**How I (would) apply this strategy/activity:**
4. Explicit Instruction	5. Meaningful Contextualization and Universal Themes	6. Modeling, Visuals, and Graphic Organizers
Clarify subject-specific use of academic vocabulary and unfamiliar cultural references before, during, and after students listen, speak, read, or write about academic concepts **Intentionally clarify, model, and explain subject-specific components and steps** for how to read or write a paragraph, essay, report, word problem, or article; how to summarize, evaluate, persuade, interpret, solve, or prove *like a historian* (or mathematician, scientist)	**Preview new concepts by referring to meaningful, authentic resources (realia),** examples, universal themes, visuals, and/or analogous scenarios to introduce specific components of academic concepts or language forms **Elicit students' prior knowledge; foster motivation to respond** through culturally and linguistically responsive resources and high-interest or authentic tasks that put academic concepts or skills into a meaningful context	**Demonstrate new concepts or skills whenever possible;** model the specific *how-to* of any literacy-based task **Increase students' focus as part of transferring knowledge;** Use visuals, advanced organizers, or graphic organizers; graphically organized information helps students to learn and reinforce knowledge of ideas, the conceptual patterns, importance of, and relationship among key ideas
Sample Activities: How to interpret, compare, analyze, argue, evaluate; plus academic language applications, (e.g., How to write essays or report, create graphs, design and produce models, and read word problems)	Sample Activities: Socioculturally responsive texts, visuals, universal themes, anecdotes, prompts; modeling of essential concepts, skills; field trips; videos; simulations; expert read alouds; demonstrations; community connections; and mini-I-search projects	Sample Activities: K-W-L, Venn diagram, word (or phrase) wall, falling dominoes, semantic (concept) web; semantic attribute analysis: main idea and journey map, cause and effect chart, bar graph, pie charts, maps
How I (would) apply this strategy/activity:	**How I (would) apply this strategy/activity:**	**How I (would) use this strategy/activity:**

Figure 10.5a   Six Key Strategies for Secondary Teachers of English Language Learners Applications

Step-by-Step Application	Six Key Strategies
Teacher begins class by distributing an index card to each student. Each card has 1 of 10 key vocabulary words linked to today's lesson including reading excerpts from text. (The teacher has prepared three to four sets of these vocabulary cards.) • On one side of the card is the vocabulary word or phrase. On the other side is a short definition of the word and/or direct quote from text using the word or phrase, an image of the concept, synonyms for the word, a cognate of the word in the primary language of English Language Learners (ELLs), or combination of these options.	**Vocabulary and language development**
Students are asked to read both sides of their card then stand and approach another student to share card information. Students can simply read the information and/or highlight parts of card information they know or can guess about or make a prediction as to what the word, phrase, or quote is connected to in the upcoming lesson. In these *stand-up meetings,* students take turns sharing card information, repeating the exchange two or three times.	**Guided interaction** **Metacognitive reading processes**
Students are asked to quickly write from memory anything they heard about the card information during the stand-up meetings. Students are asked to join two or three other students sitting closest to them to them to share their quick write or brainstorming of information. Students are prompted to volunteer to state what was shared by their partners as the teacher records the responses onto a poster chart, overhead transparency, or PowerPoint display classifying the information into groups (circles, columns, boxes) labeled *predictions, definitions,* and/or *similar words or concepts.* Students individually copy the information in the graphic form onto a sheet of paper.	**Vocabulary and language development** **Guided interaction** **Metacognitive reading processes** **Modeling, visuals, and graphic organizer**
Teacher clarifies lesson focus; reviews key concepts previewed by students., and after sharing/modeling some examples from the teacher's life or from current events or high interest topics, asks students to write connections these concepts have to their lives or prior knowledge. (and/or) Teacher directs students to section of the text, article, or novel for today's lesson. Teacher clarifies specific grade level standard and outcomes addressing standards through today's tasks and any vocabulary pre-teaching thus far. (and/or) Teacher assigns students to use the *Double Entry Journey* format (see Chapter 9) provided with quotes that contain the academic vocabulary words, or more comprehensible synonyms of key words, previously examined by students (quote column can be pre-filled by teacher, or students can write the first few words, or phrase from the quote.) (and/or) Teacher explicitly clarifies and models steps/process for *summarizing, interpreting, analyzing,* or *generating questions* appropriate to responding to history-related text or literature.	**Meaningful contextualization** **Metacognitive reading (writing) processes** **Modeling, visuals, and graphic organizers** **Explicit instruction**
Additional scaffolds for students in earliest stages of ELD: Use more visuals, student-accessible synonyms during initial card activity; pair students w/ bilingual partners for other activities; word walls; bilingual dictionaries	

Figure 10.5b Six Key Strategies for Secondary Teachers of English Language Learners

Step-by-Step Application	Six Key Strategies
• Teacher begins class by displaying 8 to 12 words or phrases written in large print on a poster chart, whiteboard, overhead transparency, or PowerPoint slide. More than half of the words are pivotal, subject-specific words highlighted in today's concepts both in the text and in the teacher's presentation of concepts. Other words are high-utility academic terms used in various subjects (*e.g. explanation, application, measurement, depth*).	**Vocabulary and language development**
• Students are asked to list words on the left-hand side of a *T-Chart* (i.e., two columns they can draw onto a blank sheet of paper) or a sheet provided by the teacher. • On the right-hand side, students write the definition or write a sentence using the words or other words they know that have parts of the featured words or are similar to any words in the phrases. Invite English Language Learners (ELL) in earlier stages of language development to work with a partner. Information noted on the right does not have to be connected to the subject matter of the class at this point.	**Vocabulary and language development** **Metacognitive reading processes** **Graphic organizers**
• For classes with large numbers of kinesthetic learners, have students stand up and share three ideas from their papers with other students in different parts of the room (similar in fashion to the stand-up meeting). • After students return to their seats, they are called on to share their understanding of the words. Teacher records student responses on overhead transparency, poster chart, whiteboard, or the like. • Teacher explicitly clarifies the words and phrases, specifically, what they mean and how they are used for the subject matter. Students can take notes, adding them to their circles, boxes, or as a third column	**Guided interactions** **Modeling, visuals** **Explicit instruction**
Option 1: • Teacher begins an *instructional read aloud* from the text excerpt (chapter introduction, section of text) that explains a concept that refers to those words. Excerpt for instructional read aloud should be one that highlights the most essential scientific process or concept, steps for solving certain types of problems, building or designing conceptual models. Stopping points for the instructional read aloud should be those that lend themselves to students using metacognitive skills (i.e., thinking-skills) appropriate to the subject matter. Example: *Summarizing* key points describing how to solve certain math problems involves a type of listing of steps using transitions, "First you . . . then . . ."	**Metacognitive** **Reading processes** **Meaningful contextualization** **Guided interaction** **Modeling** **Vocabulary and language development**
Option 2: • Teacher explains and models the reading process, *question-answer-relationship* (QAR). Teacher clarifies each step of the process displaying and using an excerpt from the sections students will read to apply the QAR method. • Students engage in the QAR process individually or with a partner. Students share questions and answers they've written as a follow-up to their guided reading task.	**Metacognitive** **Reading processes** **Meaningful contextualization** **Guided interaction**

Additional English-language development scaffolds: Pictures of words or concepts to help students generate known words in first or second language; bilingual dictionaries; word walls of English sentence frames, transition phrases, words describing symbols, or other references to symbols (e.g., = [the equals sign] *is the same as, is equal to, is equivalent to,* and *equals*)

Figure 10.6 Planning Guide: Applying the Six Key Strategies

Six Key Strategies for Secondary Teachers of English Language Learners	*Unit-Specific Applications, Activities, and Resources*
1. Vocabulary and Language Development How will I do the following? Intentionally teach prerequisite vocabulary essential for this lesson or unit of study Support English Language Learners (ELLs) to develop foundational language and vocabulary that most of my native English-speaking students have	
2. Guided Interaction How will I do the following? Ensure that students are engaged in productive group work with clear outcomes and types of support for using academic language to express their understanding of academic concepts	
3. Metacognitive Reading Processes How will I do the following? Intentionally engage students to learn and become more aware of their use of a variety of metacognitive reading processes that reflect the skills of proficient readers	
4. Explicit Instruction How will I do the following? Ensure students know how to complete academic tasks, step by step, for a variety of critical-thinking skills and writing applications (e.g. how to summarize text ideas *like a scientist*)	
5. Meaningful Contextualization and Universal Themes How will I do the following? Elicit students' prior knowledge with socioculturally responsive resources, realia, visuals, alternative texts linked to essential concepts, providing them with a *whole*-picture view of a concept or literacy skill before teaching its parts	
6. Modeling, Visuals, and Graphic Organizers How will I do the following? Represent essential concepts and skills through modeling, demonstrations, and examples of work that meet standards; which visuals and graphic organizers will help to strengthen students' background knowledge or conceptual model of an idea, principle, process, and system, relationship among ideas, hierarchies, procedure, or chain of events	

Assessment of Student Learning

Monitoring Students' Progress

My students didn't do as well as I had hoped they would on the unit test. How can I know what students really understand while I'm teaching important concepts?

Considering ways to challenge and engage adolescents to learn key concepts has long been the centerpiece of lesson planning. For many secondary teachers, designing tests or assessments were at one time relegated to a task more akin to an afterthought. ("Now then, how will I test students on what I've been teaching them?") Assessment is now more widely recognized as an equally critical component of the initial planning and designing of instruction (McTighe & Wiggins 2004). Consider the role and impact of assessment on planning a unit of study as well as day-to-day lessons.

Formative assessments (done as students are actively in the process of learning new content) give you quick, useful information about what your students currently understand. The results of formative assessments can inform you about a possible need to modify your instruction sooner than later and, thus, improve students' chances of learning targeted concepts. Supporting students to consider what each assessment task indicates about their understanding of certain concepts supports them to monitor their progress. In monitoring their performance on benchmark tasks and related assignments, most students take greater responsibility for their part in the learning process.

Summative assessment indicates how well students have understood the breadth of subject matter concepts associated with a unit, concepts studied throughout a quarter (midterm test), trimester, or semester (final). A summative assessment can be given at the completion of instruction for a certain set of concepts, benchmarks, or unit. They are also given at the end of each of a school's major grading periods.

In this chapter, we begin by discussing the overall purpose of assessment. Then, we look in more detail at some of the distinguishing features of formative and summative assessments. We consider some of the key differences between these two types of assessment and pose the critical question, "Why is the end of the unit (or chapter) test not enough"? In the section that follows, we delve into the topic of learning outcomes and evidence, offering examples of formative assessments from across the content areas with corresponding outcomes and evidence listed for each example. Finally, we examine the ever important link between assessing content knowledge and students' literacy skills.

THE PURPOSE OF ASSESSMENT

Why should I assess?

The word *assessment* is derived from the Latin word *assido* or *assidere*, which means to sit beside. When you assess students' work you are, in essence, *sitting beside* them, viewing their perspective when encountering new content. Whether teaching large numbers of students or fewer students in smaller learning communities, it is important and possible to assess at least trends for how and to what degree students are effectively learning targeted concepts. Tasks designed and assigned intentionally as assessments can reveal students' level of understanding of concepts as well as the depth of their related background knowledge. Assessments also reveal trends in students' misconceptions about ideas or inaccuracies in their understanding of subject-specific terms, general academic language, and application of procedures. Assessments also indicate the effectiveness of your skills in planning and designing instruction. Such information may help you to analyze the effectiveness of the resources you use as well as the clarity of the way you convey information to different groups of students.

General Principles for Assessment

- *Consider instructional objectives.* Based on your overall curriculum unit goals, what are the essential concepts and skills you want students to understand and apply? Assess these in both an ongoing and summative manner.
- *Match assessment format to instruction.* Assessment tasks should reflect the types of strategies used to teach the content. For example,
  - If you used graphic organizers to categorize, classify, or identify information, then directing students to demonstrate their knowledge using familiar graphic organizers as appropriate.

○ If students were encouraged to think divergently about new ideas presented in readings, lecture, or discussion, you might assess them through a writing-based assessment that allows them to debate ideas or compare and contrast them to related ones.

○ If you engaged students to learn about concepts based on your pre-assessment of their various learning styles and multiple intelligences, you might design assessment tasks that allow them to demonstrate their learning based on these same modalities.

○ If during guided practice students were asked to solve word problems or recall or match vocabulary with examples, then a quiz with short-answer questions and/or multiple-choice statements makes sense.

- *Demonstrate consistency and predictability.* Some culminating assessments like projects and presentations are intended to be unique and offer students choices in how they present their knowledge. However, the majority of your assessments should be somewhat predictable and consistent. Consistency supports students in knowing what and how to study for tests. If students know that you will likely direct them to match terminology or write summary paragraphs about key concepts, they can better anticipate how and what to study.

Monitoring Student Progress

First Week Assessments

During the first couple of weeks of the year, lessons, writing prompts, and other activities should be designed primarily to help teachers see what the students already know. What is their prior experience with the content? How well can they read and comprehend the text? How are their writing skills?

You want to get a feel for proficiency with academic English for both English Language Learners (ELL) and native English speakers. You are also scanning for evidence of higher-level literacy skills, such as summarizing, presenting opinions, describing, following written directions or procedures.

What Counts and How Much?

Let students know how often you will be assessing their progress, what percentage of these assessments will count toward their quarter/semester grades, and what weight you place on the assessments regarding their overall grade. You will need to decide what percentage of each of the following will contribute toward the student's grade:

- Daily participation
- Homework
- Ongoing or weekly assessments (see samples described later in this chapter)
- Summative, end-of-unit assessments or tests
- Extra credit

It is not necessary to reinvent the wheel in these decisions. Check with your department chair or veteran teachers about how they weight their assignments.

Inform students of percentages early in the quarter. If possible, include this breakdown in a letter home to parents, on an informational sheet available for back-to-school night, or as part of your semester syllabus.

Communicating With Students

Set aside time for short, two-minute conferences with students to share their individual progress, sometime before report cards. For teachers in large schools, some with upward of 160 students, this might appear daunting. Set aside time during guided or independent practice time to speak with six to eight students a day for a week. Note their areas of success and make suggestions as to areas for growth. If students need additional support, make an appointment to meet for extra help at lunch or after school.

Teachers who use a software program to post grades sometimes opt to print out the results of student progress and post them in class. Consider student privacy and sensitivity to sharing this information. You may print this information and announce that this is available for students after class or during independent class work time. You may also code student achievement scores so students can only access their scores

FORMATIVE AND SUMMATIVE ASSESSMENT: WHAT IS THE DIFFERENCE?

Why is the test not enough? Why does it matter to know students' progress as they go along?

Formative Assessments

Every assignment you give students gives you some assessment of their progress and comprehension. You can choose to review and grade some assignments with more importance than others. In choosing key formative assessments, think about how well the assignment shows what the students have learned from the key concepts in your curriculum unit. Summaries, lab reports, and select problems of the week can each give you a snapshot view of student progress.

Summative Assessments

The focus on standards-based instruction stresses the importance of designing the summative assessment or final examination before you begin the first day of a curriculum unit. Ideally, by the time the final test comes around, the students should already know the concepts that will be tested. They will know the way they will be expected to demonstrate their knowledge and skills. The summative assessment for a unit is often a remix of various formative assessments or tasks that were given to students throughout the term. The summative assessment can take the form of a test, project, presentation, or some combination thereof. A summative assessment may take the form of a

(a) multiple-choice test, (b) series of math or science problems, (c) final paper, (d) series of short essay questions, (e) multicomponent project, (f) demonstration, (g) simulation of skills or procedures, (h) an essay, or (i) a combination of some of these assessment forms.

Remember the General Principles of Assessment

- Make sure the assessments match up with what you want to teach and how you are teaching.
- Let the format of the assessment be predictable and consistent so that students can concentrate on what they have learned.
- Let students know the value of the assessment related to their grade.

LEARNING OUTCOMES AND EVIDENCE

How do I choose outcomes and look for evidence?

In Chapters 5 and 6 on lesson planning, we talked about the *backward-design* approach beginning with learning outcomes first rather than the minute-by-minute progression of a single lesson plan:

- What is it you want your students to know or be able to do?
- What evidence, product, or assessment will show you what students are learning?
- What resources, learning activities, direct input, guided practice, and independent student tasks will be incorporated into a series of daily lessons for this unit of study?

In deciding what to teach, these are the key questions you will ask yourself over and again. Figure 11.1 provides examples of formative assessments showing outcomes and evidence in a variety of content areas.

Learning Outcomes

In this case, each of the content area outcomes was taken directly from the California State Content Standards. Each state will have similar standards to both guide and hold teachers accountable. It can be helpful to sit down with department colleagues or your mentor teacher to study, prioritize, and sequence a path through these standards.

Evidence

Traditional thinking has led us to believe the best way to measure student learning in secondary schools is by the final exams. Either the students learned the material or they didn't. It was considered as simple as that. Intentionally designing and assigning certain tasks as formative assessments is a shift in this way of thinking. You'll notice that the formative assessment examples we have listed are many of the learning activities and student tasks you've already been implementing. The difference we emphasize here involves the intention with which you plan and analyze the results of these student tasks (i.e., formative assessments). By analyzing evidence of your students' strengths and instructional needs as part of an ongoing process, you will be better informed about how to fine-tune your practices in ways that will significantly increase your students' academic success.

Figure 11.1 Examples of Formative Assessment

Content Area	Outcomes *What do you want students to know or be able to do?*	Evidence *What product or assessment will show you what students know?*
Math	Students solve equations and inequalities involving absolute values.	Problem of the week, quizzes, cooperative group poster, create own equations, summary paragraph on process
	Students make decisions about how to approach problems (mathematical reasoning).	Authentic problem solving project (environmental quality, economics, and other global issues); poster presentation; descriptive paragraph, bar graphs, comparison charts
Science—lab sciences, health, and agriculture	Students know how to solve problems involving distance, time, and average speed.	Lab report, science project, descriptive paragraph, poster presentation
	Students will be able to describe key elements of nutrition and related diet.	Poster presentation, sample meal, analysis of school meal, essay
Language— English, world language, and English-language development (ELD)	Students compare and contrast the presentation of a similar theme or topic across genres.	Venn diagram, comparative essay, dramatization, poster presentation, literature log, character journey map, retelling
	Students relate a clear, coherent incident, event, or situation by using well-chosen details.	A sequence of writing drafts, demonstrating skills progression, student's self-evaluation on rubric, weekly writing samples focused on specific writing standards
History, social science	Students analyze the multiple causes, key events, and complex consequences of the Civil War.	Sequential timeline, research report, cooperative group jigsaw synthesis, poster or PowerPoint presentation, flow chart, short essays
	Students analyze the effects of the Industrial Revolution in England, France, Germany, Japan, and the United States.	Venn diagrams, cooperative group-written synthesis, PowerPoint presentation, research paper, dramatization, short essays, debate from perspective of historical figures, decade posters or newscasts

Content Area	Outcomes *What do you want students to know or be able to do?*	Evidence *What product or assessment will show you what students know?*
Fine Arts—art, drama	Students use artistic terms when describing the intent and content of a work of art.	Art show review, oral presentation, quiz, weekly writing samples on a range of art pieces
	Students create characters, environments, and actions that exhibit tension or suspense.	Improvisational or practiced demonstrations, writing a script or screenplay
Applied arts— business, computers, shop	Students plan and conduct multiple-step information searches by using computer networks and modems. (also in language arts)	Sequential diagram of information chain, annotated bibliography of Web-based sources
	Students diagnose and repair difficulties in small engine carburetor systems.	Diagnose and repair a variety of small engine carburetor problems
Physical education	Students demonstrate fundamental gymnastic tumbling skills.	Demonstrate progress in gymnastic skills based on weekly goal setting; demonstrate skill
	Students describe leadership roles and activities in the context of team games and activities.	Oral presentation on leadership roles, paragraph summary, observation of practice in a leadership role

THE LINK BETWEEN ASSESSING CONTENT KNOWLEDGE AND STUDENTS' LITERACY SKILLS

Why would I be concerned with literacy skills if I am not an English or literacy development teacher?

Based on formative assessments, you may find that you have students who show great enthusiasm for and make progress in learning subject matter concepts, and yet these same students may perform poorly on the final test. It is key to learn why this is the case especially for students who are learning English as a second language (ESL) or students who continue to struggle with their use of academic English. Subject matter teachers should differentiate assessments such that, as much as possible, the directions for and the assessments themselves will allow all students to demonstrate their knowledge of academic concepts regardless that some are not currently proficient in academic English literacy skills. (The exception to this practice is those teachers who are specifically assessing student progress in learning ESL or developing remedial reading skills in English.)

With so much content to teach and so many students to serve, secondary teachers tend toward designing multiple-choice assessments that are easy to grade and give a quick picture of progress. We encourage you to consider these additional questions in preparing to assess students who are (1) acquiring ESL,

(2) nonproficient readers and writers of academic English, and/or (3) acquiring academic English vocabulary.

- Is your assessment format designed so that students can independently determine the task you want them to perform when reading directions?
- Have your students been given prior instruction in the vocabulary words you use in your directions, graphics, or description of essential concepts?
- If your class is *not* a language-arts-based class, to what degree will you deduct points or credit for incorrect spelling, faulty grammar, and punctuation? How much will you deduct if it *is* a language arts class?
- Will your test include a visual representation of word choices in vocabulary-based assessments? Namely, rather than fill-in-the-blank with no word bank option available, you can include an array of words from which they can choose to fill in or match correct terminology.
- Is the language you use in the test free of idiomatic phrases that might be challenging for students acquiring English? If idioms were necessary to the context, would you be willing to include a sheltered definition of these phrases in the margins?
- Will your assessment tasks have sample problems or models for students to consider? Or will your assessment tasks be somewhat familiar to students by the time they attempt summative tests?

While ESL and remedial English teachers have the direct charge of teaching English skills, many content area teachers believe it is equitable to give a dual grade on assignments, one that reflects students' understanding of content and one for their academic language proficiency. These same teachers have found ways to integrate a level of foundational literacy and content literacy development instruction into their subject matter lessons. This instructional approach is, perhaps, one of the most important shifts in the last decade's focus on standards-based instruction.

This final point emphasizes the importance of considering differences between what you are testing as far as subject matter concepts and the English-literacy skills of your students. Given the rising numbers of teenage students who speak social as well as academic English as their second language, this is no small point. Among these students are immigrant English learners and students born in the United States who are still acquiring academic English. Math, science, social studies, and other teachers across the disciplines are experiencing the need to explicitly teach vocabulary and specific skills related to expository writing and reading comprehension (see Chapter 9 on reading strategies). Regardless of their current academic language proficiencies in English, remember that adolescent students have lived in the world and with words much longer than their younger counterparts. Limited proficiency in the language of instruction does not equate to limited understanding or lack of background knowledge. It is important that secondary teachers understand these distinctions as they plan how to assess student learning.

12

Communication With Parents

Maintaining That Vital Link

I have 160 students. Am I really expected to have a relationship or make contact with all of my students' families?

Communicating with the parents or guardians of your students can benefit everyone involved. Some of your students may come from sociocultural and language backgrounds that are different from yours, and family members can provide tremendous insight into your students' world, the various life experiences, and the skills they bring to your classroom. Also, the more you know about the social, historical, and economic dimensions of the surrounding community the more effectively you can make connections between what you want to teach and what students may already know.

Parents appreciate knowing about their students' progress and how they can help and support their student to be successful in your class. Communicating with parents means utilizing several ways of sending information out, as well as receiving information. In addition to back-to-school events, progress reports, and announcements, your school may have different templates or guidelines available to you regarding how to inform parents about what their students are studying and how they are progressing. These resources are typically available in both English and in the various home languages of parents who do not speak English as their first language.

Expect that parents' involvement in their students' schooling will differ. Some parents become involved only when learning their student is academically at risk. Other parents are very much involved in their students' academic progress, after school activities, and schoolwide events. Still other parents may have a high level of intimidation about any sort of school involvement. They may attend back-to-school night functions or parent conferences when requested to but little else. As mentioned earlier, parents of teenage students may have younger children at home and have shifted their school-related focus on them. Talk with your school's parent liaison, your mentor teacher, or other experienced teachers to learn more about ways to communicate with parents more effectively. Make sure you plan to participate in every one of your school's scheduled family-related events. Let your students know that you look forward to meeting their parents at these events and that you'll be communicating with them about their progress throughout the year.

Other than schoolwide events, what else might you do to communicate with parents? How do you reach parents when you have so many students? This chapter provides some practical resources to help you get started, and it answers the following questions:

- Why is it important to be in contact with parents?
- Are there any special times that make parent contact easier?
- When are the best opportunities for parent contact?
- How do I best reach out to parents who do not speak English or have a limited formal education?

WHY IS IT IMPORTANT TO BE IN CONTACT WITH PARENTS?

Many beginning secondary teachers have confirmed their reluctance contact the parents of their students. The thought of maintaining a system of ongoing communication with so many families usually stops well-intended teachers from beginning the effort. In addition, if students are exhibiting the type of at-risk behavior that warrants parent contact, teachers may fear that their teaching practice may be misrepresented by some students to their parents. However, consider the following positive aspects of establishing and maintaining communications with parents:

- *The recognition of establishing your professionalism and availability.* Sending home a letter to parents introducing yourself, a brief description of the course (one paragraph), and how and when to contact you demonstrates your willingness to be a partner in their students' educational success. Including highlights of your instructional year lets them know very quickly that you are prepared and professional (see Figure 12.1 for a sample letter). Some parents do not respond as much to print, but with enough school-based outreach, they will come to an open house or a dinner or barbecue-type event. These parents will also value hearing you talk about your teaching history, your goals, and your expectations for their student.

Figure 12.1	Sample Letter

September 2008

Dear Parents and Guardians,

I look forward to teaching students at _____ High School this year. Your son/daughter is enrolled in my _____ class during _____ period this year/semester.

Attached is a copy of my syllabus, or plan for the year. Included are my expectations for homework and classroom behavior. Each day, students can expect the following:

- An agenda of class activities and assignments will be posted.
- Key concepts for the day will be identified.
- Opportunities to clarify, practice, or extend concepts will be provided.
- Homework will be assigned and reviewed.
- Tests or quizzes will be given every _____.

Feel free to contact me during my prep period, which is between _____ (time) during _____ period or after school between _____ (time) with your questions or concerns.

It is my hope that your child will be challenged and enjoy this class. I look forward to meeting with you during our all-school events or individually if the need occurs.

Sincerely,

_____
(your name)

_____ Extension _____
(school phone number)

School e-mail address: _____

- *The ongoing benefits of establishing expectations early.* Attached to your introductory letter can be a brief course syllabus including a description of your expectations for homework and classroom behavior (see Figure 12.2 for a sample course syllabus). This information should convey to parents and administrators your guidelines, rules, and consequences related to absences, tardies, late or missed assignments, expectations about materials, and general classroom rules. For the majority of students, this information will give them enough direction to stay on task and be successful in your classroom. For more reluctant or resistant students, this information will lay the groundwork for any occasions where they or their parents may want to challenge your interventions or warnings regarding their progress or behavior.

Figure 12.2   Sample Course Syllabus

Course Title:

Instructor's Name:

Course Description: (Besides a description of your curriculum, you may want to include whether this satisfies graduation or university admissions requirements.)

Course Outcomes and/or a few of the Essential Content Standards Addressed:

Description of Typical Instructional Methods or Approaches: List typical daily activities or sample activities students will experience (homework review, guided note taking, responding to textbook information, cooperative activities with peers, experiments, comprehension activities through writing, quizzes, reports)

Grading Policy: (What percentage of students' quarter grades are linked to homework, in-class participation, extra credit, tests, projects, and daily assignments? Some teachers cite their expectations for student behavior in this section.)

Homework Policy: (How much homework is assigned weekly? What are expectations in relation to the quality, time spent, and due dates?)

Absences and Late Assignments: (What should students do or expect if they are absent or have late assignments?)

Makeup Options: (Will you have makeup options for missed assignments or tests?)

Progress Reports: (List the date when progress reports are submitted.)

Teacher Contact: (How can parents reach you? Are there special-conference days or minimum days for this purpose? When is the best time to reach you? Include school phone and your extension and/or your school e-mail address.)

- *The value of setting behavior standards that include students, teacher, and parents.* While establishing communication with the initial letter and syllabus, you have set a standard for yourself in relation to maintaining an effective learning environment for students. The classroom management challenges of first-year teaching may indeed be *decreased* if you can take the time to explicitly determine your expectations for student productivity and behavior. Consult with veterans in your department and your beginning-teacher mentor for some ideas regarding these initial communications with parents.

ARE THERE ANY SPECIAL TIPS THAT MAKE PARENT CONTACT EASIER?

Consider the following suggestions regarding ongoing communication with parents:

- *Introductory letter.* An introductory letter that accompanies a course syllabus establishes your initial contact with parents. This letter can also include expectations for homework, assignments, and other classroom procedures.
- *Signature request.* Whenever possible, have all documents signed that go home. It is important that you document that parents have seen what you have sent to them.
- *Translations.* Ask your department chair or office manager about available support if you need help translating parent materials into their home language.
- *Proofread.* Make sure to proofread your documents for any misspellings and other errors and, if possible, print them on school stationary. Remember to put your best professional foot forward.
- *Contacts regarding behavior or unsatisfactory progress.* It is critical to have a record of a student's attendance, assignment grades, or interventions (warnings, detentions) available when you set up your appointment with a parent, speak to them on the phone, or actually meet with the parent. Organization pays off when looking to work collaboratively with parents to support an at-risk student. Figure 12.3 provides a format for records of calls to parents.

Figure 12.3 Record of Calls

Quarter: 1st 2nd 3rd 4th (circle one) Teacher Name: _____			
Date: • Student Name: • Phone Number: • Parent Name:	*Period*	*Concern*	*Solutions Agreements*

- *Keep a file.* Keep a file or binder with copies of these dated documents, including a log of positive notes you've sent home. You may want to share the file with your evaluating administrator during conferences or with individual parents to review aspects of your program. You may want to use an *interventions log* for each student who habitually does not follow your expectations (see Figure 12.4).

Figure 12.4 Interventions Log

Teacher: _____

Student Name (Period)	Warnings (Date)	In-Class Detention (Date)	Parent Contact (Date)	On-Campus Detention or Saturday School (Date)	Administrative Intervention (Date)	Other Actions (Date)

- *When administrative or other support is advised.* When attempting to support a student who is at risk because of habitual absences, missed assignments, or inappropriate behavior, it is advised that you inform an administrator or the student's counselor about the situation prior to a parent conference. In this situation, the student's attendance and assignments should be posted in your grade book, as well as records of your previous interventions. In some cases where the parent has expressed some negative comments about your expectations or policies, you may want to have a supportive administrator, student counselor, or your beginning-teacher mentor present to help keep the conversation neutral and professional.

WHEN ARE THE BEST OPPORTUNITIES FOR PARENT CONTACT?

Consider these key opportunities and situations for making parent contact:

- *First week of school.* Distribute your introductory letter and syllabus to parents during the first week of school. You may also include your discipline and grading policy or other expectations as a part of this first communication.

- *Back-to-school night.* Parents will be invited to come to school to meet with their students' teachers. This is *not* a night for extensive conferencing about an individual student. You may want to make an appointment if a parent requests one, or have your contact information available. Most schools format this evening so parents can visit each class for approximately 10 minutes. In that time, you should provide an overview for each group of parents about the courses you are teaching, a quick statement about the curriculum covered, a copy of your syllabus, a brief description of typical classroom activities, and any information about homework and larger projects. You may want to have course textbooks and other resources on display. That evening you will simply be walking parents through the highlights of your program.

- *Anytime—on a positive note.* On a half sheet of paper, you may want to highlight for parents a current or just completed unit of study with a congratulatory note for a particular student (see Figure 12.5 for sample notes in English and Spanish). Format it with some title incorporating the school name or mascot, a descriptor of the behavior or unit of study, your name, the date, and the name of the student you are acknowledging. This can be done anytime in the year. Send home via the student.

Figure 12.5 Sample Congratulatory Notes

Dear Parents,

For the past _____ weeks, our _____ class has been studying _____.

This note is to let you know of my appreciation for your child's progress. In particular, _____ is to be congratulated for _____.

Sincerely,

_____   _____

Teacher's Signature   Date

_____

(Continued)

Figure 12.5 (Continued)

Estimados Padres de Familia,

En las últimas _____ semanas, nuestra clase de _____ ha estado estudiando _____.
Esta nota es para informarles de mi apreciación por el progreso su hijo/a ha hecho en
_____. Favor de felicitarlo/por su esfuerzo. Gracias!

Sinceramente,

_____   _____
Firma de Maestra ir Maestro   Fecha

Dear Parents,

Your child _____ has made excellent progress in completing all work in class and homework.
Please congratulate _____ for this hard work and effort. Thank You.

Sincerely,

_____   _____
Teacher's Signature   Date

Estimados Padres de Familia

Su hijo ir hija _____ ha hecho progreso excelente en completar todas sus tareas académicas.
Favor de felicitarlo/a por su esfuerzo y trabajo. Gracias.

Sinceramente,

_____   _____
Firma de Maestra ir Maestro   Fecha

Dear Parents,

Your child, _____ has made excellent progress in demonstrating responsible behavior in
class. Please congratulate _____ for this effort. Thank You.

Sincerely,

_____   _____
Teacher's Signature   Date

Estimados Padres de Familia

Su hijo ir hija_____ ha hecho progreso excelente en su portamiento y responsibilidadas en la
escuela. Favor de felicitarlo/a por su esfuerzo. Gracias.

Sinceramente,

_____   _____
Firma de Maestra ir Maestro   Fecha

- *Progress reports.* Most secondary schools will send home progress reports for students who are in danger of failing a course. The school may also send a record of the all students' current grades prior to the end of the quarter. Typically, there are codes on the progress report form that you will be asked to bubble in to explain the general progress of the student. These formal progress reports are generally sent out through the main office.

- *Prior to first grading period (quarter).* As veteran and new teachers alike begin to teach a new course of study, it may take a few weeks to finalize the value or percentages ascribed to assignments for cumulative grades, such as a quarter grade. At about the time you submit progress reports, you may want to send out a brief note outlining key projects or assignments, as well as a review of the credit ascribed to homework and quizzes. This may shed some light on the progress of all students and the possibilities for a final semester grade. You might include information about learning outcomes for the next quarter in this communication.

- *When necessary—"for your attention" forms.* On a half sheet of paper you may want to list a number of behaviors or concerns about which you would like to inform parents (see Figure 12.6). If there are serious or chronic concerns, you may want to call a parent directly. However, if you see a pattern of at-risk behavior surfacing, you may want to send a note home through the mail and make a follow-up call if you haven't heard from the parent in a week of mailing your note. Remember when you are calling a parent as an early or late intervention, you need to have available a record of a student's behavior, attendance, or overall academic progress.

Figure 12.6 For Your Attention

For Your Attention

I am requesting that we take time to discuss your student, _____

(Name)

and the following concerns regarding his or her progress in my _____ **class.**

(Check appropriate box or boxes)

- ❑ **Frequent absences**
- ❑ **Frequent tardiness to class**
- ❑ **Missing or incomplete in-class assignments**
- ❑ **Missing or incomplete homework assignments**
- ❑ **Lack of motivation, inappropriate behavior or language (circle)**

Please contact me at your earliest convenience to discuss this in a phone conversation or in person.

_____   _____

(Your name)   (Date)

Contact Number: _____

Tips for Phone Conversations

1. Stay neutral.

2. Introduce yourself and state your purpose **for the call, emphasizing your intent to support this student's success.**

3. Restate the expectation or policy related to your concern **about the student (excessive absences, tardies, dress-code violation, missing assignments).**

4. Clarify or confirm the concern with the parent: **"Can you help me understand the situation regarding his or her (absences, tardies, incomplete work, homework)"** or **"Can you share with me what you've been thinking about this or what you've discussed with your student at home?"** *Paraphrase the statements made by the parent to confirm to the parent that you are listening intently.*

5. Elicit support from the parent **for next steps for the student. At this point, you may be able to move the conversation toward solutions linked to your expectations. Stay neutral! If somehow the conversation moves in a negative direction regarding you, calmly restate policies or expectations, and again, attempt to elicit what** *both* **you and the parent can do to support this student in modifying his or her behavior. If this doesn't work, respectfully and neutrally request that you set up an appointment to review the student's work, attendance, or behavior, perhaps with a supportive administrator or other colleague on hand.**

- *Beginning of second semester.* During the first week of the second semester, you may want to send home through your students a *welcome back* type of note, outlining key learning objectives for the semester and a quick review of your expectations, as well as any modifications you have made.
- *Open house.* This event is usually scheduled in the spring and is similar in structure to the back-to-school event in the fall. During open house, parents and administrators expect that more student work will be displayed on the walls or in individual folders. Once again, this is not meant to be a time for individual conferences with parents.

HOW DO I REACH OUT TO PARENTS WHO DO NOT SPEAK ENGLISH OR TEND TO HAVE LIMITED INVOLVEMENT IN SCHOOL MATTERS?

As we have pointed out, many of today's public school students come from homes where English is not spoken. These students may be first- or second-generation United States–born, and their home life continues to be dominated by their first language. Parent involvement may at times be limited due to the demands of adults' work schedules, a need to attend to younger children at home, and in some cases, a sense that their input or interest is not authentically valued within the school community.

How do you reach out to all parents, especially those that do not speak English? First, start with the assumption that *all* parents care deeply about their children, and all parents would like their children to succeed. Different cultures have different ways of demonstrating their support. Teachers who do not come from the same cultural background as their students should refrain from making judgments about parents' values, and instead, try to learn more about their culture. For example, in some cultures, support of family members in crisis may be valued over completing homework on any given night. It is important to honor that value and show respect for the family's decisions while, at the same time, encouraging students to keep up with the class work and helping them find ways to do so.

Second, teachers need to seek out translating assistance, if needed. Many schools or districts have designated community liaison personnel that can assist with translation. If not, it is important to check with the administration or teacher colleagues to find out what resources for translation have been available in the past. Investigate these possible resources for translating:

- School/parent liaison—school or district wide
- Office staff designated for translating assistance
- Use of categorical funding from state and federal programs to pay bilingual instructional aides or other staff a stipend for translating
- Bilingual parents
- Bilingual students who are often more than willing to translate if the message home is about positive behavior or academic progress

Making an effort to *send home key communications in the home language of the family* gives the message that all families are valued and important. It also provides needed information to the parents and a window into secondary school life. The majority of immigrant parents in the United States today did not complete high school themselves and may consider it a mysterious domain. For some immigrant parents, having their children even arrive at secondary school and stay there is already a pinnacle of success for the family.

Third, keep in mind that even translated communication will have limited impact if it is not written in direct language without academic jargon. This pertains not just to parents who speak a language other than English but also to other parents of diverse racial and class backgrounds. *State—clearly and simply—what you are studying and problems or praises you wish to communicate about the student.* Phone communication with a translator is often more effective than writing.

Epilogue

Sustaining a Passion for Teaching

H ow do you sustain the passion and optimism that brought you to the wild ride of teaching secondary students? You may have started with a childhood dream of being a teacher, been inspired by a heroic teacher in a Hollywood movie or a real-life teacher who had a lasting impact on your life. Or you may have stumbled into the profession and decided to stay. No matter what brought you here, at one time or another in your teaching career, you are likely to experience not only highs but also lows. Then you will need to be prepared with practices of revitalization that will help you to return to your initial vision.

Conditions are rarely what teachers imagined. Occasionally, teachers will find themselves in a job situation as new secondary teachers where they are given a reasonable set of preps with few or no outside duties. They will have a clean, well-stocked classroom with a manageable number of students. They will feel safe and valued in their school environment. They will have the opportunity to work with a strong collegial team that assists in planning and insures that their assignment is one they prepared for. They will be given support staff, resources, and training to assist in teaching underprepared students. Their work will be guided by standards, and at the same time, they will be encouraged to teach creatively to meet the range of needs of all their students.

However, for the majority of teachers, likely including you, the conditions for success described here will not all be there all of the time. When things are not going well, you may feel ineffective and discouraged. You may find yourself blaming the system, the students, and even yourself. How do you rise above these slumps and return your initial vision? The following practices can help to restore energy, momentum, and purpose to your teaching work:

- To sustain optimism and hopefulness, it is vital to get to know your students, create real connections, and notice your impact on their lives. Although you cannot forge an instant relationship with all 180 students, you can set an intention to know more of them each year, to know what matters to them, and to know how they learn best. Even incremental changes can lead to a powerful impact on student's lives and, in turn, allow the students to have an impact on you.

- You need to inquire in your teaching practice and make a study of your work. Always be a learner. You can learn from your students, from your colleagues, and from professional development opportunities. Teaching is a fine craft, and the focus on excellence should continue throughout your career.

- At the same time that you focus on improvement, you need to accept yourself and where you are in the process. Acknowledge that in the first few years, you can't be everything. The work of teaching is complex and growing more and more so over time for experienced teachers as well beginning teachers. You need to be kind to yourself and celebrate your small successes. You need to acknowledge your incredible capacity to do well and, at the same time, not compare yourself unfairly with more experienced colleagues. It takes time to learn a craft.

- You need to take care of your health, which means getting exercise, eating well, and maintaining bonds with family and friends. You need to continue with outside interests and passions, even if it might seem, at times, you are too tired to do so. Often, this practice may seem in contradiction with being well prepared for the teaching day. Yet, the paradox of it all is, the more you keep yourself well rested and nourished, the more effectively you can use your teaching and preparation time.

- One of the greatest antidotes for any feeling of powerlessness is to take leadership. Many of the teachers we see staying vital in the profession over a long period see themselves as teacher leaders. Opportunities you find to advocate, facilitate, and be visible in your school and communities often renew energy and commitment for your work.

- You need to take the time to learn from parents and community members and to soak in the richness of the diverse cultures represented in the schools today. Learn about sources of community celebration and pride. Connect with parents on positive features about their children.

- You can learn to work with mentors, and allow yourself to benefit from that collaborative relationship. If your school district is part of a program that sets you up with a support provider, so much the better. If not, you can find colleagues that inspire you and seek them out. You can find ways to collaborate to analyze student work, plan, design, and think about practice.

- Above all, you need to keep your sense of humor and never lose sight of the goals and visions that brought you to teaching. Mandates will come and go, and policies will shift. You need to use the textbook as a tool, and never forget to think critically about what you are teaching and why. You have amazing opportunities in this work for creativity, connection, and the ability to make a significant difference. Enjoy it!

Key Resources

*Web Sites, Articles, and
Books for Secondary Teachers*

T he following list of Web sites, articles, and books provide additional resources
for your consideration. The resources are organized into broader themes
and concepts reflected throughout this book.

ADOLESCENCE, BUILDING COMMUNITY, AND CULTURALLY RELEVANT TEACHING

(Chapters 1, 2, 3)

Web Sites

http://www.teachnet.org/NTNY/nychelp/build.htm

http://www.eduplace.com/activity/

http://teacher.scholastic.com/activities/

http://www.teachers.tv/video/4946

http://www.nea.org/tools/ClassroomManagement.html

http://teachersnetwork.org/ntol/ntol_how_to.htm

http://www.rethinkingschools.org/web_resource/index.shtml

Articles and Books

Au, W. (2009). *Rethinking multicultural education: Teaching for racial and cultural justice.*
Milwaukee, WI: Rethinking Schools.

Christison, M. A. (2005). *Multiple intelligences and language learning: A guidebook of
theory, activities, inventories, and resources.* San Francisco: Alta Book Center.

Delpit, L. (2002). *The skin that we speak: Thoughts on language and culture in the classroom.*
New York: The New Press.

Newmann, F. M. (1998). How secondary schools contribute to academic success. In
K. Borman & B. Schneider (Eds.), *The adolescent years: Social influences and educa-
tional challenges. Ninety-seventh yearbook of National Society for the Study of
Education* (pp. 88–108). Chicago: University of Chicago Press.

Olsen, L., & Jaramillo, A. (1999). *Turning the tides of exclusion.* San Francisco, CA: California Tomorrow: Equity-Centered School Reform Series.

Sylvester, R. (2007). *The adolescent brain: Reaching for autonomy.* Thousand Oaks, CA: Corwin.

Wallis, C. (2008). What makes teens tick? *Time.* Retrieved January 12, 2009, from www.time.com/time/magazine/article/0,9171,994126,00.html.

TEACHING AND LEARNING

(Chapters 4, 5, 6, 7, 8)

Web Sites

http://712educators.about.com/

http://www.teachnet.org/ntol/howto/start/c13796,.htm

http://www.free.ed.gov/

http://www.teachnet.org/ntol/howto/implement/

http://www.lessonplanspage.com/

http://www.eduref.org/Virtual/Lessons/

http://www.nationalgeographic.com/education/

Articles and Books

Bender, W. N. (2002). *Differentiating instruction for students with learning disabilities.* Thousand Oaks, CA: Corwin.

Chapman, G. G., & Chapman C. (2002). *Differentiated instructional strategies: One size does not fit all.* Thousand Oaks, CA: Corwin.

Lenz, B. K., & Deshler, D. (2004). *Teaching content to all.* Boston: Pearson Education.

Marzano, R. J., Pickering, D. J., & Pollock, J. (2001). *Classroom instruction that works: Research-based strategies for increasing academic achievement.* Alexandria, VA: Association for Supervision and Curriculum Development.

McTighe, J., & Wiggins, G. (2004). *Understanding by Design: Professional development workbook.* Alexandria, VA: Association for Supervision and Curriculum Development.

Tomlinson, C. A. (2001). *How to differentiate instruction in mixed-ability classrooms.* Alexandria, VA: Association for Supervision and Curriculum Development.

Zwiers, J. (2004). *Developing academic thinking skills in grades 6–12: A handbook of multiple intelligence activities.* Newark, DE: International Reading Association.

ASSESSMENT

(Chapters 4–10)

Web Sites

http://www.teachinginfocus.com/FocusedAssessment.html

http://www.rmcdenver.com/useguide/assessme/online.htm

http://www.rmcdenver.com/useguide/assessme/definiti.htm

http://www.rmcdenver.com/useguide/assessme/gideline.htm

http://www.edutopia.org/modules/Assessment/index.php

Articles and Books

Bernhardt, V. L. (2004). *Using data to improve student learning in middle schools.* Larchmont, NY: Eye on Education.

Doty, G. (2009). *Focused assessment.* Bloomington, IN: Solution Tree.

Guskey, T. R. (2003, February). How classroom assessments improve learning. *Educational Leadership, 60*(5), 6–11.

Jimenez, R. (2004). More equitable assessments for Latino students *Reading Teacher, 57*(6), 576–578.

Stiggins, R. J. (2002, September). *Classroom assessment for learning.,* Educational Leadership, 60(1), 40–43.

Wiggins, G., & McTighe, J. (2005). *Understanding by design* (2nd ed.). Upper Saddle River, NJ: Prentice Hall.

CONTENT LITERACY INSTRUCTION AND ACADEMIC LANGUAGE DEVELOPMENT

(Chapters 7, 8, 9, 10)

Web Sites

http://www.adlit.org/

http://readwritethink.org/student_mat/index.asp

http://www.ncte.org/adlit

http://cri.cps.k12.il.us/

http://www.reading.org/publications/journals/jaal/

http://www.ohiorc.org/adlit/

http://www.a114ed.org/adolescent_literacy/

http://www.eslgames.com/

Articles and Books

Alexander, P., & Jetton, T. (2004). Domains, content and literacy In T. Jetton and J. Dole (Eds.). *Adolescent literacy: Research and practice* (pp. 15–39). New York: Guilford Press.

August, D., & Hakuta, K. (1998). *Educating language-minority children.* Washington, DC: National Academy Press.

Biancarosa, C., & Snow, C. E. (2004). *Reading next—A vision for action and research in middle and high school literacy: A report to Carnegie Corporation of New York* (2nd ed.). Washington, DC: Alliance for Excellent Education.

Chall, J. S. (1996). *Qualitative assessment of text difficulty.* Brookline, MA: Brookline Books.

Daniels, H., & Zemelman, S. (2004). *Subjects matter: Every teacher's guide to content-area reading.* Portsmouth, NH: Heinneman.

Fisher, D., Brozo, W., Frey, N., & G. Ivey. (2007). *Fifty content area strategies for adolescent literacy.* Upper Saddle River, NJ: Pearson Education.

Fitzgerald, J. (1995). English-as-a-second-language learner's cognitive reading. *Review of Educational Research, 65,* 145–190.

Garcia, G. (2003). *English learners: Reaching the highest level of English literacy.* Newark, DE: International Reading Association.

Heller, R., & Greenleaf, C. (2007). *Literacy instruction in the content areas: Getting to the core of middle and high school improvement.* Washington, DC: Alliance for Excellent Education.

Herrell, A., & Jordan, M. (2004). *Fifty strategies for teaching English language learners.* Upper Saddle River, NJ: Pearson Education.

Marzano, R. J. (2004). *Building background knowledge for academic achievement.* Alexandria, VA: Association for Supervision and Curriculum Development.

Pritchard, R., & Breneman, B. (2000). *Strategic teaching and learning: Standards-based instruction to promote content literacy in grades four through twelve.* Sacramento, CA: California Department of Education.

Scarcella, R. (2003). *Accelerating academic English: A focus on the English learner.* Oakland: Regents of the University of California.

Short, D., & Fitzsimmons, S. (2007). A Report to the Carnegie Corporation of New York. *Double the work: Challenges and solutions to acquiring language and academic literacy for adolescent English language learners.* Washington, D.C.: Alliance for Excellent Education.

Zwiers, J. (2007). *Building academic language: Essential practices for content classrooms 5–12.* San Francisco: Jossey-Bass.

Sample Class Guidelines

Algebra 1

Fall, 2009

ABC High School

Mr. Ira Newman

CLASS GUIDELINES

Welcome to the 2009−2010 school year at ABC High School. It is my pleasure to be your mathematics teacher, and I look forward to working with you. Studying college-prep mathematics can be a rewarding experience, and it is my aim to make it as worthwhile to you as possible. Because this course is a college-prep level mathematics course, I will share with you many time-proven study skills to help you learn the algebra content standards. Expect to work hard in this class. Also, expect that your efforts will be rewarded with a deeper understanding and appreciation of mathematics.

So that you will understand my expectations and grading policy, I am providing these *Class Guidelines*. They contain most of the information you need to know to have a successful year. Keep these guidelines in your notebook and refer to them from time to time to remind yourself what I expect from you.

I believe that success in high school mathematics is obtainable by everyone. However, certain ingredients facilitate success. Helpful or sympathetic parents/guardians can be a tremendous asset. Look to your classmates to help you and lend them a hand when they need it. I have worked hard to create a safe and positive working environment—help me preserve it and don't hesitate to let me know how it can be improved. Most successful learners accept challenges and are open to change. I invite you to push yourself in new directions. Working together, I see no reason why we all cannot succeed in this class.

I am looking forward to a good year.

Mr. Ira Newman

Purpose of Notes

Note taking will be a fundamental, required part of this course. Notes are a key to success in most college and college-prep courses. I will share strategies to take, edit, and review class notes.

Notes can be taken in pencil or pen. I encourage you to use a mechanical pencil while taking notes. In reviewing notes, I encourage you to experiment using different colored pens and highlighters.

We will be taking a certain style of notes called Cornell notes, which encourage editing and reviewing to foster understanding.

Purpose of Assignments

Assignments allow an opportunity to practice and investigate the material we are learning. Assignments for the each month will be passed out at the beginning of the month on class calendars. Generally, we will follow the calendar, but expect that changes may sometimes occur. Often, as you work out problems on assignments, you discover shortcuts or easier methods to solve the problems. Put these ideas in your notes! Assignments must be finished before the start of the next class period to make review time worthwhile. You can watch your teacher or classmates do problems, but unless you jump in and try them yourself, you will not learn. To get the most out each assignment, the following is required:

- Use a proper header on each assignment
- Write each problem in pencil
- Show each step, working downward instead of horizontally
- Include a sketch when possible
- Use a straightedge to draw straight lines, and always use graph paper when graphing
- Indicate the answer by circling or highlighting it
- Leave space between problems

Assignments will be informally checked and assessed daily. I will also periodically collect and more thoroughly assess assignments.

Purpose of Class Study Time

Often, we will have time to start assignments in class. Many times, we will work in pairs of groups of four during this time. I will assign groups, often randomly. Groups will change about once per month.

Purpose of Quizzes

In the middle of each unit, you will be given a quiz to measure your progress. This helps break up long chapters or units and encourages more frequent studying of notes and assignments. Each quiz will be worth 15 points.

Purpose of Tests

At the end of each unit, we will have a unit test. Tests evaluate your understanding and ability to apply the content. You may expect about two tests each six weeks, each worth 50 points.

Note: Before each test, a practice test or other review assignment will be given to help you study for the test. Use these review assignments to self-assess how much you need to study before the actual test, as no makeups will be given.

Purpose of the Final

At the end of the semester, a comprehensive final will be given. The final will cover everything studied during the entire semester. I will show you how your notebook can be very helpful to use to study for the final.

Written Work, Projects, and Extra Credit Opportunities

At times, we will investigate the subject in different ways. Even though this is a math class, expect opportunities to write or make class presentations. Every six weeks, you will have an *extra credit opportunity*. This will be especially helpful for students with borderline grades at the time of progress reports.

Odds and Ends

Expect class to last the full 90 minutes. Be in your seat and ready to work at the proper time. Do not expect to be released early.

Food and drink should be finished outside of class. They are not permitted inside of the classroom except during lunch. Help keep the class clean by picking up after yourself and/or others, if necessary.

Keep personal stereos and headphones inside your backpack during class.

Treat substitutes courteously. Know that they will do things differently and have different expectations of you. Help out. Be responsible.

Show up to class! You cannot learn the material if you do not come to class. If you are absent, use your assignment sheet to keep current. Call your study buddy to hear what you missed. Stop by and see me to get a copy of the notes you missed.

You have as many days to make up work as you were absent. If your absence is not excused, you will not receive credit for work missed.

The schoolwide attendance policy will be followed during this class. Note that if you are dropped from this class because of lack of attendance, you will not be reinstated.

A NOTE TO PARENTS/GUARDIANS

To help foster understanding of the material, parents/guardians can do the following:

- Check assignment sheets and notes to see what homework was assigned
- Quiz students on examples from the textbook
- Create sample tests for students using odd problems in the book (answers to odd numbered problems are in the back of the book)
- Provide study time in the home where everyone reads or studies with no television. Be sure to provide proper lighting.
- Quiz students from homework assignments to make sure they understood what they did
- Monitor to assure the student does not fall behind, and contact the teacher as challenges surface before they become chronic

Calculators

A scientific calculator is required in this course. Calculators and other forms of technology are invaluable for mathematicians. However, it is equally important to be able to do many types of mathematics, such as quick mental estimations, without calculators. We will have a variety of assessments during this course, some of which calculators will be required and others which calculators will not be allowed. I will always give you plenty of notice about whether calculators will be allowed or not.

Notebooks

Students will be required to keep a three-ring binder for this course. Loose pieces of paper floating between textbook pages or spiral-type notebooks will not fulfill the notebook requirement. Notebooks must be neatly organized and contain the following:

- Class assignment sheets
- Calendar pages
- Class guidelines
- Cornell notes
- Assignments
- Tests, quizzes
- Written work
- Special projects

I will have a model of a notebook to share, which will help you organize yours. Periodically, we will have time to organize and assess notebooks in class.

GRADES

Your semester grade will be based on these approximate percentages:

Tests 40%

Assignments 30%

Quizzes 20%

Notebooks 10%

At any time, you can compute your grades as follows: Count the number of points you have earned to date, and then divide by the total number of points possible. I will show you how you can use your assignment sheets to do this.

$$\text{Your percentage} = \frac{\text{your points}}{\text{total points}} \times 100$$

90%	100%	A
80%	89%	B
70%	79%	C
60%	69%	D
0%	59%	F

I am always available for extra help before school (7:30 to 8:00) and after school (2:45 to 3:15), and by appointment. Parents may contact me at the school at 555-3422, or by e-mail at inewman@ABC.newschools.k12.ca.us.

References

August, D., & T. Hakuta. (1997). *Educating language-minority children*. Washington, DC: National Academy Press.

Bongolan, R. (2005, December). *Six key strategies for teachers of English language learners*. Retrieved from http://www.all4ed.org/files/archive/publications/SixKeyStrategies.pdf

Chall, J. S. (1995). *The stages of reading development* (2nd ed.). New York: Harcourt Brace College.

Chamot, A. U., & O'Malley, J. M. (1996). The cognitive academic language learning approach (CALLA): A model for linguistically diverse classrooms. *The Elementary School Journal, 96*(3), 259–273.

Echevarria, J., Vogt, M. E., & Short, D. (2004). *Making content comprehensible for English learners: The SIOP model* (2nd ed.). Boston: Pearson.

Fitzgerald J. (1995). English-as-a-second-language learner's cognitive reading. *Review of Educational Research, 6*, 145–190.

Freeman, Y. S., Freeman, D. E., & Mercuri, S. (2002). *Closing the achievement gap: How to reach limited-formal-schooling and long-term English learners*. Portsmouth, NH: Heinemann.

Gandara, P., & Maxwell-Jolly, J. (2005). *Listening to the teachers of English language learners: A survey of California teachers' challenges, experiences, and professional development needs*. Santa Cruz, CA: The Center for the Future of Teaching and Learning.

Garcia, G. (2003). *English learners: Reaching the highest level of English literacy*. Newark, DE: International Reading Association.

Gersten, R., & Baker, S. (2000). What we know about effective instructional practice for English-Language Learners. *Exceptional Children, 66*(4), 454–470.

Heller, R., & Greenleaf, C. (2007). *Literacy instruction in the content areas: Getting to the core of middle and high school improvement*. Washington, DC: Alliance for Excellent Education.

Krashen, S. D., & Terrell, T. D. (1983). *The natural approach: Language acquisition in the classroom*. Hayward, CA: The Alemany Press.

Ladson-Billings, G. (1999). Preparing teachers for diverse student populations: A critical race theory perspective. In A. I. Nejad & P. D. Pearson (Eds.), *Review of research in education* (Vol. 24, pp. 211–247). Washington, DC: American Educational Research Association.

McTighe, J., & Wiggins, G. (2004). *Understanding by design: Professional development workbook*. Alexandria, VA: Association for Supervision and Curriculum Development.

Obidah, J. E., & Teel, K. (2000*). Because of the kids: Facing racial and cultural differences in schools*. New York: Teachers College Press.

Palincsar, A. L., & Brown, A. L. (1984). Reciprocal teaching of comprehension-fostering and comprehension monitoring activities. *Cognition and Instruction, 1*(2), 117–175.

Short, D., & Fitzsimmons, S. (2007). *Double the work: Challenges and solutions to acquiring language and academic literacy for adolescent English language learners* (A Report to Carnegie Corporation of New York). Washington, DC: Alliance for Excellent Education.

Snow, C., Burns, M., & Griffin, P. (1998). *Preventing reading difficulties in young children: Report to the National Research Council.* Washington, DC: National Academy Press.

Stanovich, K. (1986). Matthew effects in reading: Some consequences of individual differences in the acquisition of literacy. *Reading Research Quarterly, 21*(4), 360–407.

Wong-Fillmore, L., & Snow, C. (2000) *What teachers need to know about language.* Washington, DC: U.S. Department of Education.

Index

New Teacher Center
Launching the Next Generation

New Teacher Center (NTC) is a national organization dedicated to improving student learning by accelerating the effectiveness of teachers and school leaders. Since 1998, the NTC has served over 49,000 teachers, 5,000 mentors, and touched millions of students.

NTC strengthens school communities and builds school leadership through:
- Proven mentoring and professional development programs
- Online learning environments
- Policy advocacy
- Research on induction programs and teacher learning conditions.

At the heart of the work is the belief that every student is entitled to a quality education, and that by focusing on teachers, student learning improves. Ellen Moir is the organization's executive director.

www.newteachercenter.org
831-600-2200

CORWIN

A SAGE Company

The Corwin logo—a raven striding across an open book—represents the union of courage and learning. Corwin is committed to improving education for all learners by publishing books and other professional development resources for those serving the field of PreK–12 education. By providing practical, hands-on materials, Corwin continues to carry out the promise of its motto: **"Helping Educators Do Their Work Better."**